My
UNAPOLOGETIC
Diaries

Also by Joan Collins

MEMOIR

Past Imperfect: An Autobiography
Katy: A Fight for Life, A Memoir
Second Act: An Autobiography
The World According to Joan
Passion For Life: An Autobiography

NON-FICTION

The Joan Collins Beauty Book
My Secrets
Health, Youth and Happiness: My Secrets
My Friends' Secrets
Joan's Way: Looking Good, Feeling Great
The Art of Living Well: Looking Good, Feeling Great

FICTION

Prime Time
Love and Desire and Hate
Too Damn Famous
Star Quality
Misfortune's Daughters
The St. Tropez Lonely Hearts Club

My
UNAPOLOGETIC
Diaries

W&N
WEIDENFELD & NICOLSON

First published in Great Britain in 2021 by Weidenfeld & Nicolson
an imprint of The Orion Publishing Group Ltd
Carmelite House, 50 Victoria Embankment
London EC4Y 0DZ

An Hachette UK Company

7 9 10 8 6

A CIP catalogue record for this book is
available from the British Library.

ISBN (Hardback) 978 1 4746 2127 4
ISBN (Export Trade Paperback) 978 1 4746 2128 1
ISBN (eBook) 978 1474 2130 4
ISBN (Audio) 978 1474 62131 1

Typeset by Input Data Services Ltd, Somerset

Printed and bound in Great Britain by Clays Ltd, Elcograf S.p.A.

MIX
Paper from
responsible sources
FSC
www.fsc.org FSC® C104740

www.weidenfeldandnicolson.co.uk
www.orionbooks.co.uk

For Percy
For Always

Acknowledgements

I dedicate these diaries to my family, and my many friends and acquaintances with whom I have had so many adventures, experiences and fun throughout these years.

And with grateful thanks to Richard Linford for interpreting my tape-recorded mumblings, to Alan Nevins for making it happen and to Alan Samson for deciphering my hieroglyphics and patiently coaching me to pronounce the word 'unapologetic' . . .

Prologue

I was named Joan Henrietta Collins, but perhaps you may know me better as 'Alexis Morell Carrington Colby Dexter Rowan' from the TV series *Dynasty*, or perhaps Edith Keeler, the saintly missionary worker on *Star Trek*.

I was born on 23 May, sometime between the end of the Great Depression and the beginning of the Second World War . . . Oscar Wilde once said, 'Any woman who would reveal her age, would reveal anything.' So there! You can always google it.

I am a wife, a mother, a grandmother, a sister, an aunt and a loyal friend. I have three children, three grandchildren and thirteen godchildren, who range in age from nine months to fifty-seven years old, and some of whom may not even remember that I'm their godmother.

I am an actress – I don't ever refer to myself as an actor – an author, a producer, a feminist, a philanthropist and an entrepreneur. I have been married five times (and by far the happiest and longest is my last husband of nearly twenty years, Percy Gibson).

I have been in over seventy films, *hundreds* of TV shows and over a dozen plays. I have written seventeen books and hundreds of articles, editorials, diaries and even edited a magazine. But I have no mentor in my life other than fate.

I've been on thousands of magazine covers and appeared in dozens of TV commercials, as myself!

I've been called a 'vixen', a 'bitch', a 'pouting panther', 'Britain's bad girl', 'England's answer to Ava Gardner', the 'Denver Beast', the 'torrid baggage', the 'Coffee Bar Jezebel' and even the 'face of innocence' once, when I played a nun.

And now I'm spilling the beans! Well, nearly all of them. I've always been a diarist, starting at age twelve with a tiny five-year diary of the kind you'd find at Smythson's, and writing sporadically over the years. What you will read in the following pages was written when 'I felt like it' between 1989 and 2006.

I dictated most of these entries in real time, into a mini tape recorder, every night when I came home. There is no rhyme or reason why there are gaps of years between entries. I do know that interesting events happened in those gaps, but I guess I wasn't in the mood, or I couldn't find my tape recorder, or maybe the tapes ended in the same place as Richard Nixon's lost eighteen minutes . . .

Anyway, here they are, with NO apologies to anyone mentioned in them. Enjoy!

Diaries 1989-2006

March 1989

I was looking forward to the final days of *Dynasty*. The show had gone so rapidly downhill both in ratings and audiences that it had turned into a joke, and impossible as an actor to take seriously or to make any sense of the puerile plots and dialogue. It had become embarrassing to play, and the audiences knew it too. Although I adored playing Alexis, I knew that all good things must come to an end.

I had been hurt that, after difficult negotiations, I had finally succeeded in getting pay parity with John Forsythe to $120,000 per episode. However, just before we started shooting, I was informed that they couldn't afford to pay me for the whole season so I would only be in half the episodes! John of course would be in all twenty episodes – so much for sexual equality in the industry. While I was now apparently the highest paid TV actress in the world, it was a purely Pyrrhic victory since I would effectively earn the same as before. (Still, half the work!) without Linda Evans as Krystle Carrington, who had left the sinking ship last season, and with Alexis only appearing in half the episodes, the show was destined to decline.

To add insult to injury, I was hoping for a future lived on lovely residuals like the actors on *Dallas*, *Golden Girls* and others did. But on the last day of shooting a jobsworth lawyer working for Aaron Spelling [*Dynasty*'s producer] came to my dressing room to insist I sign away all of my rights to future showings of *Dynasty*. 'Serials don't sell on syndication,' he spouted. 'John and Linda have already signed the waiver, you will all get three weeks' salary as a bonus, but no more.'

'That's it? No residuals at all?' I asked.

'None,' he said.

I demurred, thinking that was not enough pay for play after nine years of solid slog in this show. But it was a 'no-go' – he was adamant and so was my agent. So, after believing that *Dynasty* would be my annuity, I now realised I needed to think about what I should do about my future. Thus, it was the theatre I wanted to return to. I had been thinking about it for several years – it was, after all, originally the reason I wanted to become an actress – and the thought excited me. No more tacky dialogue and 5 a.m. calls. Noël Coward here I come!

April 1989

Packed up my tiny *Dynasty* dressing room. It was about the size of a cupboard. This is where I had put on my make-up, done my hair, dressed in those fabulous gowns and had my lunch for nine years. As I gazed at the empty four walls with their peeling paint and nail holes, I thought, 'So much for the glamour of showbiz!' My best friend and at the time assistant, stand-in and occasional background player, Judy Bryer, helped me and a week later I was off to London, and hopefully the West End and a new life!

Monday, 8 May 1989

Lunched at the Savoy with my agent Peter Charlesworth and West End producer Michael Codron. Codron wants me to appear in a play called *What the Butler Saw*, in which I would play a nymphomaniacal wife who appears clad in a mink, wearing only black underwear underneath. Well, thanks a heap! It has all the shades of *The Bitch* and *The Stud*, and I think I've gone beyond that – certainly hope so!

Codron is charming and amusing – whitish-grey hair and a very tanned face. As with many 'show girls', he admires me and wants to do something else since I'm not keen on what he's suggesting, even though Coral Browne had a big success with it a few years ago.

I told him that if I were to do a play, it would be one that I wanted to do for years: *Private Lives*. He seemed interested but asked if I was up to the fight scenes, remembering the debacle of Elizabeth Taylor and Richard Burton on Broadway and how they *threw* themselves all over the place and Liz got hurt. We left it that we'd both give some thought to this idea!

Tuesday, 9 May 1989

Charlesworth rang and said that Codron was mad about me and very enthusiastic about doing *Private Lives* and who did I want to play opposite me in the role of Elyot?

May to August 1989

I want Leigh Lawson to play Elyot in *Private Lives*. Codron not too enthusiastic but I thought he was wonderful in *Merchant*. We all had lunch at Orso's and Codron finally bowled over and agreed. Then Lawson wants his wife Twiggy to play Sibyl. Codron says no, I like Twigs but she's too cockney for Coward, so 'bye-bye' Lawsons.

Next stop Tom Conti. He says he's very interested. We lunch

at the Savoy with Peter and Michael. Tom seems somewhat dour and taciturn and I do not see charisma or chemistry between us. Peter doesn't agree but Michael is of two minds.

However, Tom solves the problem – he passes. He wants to do the movie version of *Present Laughter* (which incidentally doesn't happen. Rather like my projects this year!).

We then put everything on hold as I go on holiday and a tour of Australia for my new novel *Prime Time*. I am anxious that my great friend Edward Duke plays Victor.

Friday, 13 October 1989

A day at Houghton Hall, one of the great stately homes in Norfolk. Went with Charles Cholmondeley, who is lady Sybil Cholmondeley's grandson, and Robin [Hurlstone, JC's then partner]. Left at ten thirty in a stretch limo, armed with the *Spectator*, *Bookseller* and *Daily Mail*.

The latter has an extremely bitchy article about me by a white-faced, saggy-breasted Fleet Street hag about last weekend's 'Cartier Millions Ball'. She referred to Ned Ryan as 'a walker Joan shares with Princess Margaret' and then to Ira von Fürstenberg as the 'end of an Ira, searching for her lost youth' accompanied by a photo of her 'toy-boy' and other tacky slime. Therefore, it was wonderful to leave the modern world and go back in time for a visit to Lady C.

The house is of imposing stone, built in 1726. The butler showed us into her sitting room, where this tiny ninety-five-year-old lady sat beneath a staggering life-sized portrait of herself by John Singer Sargent, painted in 1920. She is amazingly sprightly, bright and amused by life, although only yesterday she came out of hospital for a minor leg operation. She walks with two sticks and is about four foot eleven, and quite bent. Her hair is white, with perhaps a faint blue rinse, and bald patches on top with age spots, but her hands look thirty years younger. Apart from a deaf aid she appears to have 95 per cent of her faculties.

There were fifteen amazing Sargent pictures in her sitting room, her little dachshund Lena, a big TV and a video machine (which she says she doesn't know how to work, and neither does the butler!). Lunch, in what used to be the main hall, was served at a round table and she sat me on her right. Another older couple – Bill and Pat – were there; and Todd Bruno, an American deer expert, who was taking care of her herds of white deer under the instructions of her other grandson, David Rocksavage. She chatted away, very knowledgeable about art, music and current events, while sixteen-year-old Lena sat under the table.

The pudding, a raspberry puree with clotted cream, was served in glass bowls on the most exquisite eighteenth-century Sèvres china from Sir Philip Sassoon's collection. Charles said this was the first time he had ever seen it! The wine was pre-war Chateau Lafite – delicious! She urged us not to waste it. After lunch, we drove, in the freezing cold, with Bruno to see the baby llama and the deer (having something nasty done to their nether regions).

We rushed back to meet Lady C, who took us on a tour. Downstairs is quite gloomy. Although it is supposed to be one of the five greatest houses in England, it seemed draughty, prefabricated, sort of empty, cold and dull. But upstairs was magical – each room more gorgeous than the last. Sybil Cholmondeley walked us through herself, followed by the faithful Lena, who, being incontinent due to her great age, did small wee-wees and left small droppings on the rare carpets. Charles and I became hysterical but Lady C did not notice. Her hearing aid makes a strange buzzing noise when one is close to it. Every room contained furniture which had been there for 250 years, covered, in many cases, with gorgeous teal-blue, green and scarlet velvet.

When we came to the yellow drawing room, hung with delicate brocade, I gasped in admiration at another portrait of her that Sargent painted in 1913, when she was nineteen, on her honeymoon. She had such a strong, wilful, beautiful face – lovely by today's standards too. Strong brow, black eyebrows like wings, black hair. She wore some kind of loose wrap in the portrait. She said that Sargent wanted something different than 'just a gown'. He was a good friend and the portrait took three months. Charles said it was worth about two million. There was also a very famous Oudry of a hanging duck, a silver candlestick and a candle.

Sybil Cholmondeley died three months later – I was very happy I met her, had a chance to see one of the last stately homes and meet a great lady.

Friday, 1 December 1989

Lunch at Scott's with Michael Codron and Edward Pether-bridge. He is very dry and dusty – no humour that I can see and neither sexy nor attractive. Perfect for Elyot (not!). I am sick from three weeks of beastly flu. When I leave, Edward makes a big fuss about losing a silk scarf that his wife gave him – well, really! Like, I took it? Michael calls me – it's a pass, or as they say in the business: *Pasadena!*

Thursday, 14 December 1989

Tea with Codron and Christopher Godwin, who wants to play Victor. He seems nice but I still want Edward Duke.

Friday, 15 December 1989

Drinks at Eaton Place with Codron and Simon Williams. I adore Sam (Simon's pet name) but he feels I need a really strong charismatic man for Elyot. Too bad – Sam was great in *The Last of Mrs Cheyney*.

Tuesday, 13 February 1990

Lunch with Elspeth March [actress] at Mimmo's. She loves the idea of Keith Baxter, who we are seeing *ce soir*. Fingers crossed. Elspeth says he's a poppet.

Peter Charlesworth and I wait, giddy with anticipation, at Orso's for Keith, who is in a play he wrote – *Barnaby and the Old Boys*.

He's charming, Welsh, beautiful voice, very full of anecdotes. Reminds me slightly of Richard Burton. He looks a little older than we thought, even though he's fifty-six. His hair is grey, and I liked him.

Wednesday, 14 February 1990

Called Michael Codron and told him I'll agree to Keith Baxter for Elyot as long as I can have Edward Duke for Victor. I feel they will balance beautifully – one younger, one older. Hope it works. Leave for NY.

Monday, 12 March 1990

Carl Toms, the designer who will do my costumes for *Private Lives*, came to talk. A real poppet. I love his ideas. We go through many of the 1930s books I bought in Paris and he goes off to do sketches.

Tuesday, 13 March 1990

Sarah Crowe is cast as Sibyl. I don't know her, but I hear she's a good actress and very pretty. Michael Codron jokes that she and I are the only heterosexuals in the *Private Lives* company. Oh, my God! It's true!

Friday, 16 March 1990

Lunch at Orso with Michael Codron and Tim Luscombe as potential director. I like Tim – he's young but bright and enthusiastic. I think he'd direct the play with integrity and humour.

Monday, 26 March 1990 – Los Angeles

Take Edward Duke to Swifty Lazar's Oscar party at Spago. One of the most 'in' events in Hollywood, an invitation is highly coveted and I was delighted to have always been asked, even though many people higher in the Hollywood hierarchy than I didn't make the cut. Edward, normally cool and sophisticated, was gobsmacked watching Gregory Peck, Kirk Douglas, Billy Wilder and dozens of the crème de la crème of Tinseltown eat the fabulous dinner prepared by Wolfgang Puck. We had an absolutely terrific evening, even though Tony Curtis kept table-hopping and getting in front of the TV screens while we were trying to watch the brilliant Billy Crystal hosting. I wanted Kenneth Branagh to win for *Henry V*, as I loved working with him on *In the Bleak Midwinter* last year, but everyone thought Daniel Day Lewis deserved it for *My Left Foot*. Sad that Pauline Collins didn't win Best Actress for *Shirley Valentine*, but Jessica Tandy did for *Driving Miss Daisy* and it was great to see an older

8

actress win. Said hello to Pauline and her hubby John Alderton, as well as many other nominees. Jack Lemmon was adorable and flattering to me, as he often was; and Robert Wagner and I shared a joke or two as usual. Edward is over the moon that he's invited and that he will be playing Victor. His enthusiasm and excitement are great, and I'm sure he will be too.

Friday, 27 April 1990 – Destino, France

Rupert Everett comes to dinner at our home in the South of France. He says I should use Philip Prowse as director. He brings out lots of tiny black-and-white photos of PP's productions at Glasgow Citizens Theatre. Apparently Philip had directed him in *Pygmalion* and *Vortex*. 'Rupie' says Philip must be assertive. This is *my* show. The public are coming to see *me* (please God!). Tell Michael Codron what *I* want. Well, we discussed Peter O'Toole and Richard Harris for Elyot but they both look a hundred years old and are probably busy. Called PC about Albert Finney, but he's in a play. Casting is very difficult.

Sunday, 6 May 1990 – England

Go for lunch to Keith Baxter's house. It's a very hot day and he's wearing just a pair of briefs and looks a bit fat. We must do something with his hair! His boyfriend Brian is there – a sweet boy. Keith plays 'Someday I'll Find You' on his piano. He has been practising and it's very good. He wants me to sing it with him but I'm not in good voice yet. Will I ever be? I like Keith – he's a great raconteur.

Thursday, 10 May 1990

Met Keith at Zoë Dominic's studio for photos for the ad of *Private Lives*. I'm not wild about my wig from Derek Easton – it's too 'mumsy'. Also, since there are no frocks yet, what they come up with is more suitable for a skinny seven-stone vestal virgin, so I wear a black 1930s dress of my own. Keith has dyed his hair and he looks good in his dinner jacket. Zoë however does not take enough photos of each set-up. Keith is a bit stiff as he's not used to posing, and dubious about photos.

Thursday, 17 May 1990

See Zoë's photos – was right, they are stiff and fake-looking. Do a series of photos for John Swannell for *Sunday Mirror*. They are so good that I beg Codron to forget about the Zoë pics and use Swannell. He agrees that Zoë's pics are bland.

Tuesday, 22 May 1990

Lunch at L'Incontro with Edward and Elspeth – he's so excited he got Victor! He does look quite a lot like Laurence Olivier looked in the 1930 production.

Wednesday, 11 June 1990

Keith and I do a photo session with John Swannell. Adrian has found a better dress. The wig is shorter and on seeing the Polaroids they are 100 per cent better than Zoë's.

Monday, 18 June 1990

Photocall for national press at Aldwych Theatre. I wasn't keen to do them, but Codron says that it will coincide with box office opening. The shoot goes well. Keith and I pose for half an hour and give them what they want, then go to lunch at Joe Allen's with Elspeth, my PR and close friend Stella Wilson, Michael, Keith and Lynn, Michael's PR girl. We wait for Swannell's photos and Michael gets more and more chippy and aggravated although we are having a great time. He explodes at last and Keith and I look at each other with raised eyebrows. Who's the prima donna here?

Finally, the photos arrive, and they are brilliant. We are all thrilled. Michael leaves to catch a train, saying that the ads for *Private Lives* will now have to wait until next week to appear.

Tuesday, 19 June 1990

Paparazzi pictures of Keith and me appear in press, with the usual shit thrown at me that 'Joan says her play is for toffs. Doesn't want *Sun* readers – she chucked out their lensman.' What crap! Apparently, Lynn threw out the *Sun* and the *Star*'s photographers by mistake, because they tried to smuggle in a journalist. The *Express* said about me, 'She was her usual prima donna self.' The Alexis syndrome! Keith says it's most unfair – wish they wouldn't make these stories up about me. Still, box office is open now – good for business.

July–August 1990

Spent this six-and-a-half-week period trying to get into shape for *Private Lives*, since I haven't done any exercise since *Dynasty* finished in March 1989. To say I am rusty is putting it mildly. Started doing push-ups and could only manage five 'girls' ones. By the end of July, I was up to one hundred a day, thirty of which were 'male push-ups'! Then swimming – puffed after one lap in July, by August I can do twenty. The pool here has such a wonderful view of the valley and the sea. Edward Duke arrived and we started learning our lines. I must say, they are quite difficult to learn – very strange grammar in many speeches. Continual use of one particular word – 'nice'. It appears fifty-five times on one page, and 'don't' five times on another.

Edward says that Coward had quite a small vocabulary, hence Amanda constantly uses the words 'peculiar', 'awful' and 'dreadful'. I suppose it's the period, but they're going to have to cut some of that.

This is the lull before the storm – hope it won't be a storm.

Codron finally took an ad in the *Sunday Times* – quite sweet. Swannell's photo is excellent. Apparently, there is great interest in the show in London in spite of the most ghastly heatwave – up to 97/98 degrees – which has collapsed everyone.

During this heatwave, darling Malcolm Fraser died of a heart attack brought on by asthma. He was a great friend who, for a bet, lent me his ex-wife's badge for the Royal Enclosure at Ascot, which created an international incident. The bet was that no one would recognise me – but they did. Pandora and Charles Delevingne and Ned Ryan were staying, and we were all desperately sad and cried most of the day.

Lisa and Philly, our staff, were cooking up a storm. They are such brilliant cooks, it's hard to believe they are only twenty. I cannot seem to lose weight, no doubt because of said cooking, but the only place it shows is my stomach. That won't look too hot in a 1930s evening gown cut on the bias. My friend Lynn Wyatt came for a couple of days to stay. According to Valentino [fashion designer Valentino Garavani] she exercises one and a half hours a day – *quelle horreur!* Twenty-five minutes is my max. She said I was doing my sit-ups all wrong and demonstrated how to. She doesn't have an ounce of fat on her. It's unbelievable considering she's had four kids and is around my age.

I shall have to starve for a couple of days next week. Amanda MUST be svelte!

Called Keith to see how he was doing with learning the lines. Tim said he would like us to be 'up' on them before rehearsals start. Keith knows the whole play! I can't believe it. I tested him with the odd line here and there and he knows it all right. Felt rather guilty. I know nearly all of Act One and half of Act Two, but I always learn during the blocking and rehearsals.

Keith also said he lost two stone on the Rosemary Conley 'hip and thigh diet'. I'm glad as I thought he needed it. He said he did it for me, as 'you're so glamorous, darling. I didn't want to look like your father.' Sweet!

Spoke to Tim – he was shocked Keith had learned the whole play. Said it made one 'too set in one's ways'. As long as I know the play, not necessarily the lines, by the first day's 'read-through', that's all right with him. Only one more day here in paradise and then rehearsals start. I'm quite excited. It's been a long wait – I hope it's going to be worth it.

Goodbye *Dynasty*. Hello *Private Lives*!

1994

Friday, 11 March 1994

Drove with Jackie [internationally bestselling novelist and sister of JC] and Frank [Calcagnini] to a lovely dinner at Barbara and Marvin Davis's gorgeous house, The Knoll. I must say they give great parties, but not as elegant as Betsy Bloomingdale's.

Greg and Veronique Peck were there, and he told me yet again how much he had liked doing his recent one-man show and that I should do one too.

Larry King always acts surprised to see Jackie and me together, God knows why. He's very weird-looking now.

Alan Ladd Jr is very dull, but then so was his dad, who I tested with when I was eighteen. And as I was taller than him at five foot five he had to walk on a raised plinth! beside me. Susan Stephen, at five foot two, got the role. I told Junior the story, but he wasn't amused.

Tony Danza was great fun. Altogether a great night and I chatted with Jackie, who told me she was in love with Frank. Hmm!

1995

Friday, 20 January 1995

The party is held in a large white bunker-type modern house in the middle of Beverly Hills. It's in honour of a well-known actor. The guest list is mostly A's with a few B's mixed in. Tony Curtis arrives, exuberant as ever, bitchily delighted to discover a tag ticket on the sleeve of my new Valentino suit as he vociferously pumps my arm in greeting. He's with his latest squeeze, Jill, who trains horses and has rather big bosoms. Tony wears a fake-looking grey curly wig and, considering he's turning seventy this year, he's lots of fun.

Ninety-nine per cent of the women are wearing black, with the exception of Shakira Caine in red, and me in white. David Niven Jr and his lovely wife Barbara, Jolene and George Schlatter, Angie Dickinson, Michael Brandon and his wife Glynis Barber, Wendy Stark and John Morrissey and Wendy and Leonard Goldberg and her sister super-agent Toni Howard, the Sidney Poitiers and Louis Jourdan. Then a flurry of excitement as the latest widow in town arrives looking like the cat that's just swallowed the canary. She has Jack Nicholson in tow, a coup indeed. An immediate hum of excited conversation begins in various corners as everyone discusses the ramifications of this latest pairing.

The waiters, some of whom wear earrings, pass Chinese hors

d'oeuvres, and we gossip and chat until dinner is called. Four tables of ten in a large marble-floored dining room, all white, very noisy, with nothing to mute the sound. It is a buffet but no one is told which table to go to, so there is much milling around and tut-tutting and whispering among the women. We'll be talking to each other tomorrow on the phone, won't we? Placement is everything in Hollywood. It shows you and everyone else your status. Good hostesses are well aware of this and consider at great length where they seat everyone. But not this hostess. At table number 1 she sits herself between Jack Nicholson and Marvin Davis, then sits Michael Caine next to the widow, then Joanna Poitier, the wife of Sidney, the hostess's boyfriend, then Mr Poitier. Table is heavily loaded in favour of 'biggies'. At the number 2 table Tony Curtis sits with his girlfriend, with supporting cast Angie Dickinson, George Schlatter, Wendy Stark and Shakira Caine. At my table on my left, a very intelligent young producer and on my right a 'B' actor whose main interest is in talking about and furthering his career. As the producer and I try to talk about a project I'm involved in, the actor leans forward eagerly as though to get into the conversation. On his right is one of the most influential and important agents in Los Angeles, but the actor is much more interested in trying to intrude on our conversation than in talking to the agent, who could probably do him a lot more good than either the producer or me.

Discuss with the producer my script, which I would like him to read. He's giving me some good advice about meetings I should take. However, the vociferous actor eagerly intrudes, and when I pause for breath, he says, 'Hey, I gotta script. It's just fabulous. Great part for me, can you imagine – John Esterhazy? Yeah, it's true, it's brilliant – it's great and it could be made for three million dollars.' The producer, ever polite, looks slightly flabbergasted but gives the actor a weak smile. At this point I leave and go to another table and sit next to George Schlatter. We drink some wine and watch Tony Curtis go to the bathroom for the third time. 'What is he doing?' I ask ingenuously. 'What do you think?' says George laconically. 'You've obviously not been in Hollywood for a while.'

People are leaving and I realise it is the witching hour and I have to get up early to prepare for the Golden Globes the following night. I go through the bar to be grabbed by Mr Curtis who, to be honest, is not my favourite person ever since he was so rude on *The Persuaders*. Dominick Dunne is regaling everyone with stories of the O.J. Simpson trial. The two men trade anecdotes until Tony tells his favourite story, the punchline of which is: 'I fucked Yvonne De Carlo!' which has everyone in stitches. A producer came up and stares fascinated down Jill's huge cleavage. I go into the powder room where several women discuss the fact that although her bosoms might be huge, when she looks down at herself she could look as though she had twelve toes.

The hostess takes me into her den, whispering, 'Would you like to see a picture of the baby?' This baby is her grandchild but is kept a big secret. Although there are hundreds of framed photographs of the hostess, her children and various celebrities strung around the house, there is not one of the baby. 'I'm frightened of kidnappers,' she whispers. I looked at her askance. 'Kidnappers, for your grandchild? Why?' She shakes her head and puts her fingers to her lips. Although the woman is a celebrity, her husband is after all only a producer. It is definitely time to leave. The waiter comes up, finds my coat and asks me if I know how to open the imposing barred front door. 'No,' I say. He opens it for me and I step out into the rainy California night. Another wonderful Hollywood evening has ended.

January 1995

At LAX airport without a boarding pass! We were followed by several paparazzi who all just put their equipment on the detector and came through snapping away with impunity. Don't think much of that security. The American Airlines representative said, 'That's the way it is here, we're not too worried.' 'It could never happen in Europe,' I said. 'We have strict security at airports.' 'Ah, yes, but you've got IRA terrorists there,' he said smugly. I hope that, since the Oklahoma City horror, security will become tighter at US airports.

Early 1995 – New York

A whirl of activity began with the live TV Regis and Kathie Lee show, then segued into an interview with Jeannie Williams from *USA Today* at the Carlyle. Then downtown to Avenue of the Americas for a video signing appearance at 'Funcoast', which was a major disaster! Since most of my signings in England have been extremely successful (a thousand books at Harrods for example), a bad signing would be only 350 people turning out. Here I sat in the middle of a huge shopping mall, on a podium on a desk in front of which were a stack of photographs of me in my exercise leotard and about seventy-five people stood below Instamatic-ing me, smiling, staring and pointing. I felt like the chimp in the cage at the zoo. It felt like catastrophe time and I was right. The video organisers had the brilliant idea that people would get a signed photograph of me, then go up three flights to the video store, buy the video and come down again to get that signed. Wrong!! They didn't. I signed only three videos, and 150 pictures!! but I posed for dozens of photographs with fans who did seem pleased to see me – 'You're so much prettier in person,' they said, and I was flattered until I remembered they kept saying that to Dustin Hoffman in *Tootsie*!

Jeffrey Lane [personal publicist and friend] thought that we should leave soon and I agreed. We then went off and did our favourite thing, shopping. Dashed into Gottex and got a few swimsuits for Acapulco and the South of France then zoomed into Donna Karan, then Judith Lieber's for bags, then SAKS, all highly exhilarating, and for me shopping is the female equivalent of fishing. Sometimes you get a catch, sometimes not. Today was a good haul. Was supposed to leave for *Live at Five* at four thirty then they changed it to four. Rush, rush, rush, rush, get there, then they change their minds because of the O.J. Simpson trial [this commenced on 24 January 1995]. Not again?! Does America think of anything else? They thought they were going to put me on earlier then changed their minds and suddenly I'm twiddling my thumbs for forty minutes in the green room. The live interview with a young guy called Matt Lauer went well finally, except for a cackling newsreader hag who sat in on our interview even though it was supposed to be a one-to-one, cracking jokes and throwing wisecracks in my direction. At one point I flirtatiously asked Matt, 'Do you know what the girls in the make-up room call you?' The newscaster quickly pre-empted my feeble attempt at gay repartee and yelled, 'Stud-Muffin!' I said to her frostily, 'Who's doing this interview, him or you?' They all laughed but it was irritating. It's difficult enough doing interviews without having other people push in on it.

Dashed back to the hotel for another interview then changed for the dinner which my good friends Blaine and Robert Trump are giving for me at the café at Mortimer's. A long table for twenty-two was beautifully set with flowers and Blaine and Robert had already arrived and were entertaining Aileen Mehle, otherwise known as Suzy, one of the most influential gossip columnists in New York. She is a lady of a certain age, but still pretty and so powerful that she doesn't have to bother to talk to someone if she doesn't feel like it. The fact that she's come to the party is a major coup in NY society

A great group of friends and acquaintances arrive. Cari Modine who looked fabulous in a short white satin Isaac Mizrahi coat. Her husband Matthew is still shooting a pirate movie with Geena Davis in Malta. 'He's been doing it for ever,' she said ruefully. Joan Rivers looked absolutely great with her new boyfriend, or 'beau' as Americans euphemistically refer to their partners, lovers or boyfriends. Nina Griscom, Renaldo and Carolina Herrera, Ann Jones, wife of rock'n'roller Mick – she's English, and enormous fun. Isaac Mizrahi, Karl Wellner, the husband of Deborah Norville, and Paul Wilmot, who's the number one at Condé Nast and Si Newhouse's right-hand man.

Everyone got along like gangbusters and also got pleasantly sloshed. The food was sensational and Robert made the most enchanting speech about me. He is such a darling man and I was absolutely mortified when I inadvertently called him Donald during dinner. 'Oh God, I'm so sorry,' I gasped. 'That's OK, Jackie!' he quipped. Then Blaine made a beautiful speech. She is one of New York's darlings of the social set and is a truly good and spiritual human being, whom everyone adores.

Wednesday, 25 January 1995

Many photographers at Brentano's and a big queue. An old man came up to me and gasped, 'When's it coming out in paperback?' I don't know which are the professional snappers and which are the fans but I posed, grinned, held the book aloft triumphantly and did all the usual things. I certainly signed about 250 copies which apparently is terribly good for that store. I was slightly disappointed, though, having signed 1,000 books and beaten the signing record at my session at Harrods last year. 'It's not the same here,' said Jeffrey grimly.

The limo drops me at Café del'Alesci on 6th Avenue where I meet Blaine and Joe Eula. He is a delightful man and a great raconteur who worked for years for *Harper's Bazaar* in the fifties, sixties, seventies and eighties doing fabulous fashion drawings. He's just had a heart attack so he's taking it easy but his zany sense of humour and bizarre wit are more outrageous than ever. Blaine as always was adorable, then Jeffrey and Cari Modine arrived looking chic as usual. She must weigh 98 pounds and she never eats!

January 1995 – Florida

Then it's over to the Disney World Theater. I am utterly astounded by the cleanliness and tidiness of backstage. All of the costumes neatly hung, no clutter, no litter, the wigs of the chorus arranged methodically and a large notice to cosmetology to 'Be Tidy'. I suppose that's a new word for make-up and hair, possibly politically correct. God knows everything else around here has to be.

Our 'Question and Answer' time on stage is also being filmed by Disney to be shown on their channel, they have cleared the stage from their five daily performances of *The Sleeping Beauty*. Totally appalled to notice that several people wander out during my riveting performance. I have to say I really hate doing this sort of gig, but it's part of the payment to Disney for them allowing us to do the fifteen satellite interviews. For free! I am asked the question: 'Miss Collins, how many people do you travel with?' I answer: 'One, his name is Jeffrey Lane. Would you like to meet him?' Jeffrey is in the wings, and I see him peeping. He turns bright scarlet and scuttles off into the bowels of the theatre. 'Come on, Jeffrey,' I encourage. 'Come on stage and meet everybody.' But he's disappeared, and I don't blame him. 'Oh well, he's shy,' I tell the crowd. When we finish, backstage Jeffrey says, 'I wish Jackie had seen you do that, it would really have been amazing.' 'She would have probably pushed you on,' I laugh. 'Don't bet on it,' says Jeffrey darkly.

A young guide wearing a tartan waistcoat then ferries us to the Legends of Hollywood shop where they have, I'm glad to see, displayed my book prominently. A large line is forming outside in the now boiling hot sunshine, and it is Instamatic City as usual. I sign about 250 books. I sign stock from the store. 'A book signed is a book sold' – I was told that by my first publisher.

We hotfoot it to the hotel to pack yet again. My clothes are a complete mess, my fingernails ripped to shreds. This packing and unpacking is getting me down. I know that everyone thinks that I travel with a huge entourage to do my hair, my make-up, my packing, and take care of my clothes. Well, Jeffrey's doing everything. I do my hair and make-up, but he is so wonderfully supportive and funny and we are having a super time.

Thursday, 26 January 1995

Arrive at airport to be told the plane to Dallas is late because of weather. Great. That's all we need. Now, I'm on my last legs. A friendly American Airlines exec comes out and tells us that although the four thirty to Dallas is delayed, there are two first-class seats left on the five o'clock. We gratefully scamper on to the smallest commercial plane I've ever seen. It's called an A80 – which I've never heard of. All the men in first class are built like brick shit-houses, all weighing at least 300 pounds! They have scarlet faces and loud voices. I wonder how the plane is going to take off. We have some atrocious red wine then the food arrives. Unspeakable steak and vile over-cooked carrots. I push mine around on the plate but Jeffrey eats everything then looks at me guiltily like a little boy caught stealing. 'I was hungry,' he says with a shy grin.

Friday, 27 January 1995

Arrived late in Dallas so up at quarter to seven feeling ghastly and utterly exhausted. I would kill for another three hours' sleep. I've got Vuitton luggage under my eyes and to my horror I've gained three pounds! How can one not on this merry-go-round?

At ABC studios to do *Good Morning, Texas!* I do the cold opening in which they get in a great plug for my book. We plug plug plug away then Robin Leach from *Lifestyles of the Rich and Famous* comes on. I adore him so we kid around with each other. Then dash over to another studio to do another interview. I'm staying at the Crescent Court Hotel, which is charming and where I stayed three years ago when I was doing *Private Lives*.

Leave Dallas on Friday afternoon after the usual mad rush and arrive in Houston. Jeffrey drops me at Lynn Wyatt's house on River Oaks Avenue and we get ready to go to the opening of Leslie Bricusse and Gregg Boyd's new show *Jekyll and Hyde*. We've all been looking forward to this for a long time as Leslie and Gregg and Frank Wilde have devoted an incredible amount of time to it. Lynn and I go to the theatre to meet the Bricusses [best friends Evie and Leslie Bricusse, composer and songwriting partner of JC's ex-husband Anthony Newley], the Schlatters, singer Robert Goulet and his wife Vera, actress Anne Archer and her husband Terry Jastrow and other luminaries.

George Schlatter jokes that he has seen me on TV so many times and clocks the fact that I had never worn the same outfit twice. 'You must travel with an entourage and sixty suitcases,' he quips. When I tell him it was just Jeffrey, two suitcases and a duffel bag, and that I did my own hair, make-up and packing, he's astonished.

The show is wonderful in the second half although the acoustics make it a little difficult to understand some of the words. The actor who plays Jekyll and Hyde, Robert Cuccioli, is quite, quite brilliant. A star if ever I saw one. He has a brooding De Niro/Pacino quality and makes the change from Jekyll to Hyde incredibly well without the aid of make-up. He has thick black hair and when he turns into the evil Hyde it falls over his face in a saturnine way.

The afterparty is on the fiftieth floor of an amazing building filled with many people we don't know. The tables are taken but we manage to grab one and hold the fort while the rest of our gang arrive. Congratulations all round are in order and it's a merry night indeed. Maxine Mesinger, the influential columnist from the *Houston Chronicle*, sits at our table in her wheelchair. She is very nice and has been writing good things about Leslie's play. When the stars arrive, they are greeted by tumultuous applause.

Robert Cuccioli comes over to our table 'You were magnificent,' I say, and he smiles and says, 'So are you.' Completely overrun by paparazzi as I am trying to have a giggly conversation with Sandra Di Portanova, Evie and Lynn, but the snappers won't leave us alone.

Back at Lynn's guest room it's difficult to find any of my things as there are many objects on every surface. But I manage to get a night's sleep until 6 a.m. when I awake to the strident noise of what sounds like a fire alarm. Go out into the corridor, which is quite creepy, and I have no idea where Lynn is sleeping. Am I in another wing of the house? Go next door and find a boys' room in which a loud alarm clock is ringing. Pull it out of the wall viciously but it still continues ringing. This must be one of those new clocks that get you up in the morning. I don't need to be up at six o'clock today, thank you. Go back to bed and turn on the television to find the most boring old American Movie Classics and fall asleep until nine o'clock.

Lynn and I go to The Grotto, a Houston restaurant where Joan Schnitzer is having a little lunch. Evie Bricusse, Ginger Mason, Jolene Schlatter, Jeffrey and Vera and Robert Goulet join us and we all have a jolly time. Spend the afternoon in bed drifting off watching TV and trying to rest.

Lynn is throwing a black-tie bash for my book tonight. Lynn and I find ourselves wearing similar dresses, me in black lace and sequin Valentino, she in black chiffon and beaded Ungaro. Lynn is in such great shape. I am sure I have gained four pounds on this tour, added to the five I already was over. It's always most difficult to lose the last few. The party is great, very glamorous. Apart from all the usual suspects, a lot of Houston glitterati showed up. Lynn had four tables of twelve. Each one had the names of one of my books, *My Friends' Secrets*, *Prime Time*, *Love and Desire and Hate* and *Past Imperfect*. She is the most fabulous hostess and the food is utterly divine. There are speeches, and then we all go into the drawing room and chat till the cast of *Jekyll and Hyde* arrive to tumultuous applause. Robert Cuccioli comes and sits between me and Evie. All the women think he is highly attractive. I tell him that he's probably going to be a major star and he is flattered and surprised. Very nice young man. That'll probably all change when he becomes famous – there aren't very many nice famous actors in my book. Then Robert Goulet sings. He modestly says that Bob and Linda (the other star) should have been singing and he should not have done it but Lynn insisted. Then Ricky Di Portanova gets very drunk and falls onto Jeffrey. This makes me laugh so much I think I'm going to split the Valentino dress. Jeffrey, as is his wont, goes a brighter shade of pink. Everyone finally leaves at two a.m. and Lynn comes up to the bedroom and sits with me and proceeded to eat about a pound and a half of butter cookies which she had cleverly secreted in a glass jar next to the chaise-longue. Totter to bed at about three, another early night.

January 1995 – Houston

Took the plane to Los Angeles with Jolene and George Schlatter and we had a few laughs. Arrived at the Hotel Bel-Air to find Judy unpacking. I have vowed that it will be a very long time before I will do any unpacking again as my fingernails are in shreds. I lounged around, had a manicure, and then Sue Mengers and Jean-Claude Tramont came over to the room and we had supper. I absolutely could not move, but God, Sue is so wickedly funny that I managed to arouse myself from my torpor to enjoy her jokes.

1996

Saturday, 5 October 1996 – Los Angeles

Arrive on the British Airways flight slightly hungover after hours of eating and drinking and sitting in those newfangled recliners which the cabin crew call 'coffins'. They are very antisocial and uncomfortable. Judy meets and greets and whisks me to the new suite at the Hotel Bel-Air. It's quite luxurious and nobody has stayed here before. Two bedrooms, large living room, all mod cons and tons of closets. Have a fairly good night's sleep but I'm still up at dawn. Luggage strewn everywhere – why do I travel with so much luggage? Outside on the patio, which hasn't been swept for about four days because of the jacaranda tree that has dropped its blossom, I inspect a huge new jacuzzi which hasn't been installed yet. Hollywood is always a mixture of total luxury and a certain amount of squalor. Nevertheless, it's a beautiful day and I start to unpack. I'm disgusted at myself for bringing all these clothes but since I've got to go to Australia, what can I do? At least there's enough space to hang them.

Judy arrives and we totter over to the patio dining room at the Bel-Air for some well-needed bacon and eggs. Girl captain informs us we can't have bacon and eggs. We've got to have the set brunch menu for $38, which is a rather complicated thing consisting of mushrooms, soups and haddock soufflés. After making slight fuss we are told we can have scrambled eggs and bacon. On the terrace below us a traditional Jewish wedding is taking place in the 85 degree sunshine. It is only when the ceremony is over and the happy couple make their way up the aisle that we realise that the bride is Chinese!

Sunday, 6 October 1996 – LA party for Star Trek

I start preparing for the *Star Trek* evening gala at the preposterously early hour of one thirty. Wear Tomasz Starzewski dress from my book party launch last month in London. Who can afford to have a different dress for every occasion – only the pin-thin actresses who are loaned them. Jeffrey Lane arrives promptly at three and off we go to Paramount for the *Star Trek* thirty-year celebrations. Our car pulls up at the red carpet where we're greeted by a phalanx of photographers and news cameras. As I face them for the de rigueur posing and pouting, the sun is so intense that Jeffrey turns bright red and I can feel my make-up sliding down my face. Usual banal questions asked: What did you think of *Star Trek*? What was your favourite moment? How the hell should I know? I never watched the damn thing. However, since I was in one of the favourite episodes, 'City on the Edge of Forever', I try to reply intelligently. Escape from the blistering heat into a cool air-conditioned tented room where dozens of people I've never seen before in black tie and for the women mostly black dress congregate.

Jeffrey and I sip white wine. I 'network' with a few people then greet Bill Shatner, Cap'n Kirk himself. He is shorter than I remember, his round pink face is sweating profusely and he is still wearing a nice curly wig. A sort of silk shirt arrangement with a built-in silk tie at the collar completes his look. Why don't American men like classic black tie? He is with a very attractive girl and we pose for smiling snapshots. I ask Bill a few questions, for example is he MC-ing, is he introducing me? He seems not to know the answer to any of these questions. In fact he seems not to know why he's here at all.

Say hello to George Stevens Jr, who is producing the show and has sent me flowers and a note: *Hey honey, we're going to be living together*. He is referring to the Sierra Towers rented apartment where I will be moving in ten days. It's still only four fifteen and the show doesn't start until five. We are given as our escort minder a young good-looking guy called Eric wearing a black satin dinner jacket, rather well cut, which he says was donated to him by Richard Tyler. At the door Jane Seymour enters with a minuscule young man either side of her. We say hello and she introduces me to her two young sons. Her body looks amazing, considering she had a baby only a few months ago. She is wearing the same dress that the *Entertainment Tonight* interviewer was wearing, a grey embroidered number.

Jeffrey and I go outside for a guilty cigarette, watched with some disdain by the people inside. Then Eric escorts us to a small covered golf cart and we are whisked to the green room. This is a tented area with a few sofas dotted around and a table with some junk food. I sit next to a most enormous sleeping man. He's spread out on the sofa, taking over half of it. He is completely oblivious to the comings and goings around him. A lady of some vintage wearing a bright red thigh-length outfit and knee-length black boots and back-combed blonde hair gushes to me how much she adores me and that she starred in one of the first *Star Trek* episodes. But who is she?

Finally it's showtime. We watch it in the green room, then I'm escorted backstage and when it's time to go on, I walk across the stage praying I don't trip. Always my nightmare. It's five twenty in LA, eight twenty in New York where the show is going out live and one twenty in London. I'm still on UK time. Get quite a few laughs when I say my piece about when people ask me am I that bitch from *Dynasty* I say sweetly, No, I'm the saintly social worker, Edith Keeler from *Star Trek*. Then it's over and backstage Jeffrey awaits. My eyes are bright red – whether from the heat or the exhaustion, I don't know. We sit in our seats next to Anne Archer, who is beautifully dressed and wearing Manolo Blahnik shoes, which I notice most of the well-dressed women tonight are wearing, and her husband Terry Jastrow. 'Why are you here?' I ask. 'With Ethel' – she gestures to the seat in front of us where Mrs Robert Kennedy (Ethel) sits surrounded by dignitaries.

The show is a great spectacle – very entertaining with wonderful clips and fabulous actors making speeches, including Ted Danson and Dr Spock [Leonard Nimoy]. A standing ovation is given to Buzz Aldrin, one of the first astronauts in space. In his late sixties, he is obviously used to being a hero and accepts the applause with charm. Jane Seymour is sitting down the row from us and I wonder when she is going to come on. Curiously enough she does not. The show ends with all of the *Star Trek* people on stage. We then thankfully go out into the balmy California night. On the Paramount backlot, the famous New York street where for some reason the asphalt is soaking wet, we are offered wine, Perrier and canapés. We are now starving. To say I'm hungry is an understatement. Take a piece of pizza and am just having an inelegant bite when I'm papped – I look over and she dashes away gloatingly. That'll give them a few laughs I suppose.

Sally Kellerman joins us. She played Nurse Houlihan in the movie *MASH* and is very attractive, in her early fifties. The three of us stand and have a long chat about women over forty and the problems they face in Hollywood. Sally is very enthusiastic about a new movie she has just made herself. 'My husband put up the money,' she says. 'It's the best part I've ever had. Now, with the success of the *First Wives Club* I think women's projects are going to be acceptable to producers and studios.' We chatter about various ideas and wait eagerly until we are allowed into the huge open area where there are about a hundred tables for dinner. The three of us sit down and start eating the rather wilted-looking salad, which curiously is topped with dried fried onions. I inspect it underneath and find shrimp. Great, that's all I need – to die from my allergy on the backlot of Paramount. A few people sit at the table that we don't know. Jeffrey whispers to me, 'This is the great table that we were promised?' Sherry Lansing comes by to say hello. She is extremely pretty and one of the true female movers and shakers in Hollywood. She can green-light a project at Paramount and has plenty of power. This does not prevent her from being really nice, really down to earth and utterly charming, unlike most of the men in the business who, as soon as they get power, turn nasty. Exchange telephone numbers with Sally, Sherry and a few others, and as we leave I ask Jeffrey what time it is, thinking it must be one o'clock. It's ten to nine, he says. 'Oh God, I can't believe it,' I say. 'It feels like three in the morning.'

Monday, 7 October 1996

Driven to the Sony studios, which used to be MGM. Cannot find the entrance where *The Nanny* set is. Finally arrive and am greeted by a woman nine months pregnant in an animal-print sheath dress. 'Hi. Brenda, wardrobe,' she says and takes me inside to show me the 'fabulous' jacket from Moschino she has chosen for me. She reveals one of the most hideous garments I have ever seen. A short ill-fitting jacket with the words 'fashion fashion fashion' embroidered all over it in different letters. 'I don't like horizontal stripes,' I joke, smiling sweetly. 'Perhaps something in red?' 'Well, you have to wear the same thing as Fran,' she says. 'And as you know, Fran is sort of a flashy dresser.' I swallow. I have a feeling I've made a big mistake accepting this show.

Go on to Stage 6 where the actors' table is set up for the read-through. Meet Charlie Shaughnessy, who's rather sweet and plays Maxwell, and Robert Vaughn, who is playing the rather boring role of my husband, Maxwell's father. Tony Curtis turned this role down, and after reading the script I can understand why. Even though there had been assurances that they had been 'tailoring this for me' they certainly so far have not. Fran Drescher arrives forty-five minutes late. She looks cute with a great figure and enormous hair. We read through, and I'm fairly appalled. The director, Dorothy, an ex-actress, assures me that 'all will change as soon as the writers see this. We really want this to work for you, dear.' After we have rehearsed and blocked I'm feeling more depressed. This is even worse than *Empire of the Ants*.

Justin Pierce [agent and friend] arrives to take me to lunch at the Rita Hayworth room at the nearby big Sony studios. It is what MGM used to be but totally unrecognisable now. I order a glass of wine and the waiters look at me as though I am a pariah. Naturally there is no possibility of having a cigarette. I complain to Justin and he assures me that this is a very good idea for me to do as *The Nanny* is so popular and it doesn't really matter what I do in it. 'It's "the Emperor's new clothes" syndrome,' he says. 'Oh really,' I say. 'Yes,' he says, '*The Nanny* is so popular that anybody who's on it by definition is going to get the benefits.' I am cynical about this.

In the afternoon, after we finish blocking, fifteen writers come on to the set and watch us 'put it on its feet'. They laugh hollowly at some of the jokes. Fran is funny, but then she is 95 per cent of the show and why shouldn't she be, after all she's the producer and the star. I wonder why the hell they are paying me all this money for this basically minor role. Back at the Bel-Air I complain to Judy, then go for a meeting in the bar with my agents Debbie Miller, Chris Barrett and Alan Margulies, and two writer-producers Jim and Bob. They pitch this fabulous idea of a glamorous woman detective. They have had a small poster made of me in a fur coat, holding a gun, surrounded by diamonds and a sort of jigsaw puzzle motif and they pitch the idea, which I quite like.

Totter back to the room and eat half a carton of chopped liver, catching the latest efforts of CBS on TV. I am totally appalled by the quality of what I see. The first is *The Cosby Show* and it's about as funny as a funeral. Bill Cosby looks seventy and Phylicia Rashad is cloyingly annoying. I do not laugh once. Have to have more chopped liver. Secondly comes a new show, *Pearl*, starring that fabulous actress and beauty (not!) Rhea Perlman. Rhea is probably fifty-five and playing an average college student. Malcolm McDowell is playing a professor. He looks highly out of place and embarrassed. I hope the money's good, Malcolm. Can hardly keep my eyes open when *Murphy Brown* comes on and Candy Bergen brings a welcome touch of class to the proceedings. Lily Tomlin comes on as her soulmate. This finally sends me to sleep, thank God.

Tuesday, 8 October 1996

Go shopping at Neimans and Saks with Judy. Try to forget about *The Nanny*. Go to Sierra Towers to see for the first time the apartment I'm going to be renting. Meet Jeffrey there with Judy. It is absolutely great. I'm thrilled to bits. Loads of closets, the most incredible view of Los Angeles. I feel that I like it better than any of the houses I had before, certainly better than Bowmont Drive, and I feel close to family as Jeffrey lives in the building as do the tall and perma-tanned George Hamilton, Diahann Carroll, Sidney and Joanna Poitier and George Stevens Jr. As David Niven Jr said the other day, 'I know thirty people who live in that building.' David lives around the corner too.

Sacha [JC's son Alexander, 'Sacha'] and Erin, his girlfriend, and Jeffrey arrive and we go off to the Academy Theatre for the premiere of *Michael Collins*, the IRA film. Am wearing long brown skirt and lace tights and brown leather jacket. Appropriate for a serious movie, I suppose. Photographers go into feeding frenzy again which is rather flattering. Hobnob with various dignitaries who are there. David Geffen, who is the producer of the film, is in front of us looking extremely casual in a Hawaiian shirt. Carole Bayer Sager, recently married to Bob Daly, arrives. She and I compare eye make-up and hair. We always thought of each other as looking similar and she often gets mistaken for me. The movie was quite confusing about what the British actually did to the Irish to form the IRA. Liam Neeson is wonderful, as was Aidan Quinn, Stephen Rea – Alan Rickman overplayed his hand as usual. Afterwards I am asked by *The Times* for my opinion: 'I believe that the British people are going to be very against this controversial subject.' I say hello to Pierce Brosnan and his beautiful pregnant partner. Hotfoot to Mr Chow, bypassing the party at Chasen's, which I'm sure will be pretty draggy. Bump into Barbara and Marvin Davis and various others.

We are expected to meet Oliver Stone at the restaurant but he arrives over an hour late. 'I had to talk to Steve and Liam,' he says. We discuss the movie ad nauseam. Oliver Stone is a very interesting man with a boyish, rather naughty sense of humour. He is fifty but acts sometimes like he is in his twenties. Erin has decorated several of his houses for his various ex-wives and ex-girlfriends and his children. His girlfriend of the evening is very pretty. Oliver says I should be working more. I totally agree with him. He says that he would like to use me in something. Where have I heard that before? 'Why don't we plot a television series for you in which you play a sort of *Charlie's Angels*-type character like John Forsythe did, but you were training three young guys how to work in the field.' 'Sounds like a plan,' I say. Everyone in Hollywood talks deals all the time. It will be interesting to see over the next few months how many deals and projects and ideas people pitch to me, about me, whatever, and what actually comes off.

We have several bottles of wine and get to talking about sex, which is a subject that Oliver is terribly interested in. I, tongue loosened by Chardonnay, tell a few stories about my naughty past, which has Sacha's eyebrows shooting up to his hairline. 'Mum, Mum, you never told me any of this!' he says. 'Of course not – you don't talk to your children about your past,' I say loftily. 'He calls you Mum?' asks Oliver. 'He's supposed to call me Mummy,' I say, laughing. We bid each other fond goodbyes with promises to meet again, another thing everybody does in Hollywood. Sacha, Kendall and Erin come back to the hotel where we open another bottle of champagne. This is not a good idea since I have to get up early for *Nanny* rehearsals.

Totter into bed and read a letter from my agent in London, Ed Victor, informing me that he really feels strongly I should accept the offer from St Martin's Press for my book even though I do not think it is enough money. He has never gotten me very good deals, Mr Victor, and I'm beginning to think his days are numbered, particularly since he referred to my novel which he has been schlepping around to various publishers as 'once a property has been around it becomes "damaged goods"'. Charming. Well *Second Act* is number 13 on the *Sunday Times* bestseller list now from number 15 last week, so it seems to be climbing. I'm going to wait and see.

Wednesday/Thursday, 9–10 October 1996

These two days seem to drift into each. Wake up on Wednesday with the world's worst hangover. Is it worth it, I ask myself. No, it isn't but we did have fun last night. Get to rehearsal and the script has changed yet again. It is a bit funnier. In the afternoon the CBS brass, plus the dozen writers, come to watch. Justin is there. 'You're funny,' he says. 'It's going to be good.' The fact that I have quite a small part doesn't seem to bother anybody. It's a hit show and that's all that counts. Judy and I go to see *The First Wives Club* at the Beverly Center – it's cute and it's great to see three women over fifty getting the approbation and success that they deserve.

Thursday, more of same except this time we have costume fittings. The wardrobe girl wants to dress me like Fran who, since she's over two decades younger and quite a bit thinner in certain places, isn't really a great look for *moi*, but I'm a sport *n'est-ce pas* so I go ahead with it. Finally compromise on a very short black-and-white pony-print skirt worn with a black leather very tight Thierry Mugler jacket which I found at Saks Fifth Avenue yesterday. They'd like me to wear my skirts thigh-length, but we compromise and go slightly lower. The second outfit is the fabulous red Chanel jacket that I found at Saks that I absolutely covet for myself. I brought an old belt from England that has Chanel written large upon it. I think it is very funny for the show. Everybody keeps on telling me how great I am in this. It could be head-turning but one must never forget that this is Hollywood. It appears that if you have been off the screen for a certain amount of time, people think that you can't cut it.

Since I've been doing it for over forty years, I find that curious. The scenes have been punched up and are funnier, so we start blocking. I'm not happy with the last scene in which I'm standing around like a spare prick at a wedding but told Dorothy, the extremely sympathetic director, and she's going to fix it.

Stay in, eat salad, read junk magazines and watch junk TV. There is so much bad stuff on the air it is terrifying. Judy calls and tells me she's spoken to Debbie Miller from my agency, who says that she's received a call from casting to say how wonderful I am. Hmm, maybe things are looking up. Watch *Friends*, a hugely popular series with six or eight thirty-somethings in it who all apparently are going on strike saying $40,000 an episode isn't enough and they want twice that. David Schwimmer seems to have the most talent, but the girls are pretty. Frankly I don't even smile. *The Nanny* is an infinitely better show and, seeing it now, I laugh very many times. We shall see, we shall see.

Friday, 11 October 1996 – taping day

Got to studio at ten and tried to get ready for the first run-through at twelve, which they also tape at the same time.

I've been given extra lines, different lines, so it's confusing. A four-camera sitcom is a nightmare. I don't think I could ever do it. In between we have to pose for photographs for *TV Guide* and also give an interview to *Entertainment Tonight*, who are snooping about on the set with their cameras subtly placed where they think we can't see them. They love to get pictures of any of us, putting on make-up or doing something untoward. We don't even break for lunch and then at five o'clock we have one hour to eat, re-tweak and then tape with a studio audience at six fifteen. Fran looks great in a series of tight, short, rather garish costumes, which suits her character. She's featuring new make-up, which is very little eyeliner and hardly any lipstick. I don't think it suits her. Renée Taylor arrives today, a hoot as ever. She's been on the road plugging her film. 'Aren't you glad I got you this role,' she jokes. 'Oh, I thought CBS did,' I say.

I feel nervous, but the taping goes as expected. The audience shriek with laughter at the most minor thing. In between, various CBS and TriStar dignitaries and important people come up and tell me how wonderful I am. This is par for the course for any actor or actress. So strongly am I identified with that one role it is hard for them to believe I can do anything else. 'Les Moonves says you should do a series.' How many times have I heard that recently? Renée Taylor informs me that she has an idea for a series. Peter Marc Jacobson confides that he has an idea for me to do a series. If one of these things come to fruition it will be a miracle.

It's a miracle!! The show is pretty good. It's Fran's show all the way with the exception of the old granny known as Yetta who has, as Robert Vaughn says to me, 'only ten lines and they're all the funniest in the piece'. Nevertheless, I had fun, and Judy and Max [Judy's husband, movie director Max Bryer] and Jeffrey and I celebrate at Eclipse.

Saturday, 12 October 1996

It's Tara's birthday [the elder of JC's two daughters] and I call her live while she is doing her three hours on talk radio in London. She's thrilled to hear from me and sounds great. Judy and I then go down to my four storage rooms on Ventura, which are jammed with the decaying junk of the past three years. I'm convinced it is all going to fit into the new apartment and look terrific. What's money for anyway? Most furnishings will need recovering for the Sierra Towers apartment which has been painted and generally tweaked. I'm very impressed by how good it looks. We measure various things and I spot a fabulous dining-room table in a shop which I covet, but it could be a bit steep at thirteen hundred dollars. On the other hand, at Harrods it would be about four thousand pounds. It's so much cheaper than England.

It's party time. Wear new red Chanel jacket as I'm supposed to meet the Davises, etc. at Spago. Nolan Miller [costume designer renowned for his work on *Dynasty*] comes to pick me up. He looks impeccable as usual. I don't want to be late. At Spago, Michael, the maître d', goes into a complete flap and looks aghast. 'Mr. Davis is coming?' he stammers. 'We don't have his very special chair!' Marvin always travels with the chair, which is larger than the average person. 'Perhaps we've come to the wrong restaurant,' I say to Nolan, who is good-humoured and laughs. Michael calls Barbara Davis and we are informed that they expect us at their house, The Knoll, on Schuyler Road. It's still only eight o'clock so we're not late. Big Mistake!

Nolan and I arrive at the lavish palatial mansion, one of the most glamorous in Beverly Hills, to greet Barbara and Marvin, Jolene and George Schlatter, and Kristina Tholstrup, who is the new love of Roger Moore. Caviar is served. Then my sister arrives with Frank Calcagnini and everybody makes really nice and tells everyone how wonderful we are. At ten o'clock the party is over and Nolan and I drive to Century City to Dani Jannsen's glamorous penthouse apartment, where she is giving a party for Clint Eastwood and his new wife, Dina. As usual at Dani's it's wall-to-wall stars and celebrities. She always pulls out some of Hollywood's finest. She has the knack. She's also a fantastic cook and can cook for a hundred people with ease. Among the above-the-title names, other than Clint Eastwood, are Pierce Brosnan, Shirley MacLaine, Jim Carrey, James Woods and James Coburn.

Other movers and shakers on the mogul side are Quincy Jones and Arnold Kopelson.

Forgot to mention: at dinner Marvin asks me what I'm doing and says that I should contact his son, John, who is doing a huge amount of movies and TV series. He informs me that I should have been playing one of the roles in John's latest movie, a role à la Sophia Loren and Ann Margret in *Grumpier Old Men*. 'So who's playing it?' I ask. 'Well I wanted Suzy Pleshette or Yvette Mimieux but they didn't want them, so we've gone with Gloria De Haven.' 'Gloria De Who? She's been out of the business for years' [actress and contract star for MGM].

The party is really wonderful. Dani's place is so brilliant for entertaining as it is one huge room with a balcony which overlooks the lights of Los Angeles so that everybody can see what everybody else is doing. Chat with Michele Lee and her husband, Fred Rappaport. Michele has just finished produ-cing, directing and starring in a movie for television which she discovered herself. 'It's the only way to do it, honey,' she says. 'You've got to find your own material.' It's for Lifetime, who I worked for earlier this year. Hollywood is an industry town and everything is geared toward the industry.

Meet Jim Carrey who is really cute and says he is an admirer of mine and I tell him I'm an admirer of his. Witty repartee. Shirley MacLaine is deep in conversation all night with somebody I don't recognise, but when we speak she seems genuinely glad to see me and I suggest that we get together, which she seems en-thusiastic about. Have a long, long talk with Quincy Jones, who is charming. We sit on the sofa while Dani's new little doggy, a mini toy poodle, frolics – I'm not much of a dog lover, but this one ain't half cute. Clint and his new wife come over. She's very good-looking and sexy and several months pregnant. A woman who knows what she's doing. She's about thirty-something and has got her man. Clint is adorable. Interesting how Dani seems to attract all of these high-profile stars. 'Jack and Sly and Al and Bobby were coming,' she says. (She's a great one for first names.) 'And Bruce and Patti were flying in.' I gathered it wasn't Bruce Willis and Demi Moore but Bruce Springsteen and his wife. We finally leave about two fifteen even though there are still quite a few people there. This is highly unusual for Hollywood as usually everyone is out of there by eleven.

Sunday, 13 October 1996

Wake up and read the *Los Angeles Times*, surely the world's most boring paper, and the *New York Times*, certainly the second. Make several phone calls to England. Talk to Katy and Tara. I miss them so much and wish that we could be together. Meet Roger Moore and Kristina in the Bel-Air patio for the Sunday brunch, which is excellent. John Schlesinger's boyfriend comes by. He used to do my make-up at Fox. Had a fun lunch in which Roger and I discuss the possibility of doing *Love Letters* in March, April and May in Washington and Florida and various other places. 'If we get enough money – and we're not going to use an agent,' says Roger, 'we're going to use a lawyer.' 'Fine with me,' says I. When we go out we say hello to Jane Powell, who looks terrific and apparently never stops working in night clubs, and her husband, Dickie Moore, who used to be a child star.

Monday, 14 October 1996 – moving day

Dash down with Judy to meet our movers at the depository in the valley where I have four 10x10 rooms crammed with furniture left over from the sale of Cabrillo three years ago. They are an hour and a half late which, putting it lightly, has me in a bad mood. The movers have to be out of the new apartment, Sierra Towers, by five o'clock. I'm sure we're not going to make it. The owner of this rather dubious group of movers gives me a version of why they're late. Never mind. Spend four hours going through every box and carton in these four rooms trying to decide what to take to the new apartment and what not to. It's a bit of a nightmare, to say the least. Plus it's bloody hot. The moving boys, all Israeli, are very sweet, and extremely helpful. Judy and I dash to the new apartment and give orders as all the furniture comes in at once. It looks absolutely wonderful, but I'm shocked to realise it's probably not all going to fit in. *Quelle horreur.* They can't finish the move because the apartment building supervisor says skedaddle. Just as well.

Tart myself up at the flat as well as I can and am picked up by David Niven Jr and we whisk ourselves to Le Dome for Roger Moore's sixty-ninth birthday. It's given to him by Kristina, who is nervous and twittery, looking rather pretty in a short very very dressy lace spangly frock bedecked with necklaces, bows and diamond butterflies. Say hello to Marvin Davis and Richard Gully, who informs me that he wrote a fabulous piece about *Second Act.* 'Well, I didn't think it was fabulous when you wrote: "Everyone knows that Joan's no Jane Austen but this is a damn good read",' I say. He splutters and stammers, but after all he is eighty-nine years old, so what can you expect.

Greet the usual suspects: the Schlatters, the Davises, and Quique and Louis Jourdan, who are so boring I cannot understand why they are invited to most Hollywood parties. Kristina is a nervous wreck, clutching my hand and whispering that this is the first party she's given for *tout* Hollywood. There are twenty-six people at a rather beautiful table.

The flower arrangements are stunning. Huge displays of

different coloured red roses, ranging from deep crimson to pale red and the whole table scattered with thousands of rose leaves. I apparently have one of the best seats between Frank Sinatra and Gregory Peck and opposite Roger, who is seated between Barbara Sinatra and Barbara Davis. Mine is not an easy draw because Frank Sinatra is not and never has been interested in talking about anything other than himself, and now that he is, to be kind, getting on a bit, his mind wanders a lot. I am quite sure he doesn't have a clue who I am. I ask about Tina, his daughter, and he babbles on about how wonderful she is and how he hasn't seen her for a long time. Luckily Veronique Peck is on his right and they know each other extremely well so she bails me out many times. Barbara Sinatra keeps a watchful eye on him from across the table, occasionally barking, 'Did you take your pills, Frank? Did you take your pills?' It's frightfully sad to see this golden icon now a befuddled old man. I prefer talking to Greg Peck who, although a little dull, is adorable and regales me with stories about his one-man show and how I should do one.

The caviar and baked potato arrive and Kristina gets up to make an emotionally charged speech about how much she loves Roger and how much he loves her and how much they have enriched each other's lives, etc., etc. We all know this, so as jaded Holywoodians, nobody really wants to hear. Basically all they want to do is eat their caviar and get the hell out of there in time to watch the ten o'clock news. After the entrée George Schlatter makes an amusing speech and Barbara Davis announces gleefully, 'Why don't we all go around the table and everyone say how we feel about Roger.' An audible sigh of horror escapes from everybody. 'I don't want to perform,' mutters Greg Peck, but around the table we go.

Everybody brings out the platitudes. Charlie Isaacs, Richard

Gully, my sister Jackie, Eddie Collins (no relation), Quique Jourdan (who says she is not able to say anything). When it comes to me I say, which I thought was quite witty but doesn't get even a titter except from Roger: 'Darling Roger, I've known you through thick and through thin, and through Tony Curtis.' (They disliked each other.) During everybody's speeches Sinatra keeps saying in a loud voice like a five-year-old: 'What's going on – why is everybody talking – is it time to leave yet?' Veronique Peck tries to soothe the savage beast's brow. Marvin Davis speaks, then Niven Jr, who is very witty, and we finally finish. I'm quite enjoying myself as Niven and I keep making silly faces at each other across the table.

Frank Calcagnini arrives late and is carrying a portable phone and talking into it. 'I can't believe you have come to a private party and are talking into a phone,' I say sternly. 'Hey,' he smiles gleefully, 'this isn't a telephone – it's a TV – I'm watching the ball game.' He reveals a tiny screen slightly larger than a postage stamp on which he is watching minuscule figures dashing about, throwing a ball. I know that Americans are addicted to Monday night football but this is ridiculous.

After the birthday cake and the de rigueur singing, there is an absolute stampede to the exit, but I can't get out as Kristina grabs my arm in terror. 'Why is everybody leaving?' she whispers. 'It's only just turned eleven o'clock.' 'That's Hollywood,' I say, and whisper to Niven, 'We must stay for a bit longer.' I still don't understand this desperation to get away from any social event, but everyone does it. Niven leaves to do escort duty with Mr and Mrs Sinatra. He comes back paler than usual and sweating. 'God, what a fucking nightmare. The paparazzi were all over us – they want to get a picture of Frank not exactly looking his best.' I realise that that is what those scumbags want. Frank Sinatra looking old and frail is definitely a big money-spinner for some greedy pap, and the tabloids buy into it. It's really so horribly sad that no one is allowed any dignity or privacy any more. Niven and I are photographed coming out arm in arm 'Newsome twosome,' he smiles. 'Oh, Barbara [his ex] will love this,' I laugh.

Tuesday, 15 October 1996

Wake up and realise this is it. Time to check out of glam Hotel Bel-Air and check into glam Sierra Towers rented apartment. Say goodbye to Frank Bowling, the affable manager, and drive fast to my new flat. I'm quite excited to see that it is looking good. As I unpack boxes with manic desperation, it's a bit like Christmas. I keep on revealing silver photograph frames, candles, little objects, clocks, all kinds of tchotchkes – many of which I wish I had given or thrown away. They've been in storage for years. But too late now, must get rid of a lot of this stuff. At two o'clock in come the Israelis, bringing loads and loads of other stuff from storage. Run around like a chicken with its head cut off wondering where it's all going to go. Have to keep on making instant decisions as they keep on saying, 'Where's this going, where's this going?' The bossy owner keeps on telling me that I can't put all my pictures in a cupboard because they will break. 'Don't tell me what to do,' I snarl in true Alexis fashion. His young assistants look shocked but pleased that I've told off their autocratic boss. The living room now looks like a mini version of the house I had at Cabrillo Drive. I'm not sure whether I like this or not. I think I like it. The bedroom, which is about an eighth of the size I had in Cabrillo, is also rather similar because of the same furniture. Saunter up the stairs at about seven thirty to share a pizza with Jeffrey in his apartment.

Wednesday, 16 October 1996

Still moving and shaking and playing Dollhouse, always my favourite thing. Take a break at two thirty and Judy and I trot down to Hamburger Hamlet to meet Bob Sidell. We have just signed a deal for me to be the spokesperson for Bob's SilkSkin cosmetics in London. I hope this will be more successful than some of the other things that I have done in the past; nevertheless I believe in his product and I'm very happy to be doing a good line of skin cosmetics. He gave me a nice cheque, which is always gratifying.

Change and get ready for Jeffrey's drinks party welcoming me to Sierra Towers. Jeffrey's apartment is dressed in its best finery. Three good-looking waiters (obviously out-of-work actors) circulate with champagne and canapés. The dining-room table is piled high with succulent dips and the party room soon fills up with the likes of Dani Jannsen, George and Jolene Schlatter, Mary Fran, Allan Carr, Alana Hamilton, Michele Lee and Fred Rappaport, Brenda Vaccaro and husband Guy, plus many others. Roger Moore and Kristina arrive, and as usual he becomes the centre of attention. It's amazing what being 007 can do to an actor even one sixty-nine years old! Roger is one of the nicest people. Possibly his niceness prevented him from becoming a great star with legs before Bond. Peter Marc Jacobson, the producer of *The Nanny*, arrives and bends Judy's ear for a long time. I muscle in to find out what's going on and he tells me that he has an idea for a sitcom that he really wants me to do and believes would be the perfect vehicle for me. It sounds rather interesting. Called 'The Diva', it is about an actress fallen upon hard times (oh no, really?) who has a son who is gay and lives with another man. The possibilities for this I can see are endless, but the political correctness in this day and age has to be addressed subtly so as not to offend the delicate sensibilities of so many.

We all get really mellow and are having a wonderful time. Get in deep conversation with Ros Kind. She's Barbra Streisand's sister and must suffer from sibling rivalry. She is prettier than Barbra but does not have the personality or charisma. 'Don't you remember when you used to play with Jason?' I signal to Sacha, waving my eyebrows madly and mouthing 'Jason'. My usually intelligent son looks perturbed. 'Yes, Jason – Jason Gould,' I stress. 'Elliot's and Barbra's son. Ros is his aunt.' Endless emphasis on last syllable and Sacha finally gets the point. He actually told me when he met Jason Gould many years ago when they were both children, Jason took him off to his mother's closet where he kept on appearing swathed in ostrich feathers and gold lamé. Sacha tells this story to Ros and it receives a weak smile.

Some of the big guns don't appear. The Davises have other plans, the Aaron Spellings have to have dinner with the Ray Starks. Nolan arrives and shrugs. 'They just didn't feel they could get out of Ray,' he says. 'Too bad,' say I. The party, which is supposed to run from six to eight, finally breaks up at nine thirty and the Bryers, Jeffrey, Sacha and Erin and myself totter down the street, yet again, to Hamburger Hamlet for a nourishing turkey burger and yet more wine.

Thursday, 17 October 1996

Wake up at three. Luckily there is a television so I'm able to see the ravishing Claudette Colbert in Cecil B. DeMille's 1930s version of *Cleopatra*. She is utterly captivating and no wonder she was a star for so long.

The shrill ringing of the telephone announces David Inman from Boxtree's worried voice from London. Have a long sad conversation. We're both depressed that my book has not got on to the bestseller list. 'Don't you realise that the public still perceive me as the woman that was categorised by Random House as not being able to write, writing gibberish and being an idiot,' I say sadly. 'There's no point in me schlepping about the countryside going to Manchester, Cardiff and God knows where and talking on television about how fine my book is and what good stories are in it. We've got to have either ads or other people saying it's good.' I am depressed. I call Katy in London and she is feeling good. We talk about the forthcoming photo shoot that she's doing.

Judy and the telephone men arrive to put in the new system. Judy tells me that the system is going to cost $2,200 dollars. 'What!!' I shriek. 'Are you mad? I'm not going to pay twenty-two hundred dollars for this. I don't want a system – I just want two lines.' Point taken, so we leave to meet Max at the Hi-Fi TV shop where I purchase within short order a gigantic TV, a new tape-deck which does everything except wash dishes, and a video plus some other charges. This comes in at $3,000. Oh well – so what, it's only money. Then we go to Nolan's emporium where I try on the dress I'm going to wear for the Carousel Ball, then see a fabulous pull-out sofa that would be perfect for entertaining, although the only guests so far are going to be Katy and Biggins [Christopher Biggins, actor and media celebrity] – I'm not Fawlty Towers.

The apartment is looking better and better and when we get back, the maid, Alicia, is beavering away, making it look even cleaner. Tart myself up in red Chanel. Lenny Gershe [playwright and lyricist, a close friend of JC] comes to pick me up. 'We must not be late for the Wilders,' he says, and off we go to Le Dome. Billy and Audrey arrive on the dot of eight. She is looking ravishing as usual, chic as a *Vogue* cover in black-and-white dogstooth Chanel with a white carnation. Although she is about seventy-four she looks divine. I'm sad to see that Billy is looking quite old, and is quite stooped. His voice is soft and he seems to have lost his zest for life. Nevertheless the evening is excellent and we talk like mad.

Don Zakarin, my lawyer in New York, calls. The other side – the enemy, those bastards Random House, have made an offer, $850,000. I know it's a ton of money that I could well do with, but I have to balance that out with the fact that they have done a great deal of damage to my writing career. Lunching with Jeffrey Archer two weeks ago I said to Jeffrey, 'Do you think the Random House case has hurt my writing career?' 'It's damaged you seriously,' he said. Well, nothing like hearing the truth. I said I'd sleep upon it, which is what I intend to do.

Friday, 18 October 1996

Started with the telephone going, the front door opening, and streams of people coming in to hang pictures, position furniture and put up shelves. A total madhouse and by the end of the day I could barely stand up. Met Roger and Kristina and Sacha and Erin at Le Dome again for dinner, which was nice, then went up to Allan Carr's house, where he was reopening his Egyptian disco from the seventies. The parking lot girls were extraordinarily rude and while Sacha was dealing with them, I went in. Allan waddled over and said, 'How well do you know your son's girlfriend Erin?' He sounded so unusually aggressive that I was rather surprised. Allan is usually sweet and laid-back. 'I know her quite well, why?' I asked. 'Because she's asked three girls here – they've crashed my party and I'm absolutely furious.' His body was quivering with rage and there's a lot of stuff to quiver. When Erin and Sacha came in, he confronted her and he pointed to one of the girls. 'I've never seen her before in my life,' said Erin extremely coolly, very calm and ladylike. Allan sort of mumbled a vague apology, but Sacha and I were seething with rage. Jeffrey was there and the rest of the party were people that one would avoid at all costs. Went down to the Egyptian disco where a large black lady with short cropped yellow hair was singing along to the seventies sounds. The disco was all done in rather old-fashioned flashing lights and satin cushions – not a fabulous scene. Jeffrey, Erin and I did some disco dancing. I can't believe I really used to love this sort of stuff. There were a few nonentity-looking people jumping on the floor. In no way did it have the flavour of the sixties, seventies or even the eighties. We got out of there as soon as we could. Not before Allan and Robb gave us a quick tour of the house. Allan was apologetic, as well he might be. Jeffrey took me back home and we were appalled at the fact that Allan had been so rude.

Saturday, 19 October 1996

Wake up to the most unbelievable sound. Feel as if I'm a child in air-raid Britain as the loud siren is going off all over the city. Call down to the concierge, who doesn't know what it is. Call Max and Judy, who say that probably some alarm has gone off. This is my morning to lie in. Oh well. C'est la vie. Maybe one of these days I'll get a good night's sleep, I haven't had one since I've been in LA.

Jeffrey and I go into various antique shops around Melrose. Everything is so much cheaper than London. And there are some very good bargains to be had. Meet Judy and go to a screening at the Academy: Geena Davis in *The Long Kiss Goodnight*. It is nothing but violence and special effects. Then we dash to the Screen Directors Guild to meet Max and see Anthony Hopkins in *Surviving Picasso*. He is absolutely wonderful and the film is a delight.

In bed by eight thirty to get an early night. The wind is howling like a banshee and the building starts creaking as though I am on a schooner in the middle of the Atlantic. It is quite terrifying. Call Jeffrey, who assures me that this is perfectly normal for this building – great. Finally, at half-past nine, I call one of the maintenance men to take a look. Manuel smiles sagely as he comes into the bedroom and he listens to the creaking of these ancient timbers. 'Ah yes, this is perfectly normal,' he assures me. I try to get to sleep by covering my head with pillows and my ears with plugs and finally succeed.

Sunday, 20 October 1996

Lunch with Peter Marc Jacobson, Fran Drescher's husband, at The Ivy. He's very enthusiastic about this idea he has for a sitcom for me to do called 'Diva'. Naturally, it's about an ex-actress, the one who has a gay son. It's quite a good idea and I express approval. Peter is very powerful now since he is the producer of *The Nanny*. I'm cynical about anything in this town as everybody has a deal, but if anybody can get anything off the ground Peter Marc Jacobson should be able to. He is attractive yet there is something bland about him.

Call Don Zakarin to discuss the latest offer from Random House concerning the settlement. They want to offer $850,000, which I do not consider is fair enough considering I've spent close to $600,000 on lawyers' fees, not to mention the tremendous damage done to my writing career. We decide we will not accept their offer but will settle for a million and a half. See what will happen.

Jeffrey picks me up and we go to Alana Stewart's in Brentwood for a small, very fun dinner with her and her new boyfriend, Joe, Wendy Stark and husband John Morrissey, and a very amusing agent called Michael Black, who tells hysterical stories about Bette Davis. Sit around the dinner table until half-past ten telling stories and really enjoying ourselves. It's practically unheard of in Hollywood to do this, as everyone wants to escape and nobody really has that much to say to each other. Joe tells very funny stories about Danny Aiello and Joe Pesci. John Morrissey keeps on staring at me and saying how great I look. Probably because I'm looking younger, wearing a black leather jacket, black jeans, white shirt and quite simple hair. Youth's the thing in Hollywood!

Monday, 21 October 1996

Huge excitement as my giant Sony 21-inch screen arrives and is installed. It certainly makes a difference. Another day of putzing around the apartment and going out and buying various things. It's beginning to look really fabulous. Gary Pudney picks me up and we go to Mortons for dinner – the de rigueur Monday nightspot. It's full of bigwigs and studio heads, most of whom I don't recognise. 'That's Ted Harvard sitting behind you,' says Gary. 'He's now head of ABC – don't you remember, we had lunch together when you were doing *Dynasty*. He likes you a lot.' 'He doesn't seem to know who I am now,' I say jokingly. There's a kerfuffle at the door as the Marvin Davis entourage enters. Barbara does the room, stopping at every table. I don't understand how everyone recognises each other since everybody looks so alike. Gary is cooking on all levels now that he's out here, although, as he says, 'Get all the money you can and sock it away so you can go and live where the real people are – the other side of the Atlantic.' He's right – there's a barrenness to life out here, particularly some people. True friendships are rare, and I consider myself lucky to have a handful of close friends.

Tuesday, 22 October 1996

Another day of handymen, getting this apartment looking good. Jeffrey picks me up at six forty-five and we go to a reception for Michele Lee for Power Women in Films. She has pulled out quite a few faces: Allan Carr, Suzanne de Passe, Joan Van Ark, Donna Mills, the director of *The Nanny*. Michele has produced, directed and starred in a television movie for Lifetime. Having producer Fred Rappaport as a husband has not hurt Michele's career one bit. He is important and rich enough and can push her to get projects. Met Jim who works at Disney Animation. He was very complimentary about me and asked me if I had done any voice-overs for animation. I said, 'No, but I would certainly like to.'

The movie was OK, slightly over the top and quite boring. Afterwards schmoozed again with this, that and the other, and Jim asked me if I would be interested in doing something for a Disney film they are making. 'Yes, of course.' Debbie Miller, my agent, was there so she was able to get in on the deal, which I'm sure won't happen.

Had a turkey burger at Hamburger Hamlet with Jeffrey, Allan Carr and his boyfriend Robb. We were descended upon by Ruta Lee and Toni Holt, two ladies of a certain age – even older than me! – and who definitely wear more make-up. They had just come from seeing Jerry Lewis opening in *Damn Yankees*. 'Can you believe it – none of the Hollywood contingent was there,' they said, twittering around us like so many birds of plumage. 'Did you enjoy the show?' I asked. 'Oh, we didn't stay to see the show,' they said. So much for Hollywood. 'I may have a surprise for you,' said Allan, referring to a movie he's doing. If any of these offers I seem to get on a daily basis materialise, I shall be one very productive woman. But I won't hang by the thumbs.

Didn't take a sleeping pill so I was awake too early the next morning. I have never slept as badly as I have in this apartment. Got ready for a photo shoot at CBS for *The Nanny*. Tony, who shot lots of photos on *Sins*, was very enthusiastic and I twisted and turned and posed and strutted while CBS executives came down to gush about how much they loved me and 'needed me on the network'. It is quite extraordinary actually. Does everyone get this treatment?

After Nolan's for a fitting, drove to the old MGM studios. Went into the old Irving Thalberg building, now Sony. Japanese-owned. Met Justin Pierce and we went to Barry Josephson's office. He is the head of all product at Tri Star and a very big wheel indeed. We had a meeting about my playing the Endora part – the mother of the young witch – in a TV version of *Bewitched*. It sounded really exciting and something I would love to do as she is the kind of character that I know I can do well. As we left, Josephson seemed extremely enthusiastic. Aren't they all? And when we parted, he said, 'You are so beautiful.'

'How do you think that meeting went?' I asked Justin. 'It is good, it's good,' he said. They're always good, I thought to myself.

Nolan picked me up at eight o'clock and in our best bib and tucker we segued to Yvette Mimieux and Howard Ruby's fantastically palatial and beautifully decorated house in Holmby Hills. Yvette has got enormous charm and is an incredibly romantic girl. She showed us the new chandelier which she had hung in the garden in a tree where she and Howard dine à deux. The dinner was for Boaz Mazor, who works for Oscar de la Renta, and is most amusing and entertaining. Betsy Bloomingdale [socialite and philanthropist, widow of Alfred Bloomingdale, heir to the Bloomingdale's department store fortune] was there looking fabulous and elegant as usual. As were Mary [Hayley] and Selim Zilkha [Iraqi-born British entrepreneur] and Barbara

Thornhill and her husband Gary Wilson. I thought the food was pretty average but it was an elegant 'Hollywood evening' as opposed to the do-it-yourself jeans and T-shirt. I like Yvette and she uses her money to good advantage.

Finally took a sleeping pill. If I don't get some sleep I'll probably have a breakdown.

Thursday, 24 October 1996

Meet Sacha and Erin at The Ivy. Supposed to be joined by Gary Pudney, but he doesn't call or show. That's Hollywood folks. At the next table is Jennifer Aniston, the current crème de la crème heartthrob of *Friends* on TV. I've never seen such slender arms. Also at the next table is an unrecognisable Cheryl Tiegs. Why do women over forty think they can go around wearing no make-up. I looked at Erin and say, 'No woman over thirty should ever go out without make-up – you're a girl after my own heart.' Jeffrey joins us and we discuss Sacha's upcoming *Vanity Fair* layout, and his exhibition which he is planning on 1 February. We swap Polaroids from our various shoots yesterday. His is absolutely fabulous from *Vanity Fair* and for the first time in a photograph I can see the incredible combination of Tony and me in his face.

Dine with Jeffrey, Debbie Miller and Chris Barrett, my agents, and Mark Paresio, a new literary agent at Metropolitan. Drai's restaurant is buzzing. Thursday night must be the night to be here. Joanie Schnitzer is sitting with Boaz. Plus the usual suspects. We have a fun dinner in which yet another television idea is pitched to me by Mark. This one I really like more than anything else. It's a one-hour drama called 'Georgetown', set in Washington with all its political plottings and plannings. I would play a Pamela Harriman type. It sounds fabulous. I would make a good Pamela Harriman, although I don't think that I possess her Machiavellian way and manipulative spirit. The usual paparazzi are outside. I am wearing my new simple look. Since Hollywood has embraced this in a big way, you leave the pearls and the glitz and the diamonds and the big hair at home. This is a bit difficult for me as I rather like it. I notice Joanie Schnitzer hasn't left hers at home.

Friday, 25 October 1996

Woken at five thirty by the most godawful creaking and blowing around the building I have ever known. It is really like being on the high seas and I don't like it one bit. I don't know how I can continue living here if this goes on. The noise is frightful and the walls sound like the masts of the schooner. I am furious that I am awake. Watch the channels and then spend the morning exercising. I'm trying to get myself ready for Australia but can't concentrate because of this noise and feeling of insecurity about the building. It's clear as a bell outside – I can practically see all the way to Catalina and downtown LA the other side, but the noise continues. Speak to Jeffrey about it and he said he was awake at three thirty. 'Ignore it,' he says. How can one ignore it? In a town famed for its earthquakes, one is never completely at ease. In any case to have a building shaking, rattling and rolling does not a happy camper make.

Went with Judy to Disney Studios and met Jim again. The studio is immense and sprawling with its own Disney shop that sells the usual Donald Ducks and Goofys. People sure do like to buy crap here. Into the recording studio, where one could put half of Pinewood Studios. Talk about high-tech! A little girl is doing a voice-over for the princess and they quickly stop all proceedings and get me set up. I read a rather unfunny prologue:

'Once upon a time there was a princess and a peasant' – that sort of thing. They are vociferous in their enthusiasm, but isn't that always the case here? Nothing is ever just OK, it's always absolutely wonderful or great or fabulous!

Jeffrey tells me about the man who pitched the CBS idea. 'They love you,' Jeffrey says. But they have a similar idea for Julie Andrews. They've got a deal with her. Typical. It'll be interesting to see how many of these irons in the fire get hot. In the afternoon called Peter Marc Jacobson re his pitch on Sunday. Bottom line is he hasn't pitched it yet – he's still working on his own deal. Two down, and two to go!

Get ready for the Carousel Ball. Nolan comes to pick me up in a white Jensen Chevy, which looks fine – very forties. We both have a stiff vodka on the rocks before we go. Outside the Beverly Hilton, the usual screaming fans and screaming paparazzi. They scream my name so loudly that my ears hurt and the flashbulbs are so dazzling that one could go blind. Nolan is very good-natured and smiling. Well, natch, I'm wearing his dress and give him credit all the time. 'You've brought glamour back to Hollywood,' screeches Roger, one of the nicer paparazzi. He has said this at every event I've been to. All of the interviews, from E!, *Entertainment Tonight*, Reuters, etc., all ask the same banal and stupid questions. 'So what brings you to an event like this, Joan?' I am never stumped for an answer. They are so stupid I am gobsmacked. Then they've got this new little ploy in which they say, 'So give us your take on what is the best and the worst of entertainment in 1996.' What am I, a MORI poll?

Nolan and I fight, yes literally fight, our way through several rooms packed with gawpers and smartly dressed, facelifted, toupee'd, overly tanned, skin-stretched Beverly Hills matrons and their partners to the back room where the Davises are having a 'photo opportunity'. Say hello to Joanie Schnitzer, Boaz Mazor,

Sidney and Joanna Poitier and Pamela Stephenson. All of us are wedged outside the room from where I can see the following luminaries inside talking to each other: Geena Davis and her husband Rennie Harlin and Brooke Shields. Well since they're all over six foot, it isn't too difficult to see them through the crowd. Shirley MacLaine is chatting to Kevin Costner, who is really cute, if a bit thin on top.

We go in and get a vodka and Rod Stewart comes up with his gorgeous wife. He is very funny, charming and witty, more than you can say for most here. Within twenty seconds of him and me talking, Barbara has zoomed in like an eagle to its prey and almost elbows me aside to get her photo opportunity with Rod. What is so amazing at these occasions is that it's flashing the molars at the camera and saying, 'Darling, you look wonderful', and frankly my dear, nobody gives a damn. Except for the odd person like Shirley MacLaine. We chat and she is really sincere and interesting. She says, 'Isn't it unbelievable that Goldie, Bette and Diane are in the biggest hit of the year and they're not even getting scripts.'

'It's really tough for women over forty in this town,' I volunteer.

She looks at me with a pitiful sneer. 'Honey, you don't know the half of it – it's not just tough, it's impossible,' she says.

'Gary Pudney said he had something he would love us to do together,' I volunteer again.

'Yes, I know, he's over there.' She gestures to a seething mass of people but I can only see Raquel Welch undulating in a too-tight red dress.

Shirley says that while I'm in Australia I should call her friend, Andrew Peacock, who was Liberal Party leader there twice and who she is rumoured to have had an affair with. We go into the Grand Ballroom which is just packed. They must have made over two million dollars for the charity. The Davises really do pull out all the stops. On the way to our table we stop to greet Sophia Loren with her son Eduardo. She's looking very good in a very tight-fitting copper-laced Nolan, but she has very odd teeth. They look like they've been carved out of ivory and are very big! There are so many people in this town with shocking teeth. I think dentistry is better in England. Sophia is the only other woman there who is clever enough to wear a hairpiece. We exchange compliments about Nolan and how wonderful he is, and Marvin's son, John, cracks a few jokes to Nolan about 'You better get her dresses in time for the picture.' She is making a picture for John Davis.

We wend our way towards table number 7, which to our horror we find is right next to the podium beside the band and seated at it are five smiling Arab gentlemen, some of whom look vaguely familiar. 'I'm a friend of Viviane Ventura,' gushes one. 'How fabulous,' I gush back. One of them is Prince Thingamy something and the other owns Saks. But Nolan and I don't know them so are not well pleased to be seated here. Raquel arrives with her boyfriend, who looks uncannily like Pierce Brosnan. When I mention this to him, he says arrogantly, 'Yeah, but I'm better.' Unbelievable, the egos of some people. Raquel is wearing the most awful rhinestone necklace, bracelet and earrings and she is not exactly svelte, although her skin is good. She sits next to Nolan. I'm dying for a cigarette, even though we've only sat there for two minutes, so Nolan and I dash to the bar and have a cigarette and a vodka and talk about how ghastly the ball is so far. In the loo I see Melanie Griffith in a fabulous strapless black-and-white dress. 'Didn't you just have a baby?' I ask in complimentary amazement. 'Yes,' she smiles; she has nice teeth. 'You look fabulous,' I say. I must stop telling everybody they look fabulous. But I don't want them to stop saying it to me. It's the buzzword – 'You look great – you look fabulous. How are you?' 'I'm good.'

Back to our seats. Barbara Davis comes on stage and gives an extremely long speech which begins by her saying, 'George Schlatter told me to make it quick.' 'She certainly didn't listen to him,' whispers Nolan. It is the same speech I have heard two years ago at the Carousel Ball, but it is really moving. Then Sidney Poitier makes a long speech. It is now ten and we've been here for almost two hours. Jay Leno comes on. I happen to think he is one of the unfunniest men in America as well as one of the most unattractive. He is also wearing more make-up than me and Raquel put together. But everyone thinks he's funny, even though I cannot manage a twitch to my facial muscles. He introduces John Travolta, who is adorable and charming and makes an extremely short gracious speech which leaves us all wanting more, and then introduces the Bee Gees. On they totter; one of them, Andy I think, has got those dreadful teeth again. But this time they are sparkling white. Instead of doing what we'd all like to hear – some medleys from *Saturday Night Fever* – they do three dreary old songs. Yawn, yawn.

Then on comes some faceless woman that nobody's ever heard of and sings a dreary song, and then on comes Penny Marshall, who played Laverne in *Laverne and Shirley* and is now the numero uno directrice in this town. She is wearing the most ill-fitting black dinner jacket, a pair of dirty black and white sneakers, laces undone. She is, to be kind, pushing fifty. She wears a creased shirt and her long blond hair hangs unkempt. She is a proud lesbian and she has one of those high squeaky voices that make Fran Drescher sound gruff. She introduces Whitney Houston, but then announces that Whitney has laryngitis. A collective groan goes around the audience. Whitney is who we really wanted to see. Instead we are treated to a ten-minute film clip of Whitney singing. Not quite the same. But then Whitney comes on. She is extremely gorgeous, elegant in a skin-tight, obviously Hervé Léger dress. Her voice is husky, so she obviously does have laryngitis, but she sings it pat.

It is so cold in the ballroom you could hang meat. Raquel has borrowed the Pierce Brosnan lookalike's dinner jacket. When I ask her conversationally where she met him, she's snappy and irritable and doesn't want to answer. Dominick Dunne drops by and tells us a bit about his new book. 'What's it about?' smiles Raquel, flashing the molars. 'The O.J. trial,' says Nick. 'Ooh, is there a part for me?' asks Raquel eagerly. Nolan and I raise eyebrows. Then life comes on stage as Rod Stewart bounds on in a blue satin jacket and waistcoat, spiky hair, tight trousers and energy to burn. He's fifty-something but is absolutely fabulous and everybody really enjoys him. As the show comes to a close, the collective crowd stands and bursts into applause. It's ten thirty – late for this town. Nolan and I cleverly go the back way via Trader Vic's where we see David and Barbara Niven and several other people with their 'goodie bags' on the ground. They are rummaging through, taking out what they wish to keep. We didn't get a goodie bag but I don't care. I'm just happy to be out of there.

Nolan and I come back to the apartment and have another stiff vodka and he proceeds to tell me about various secrets which, dear diary, I repeat only to you. Ha Ha.

'Elizabeth is such a mess,' he says sadly. 'She has nothing to live for. She doesn't care about anything – she's so fat that when I see her I want to cry. All her beauty has completely gone and she just lies around and does nothing.'

'What about her grandchildren and children?' I ask.

'Oh, they're around,' he says. 'But she's just not interested. She's just not interested in anything.'

'What about her sixty-fifth birthday celebration coming up?' I ask.

'She doesn't want to do that,' he says. 'She's just doing it, I guess, for something to do. I don't think she's going to work again. I tell you, Joan, it is so, so sad.'

'Well, Sophia seems in good shape,' I volunteer.

'Yes, she is,' he says. 'But she is always being told what to do by her sons. For example, they'll say you can't wear that, you can't look sexy, you're sixty-something years old, you can't do that.'

'Wow, if my kids said that they'd get an earful.'

'Well, she lives for those kids,' he says.

'That's very sad too.'

We ruminate some more about the fate of over-fifties actresses and finally end the evening. He's such a darling and one of the true friends that I have in this town that I can rely on.

Saturday, 26 October 1996

Stella Wilson has not been able to take the flight to Australia. She is stranded in London. BA has not been able to take off for some mechanical reason. Great. We have all sorts of dramatic conversations and I get a fax in the middle of the night that she is going via Perth. It's twenty-three hours on a plane for her, poor thing. It's only fourteen for me. Only! Ha! I'm woken up horror of horrors yet again by this bloody creaking apartment. It's driving me crazy. It's also very frightening. It's five o'clock and the wind is whistling and all the walls creak. Turn on Turner Classic Movies and get Elizabeth Taylor and Peter Finch in *Elephant Walk* and fall into a fitful sleep.

October/November 1996 – Melbourne

Sometimes I feel that my life is one step forward, two steps back. I have been here for five days in Sydney, Brisbane and now

Melbourne working my ass off with television interviews, radio and most of all literary lunches and dinners in which I have sat and talked and made jokes and conjured up as many amusing anecdotes as I possibly could. Basically trying to enchant the five hundred-strong audience. Today I did a very good signing at Myers. There were six or seven hundred people there. Channel 10, the news programme, was shooting the entire thing – the huge crowds, the gushing fans, the whole over-the-top bit. Tonight Stella and I were watching the five o'clock news. They showed Priscilla Presley who is also here in a shop signing her perfume. The news said that thousands of people were there for her then showed a shot of me with the last twelve stragglers who were at my signing at the end of it. The announcer laughed, 'Joan Collins had so few people at her turnout that she left an hour early!' I simply could not believe it – neither could Stella. It's the most unkind and unjust kind of publicity, deliberately done to put me in a bad light. The press reports said that 'I was cool to my fans', when my face is stiff from smiling at the hundreds, nay thousands, of people whose books I have signed and whose hands I have shook. As I sat on the stage tonight talking to this Ernie Sigley and being as funny enough and genuine enough to elicit an excellent response, I suddenly felt like some kind of a whore. What am I doing this for? Harper Collins, my publishers, never even sent me flowers! It is really a drag. It's hard enough to write books, let alone schlep all over the world plugging them. Talked to Ken Follett in Sydney who was here promoting his book, *The Third Twin*. 'It's a rat race,' he said. 'It never stops but you've just got to go on and do it.' I don't know if this is really what I want. It's acting I like. Although I love writing books, the combination of being a high-profile celebrity actress and author obviously rankles with some people. I'm upset that my autobiography *Second Act* does not seem to be doing well in the bestseller list in England. Nobody can understand why. I understand it too well. It's Random House's fault for the outrageously slanderous things they said about my writing when they sued me.

On an upbeat note, other than the fact that Australia has been fun, I got an ecstatic fax today from both Justin and Jeffrey in LA both saying that *The Nanny* ratings had gone through the roof, like a 10 rating and a 17 share, which is fantastic. 'The best they've had at CBS since September,' said Justin. Had a long talk with Justin who said the time was right to get one of these series off the ground. I know that he is right, but I just wonder if I'm still on this bad luck phase. I try to think exceedingly positively about everything, but I know that there are things against me. Alexis. My age. My so-called celebrity reputation as a difficult bitch (thanks, *Dynasty* producers). My reputation, according to many people, that I can neither act nor write. That's really a great thing to have to carry after forty years. More than forty years of hard slog in this business. In Sydney had the usual dinner with the usual bunch of people who are all excited about future projects with me. Brian Walsh, who is one of the heads of publicity at Fox Tel here, and Kirn Williams, who is the head of Fox Tel. It's always extraordinary to me how these people have this incredible enthusiasm when they're with me and yet it all evaporates as soon as I leave town. I wonder what's going on in Hollywood. Spoke to Lance [Reynolds, entrepreneur and friend], who's ecstatic about the *Nanny* rating and wants to push with the Patricia Kluge group for *Prime Time*. I told him to go ahead. I tell everyone to go ahead. Surely *one* of these things will happen? Fax from Charles Duggan [theatre producer] that he's still working on *Love Letters* for Roger Moore and me. Wonder if that will happen.

Great news from Don Zakarin in New York. Random House want to settle and have offered 1.1 million! We don't think this is enough since I'm in the hole for six hundred thousand in legal fees, not to mention the aggravation, and total loss of reputation that I think I've suffered from those sonofabitch bastards.

After today's signing went to the Melbourne national gallery and looked at some of the most beautiful paintings from the William Paley collection. Matisse, Monet, Picasso. Absolutely exquisite. They also had some fabulous old masters, Gains- borough, Romney etc. It was very calming to walk around there for an hour, even though I kept on getting recognised. I have a wonderful bodyguard called Johnny Santo. He looks like he sounds. Short, dark and wiry, and I wouldn't want to mess with him in a dark alley. He keeps an eye out for me all the time and he really is a hotshot at his job.

Sunday, 3 November 1996 – London

Finally got home after several days of pure slog. The Australian papers seem to like printing lies like saying I wasn't charming to my fans. Some of the papers said I acted like a stuck-up bitch. The most aggravating thing was Channel 10, who photographed my signing session at Myers for an hour which I thought was strange, then proceeded to show it on the night's television when there were only about twenty people left and compare it with Priscilla Presley's signing of her perfume, when of course she had loads of people, as did I. The news took great delight in saying that I had a very low turnout as compared to Presley! They really are complete fabricators but I console myself with the fact that they are also saying this about Princess Diana, that she had low turnouts of people, which of course is not true. It is utterly exhausting this constant telling of anecdotes and sitting on the stage and being cross-questioned about every story in my book, of which there are many. Having to remember them and repeat them. I am not a stand-up comedian, but this is what I appear to be doing, as I am having to entertain a roomful of 500 people. After that I have to sign all the books for the fans. They are all incredibly supportive and tell me that I am an inspiration, and how much they adore me or their mother or their daughter adores me or why don't I come back to television. Blah-blah-blah! This is very encouraging. However, on a less encouraging note Peter Marc Jacobson and Fran have just broken up! Typical. So now, of course, he's too strung out to pitch our series, 'The Diva', to CBS. Spoke to my agents who pitched the idea of 'Joan', the hour-long thriller series, to Leslie Moonves at CBS. He passed on the idea, which I figured he would anyway. Debbie Miller said that he would like to slot me into an ensemble series. We'll see. It's obvious that I still have pulling power on TV. It just astounds me that the networks don't seem to want to harness this. We'll see what happens.

Monday, 4 November 1996

Had lunch with Katy [Katyana, JC's younger daughter] at Scalini. The contrast between here and any Los Angeles restaurant is quite marked. The noise level here is so high that one can barely hear oneself talk. Everyone's squawking, staring, telephones are going off and it's like the bloody League of Nations. Can't really talk to Katy as it's pretty stressful. Bump into Madeleine Lloyd Webber on the way out towards Harrods. Don't recognise her, which goes down well, but the wind was blowing so much I was trying to hold on to my hat. She was very charming and said she and Andrew would be in New York when I was there. Sue St Johns [a close friend] and I have dinner at nine at The Ivy. It is quite jumping. Everybody comes in from the John Swannell showing. I haven't been able to go as there have been things going on all day. Had a meeting with Lance and Tom. Lance seems to think that *Prime Time* will be going and wanted to know my 'window'. At the moment it's not so much of a window as an enormous sheet of plate glass over my entire professional life! At The Ivy, Adrian Gill and Nicola Formby are there with Paul Raben at one table. At another is Nicky Haslam with various London jetsetters including the ubiquitous Tara Palmer-Tomkinson, the current 'It' girl of London café society. Why, I fail to see. She is plain, veering towards horsey, and eagerly informed me she had done a layout with my Tara last week who had 'taken her in hand'. The Ivy is really the best restaurant in London and we had great fun.

Tuesday, 5 November 1996

Lunch with Evie and Leslie at Mimmo's in the front section. The back part, Mimmo's pride and joy, is just too noisy, filled with boring businessmen. Caught up on all our news. Then went home and tried to get over the jet lag. Packed for Paris and then sashayed to Theo Fennell's opening of his new jewellery store. It is the old Meridiana restaurant and Theo and his partner, Richard Northcott, have spared no expense. It is dazzling. Dozens of friends to greet including Lily Mahtani, the Delevingnes, the Bricusses, Fiona Fullerton and Susannah Constantine, Charlie and Tita Carter, Will and Sue Boyd and darling Nigel Hawthorne [actor best known for his portrayal of Sir Humphrey Appleby in *Yes Minister* and *Yes, Prime Minister*] with his partner Trevor Benton. London's usual social subjects were there, including Tamara Beckwith, Tara Palmer-Tomkinson, Mogens Tholstrup, Tim Jefferies, Koo Stark, the ubiquitous Linleys as in David and Serena, Isabel Goldsmith and Lucas White, Gordon White's son, now one of London's most eligible bachelor boys. Robin, the Fennells, the Bricusses and Nigel and Trev went to Daphne's, which was swinging. Mogens was there with nineteen-year-old Yvonne Hervey, Marchioness of Bristol (Robin used to be extremely close to her father the Marquess of Bristol). And in a corner was Goldie Hawn with someone who seemed excessively thrilled to be in her company.

Wednesday, 6 November 1996

The crack of dawn came far too early as Stella and I pull our ragged selves together and rush to Paris to launch *Too Damn Famous*, which translated into French is *La Gloire et Les Larmes*. Arrived in Paris at twelve thirty and had to wait forty-five minutes for the luggage. Paris, as usual, wove its magic on us and the Ritz was as ever welcoming, warm and wonderful. We have connecting rooms which the publishers are paying for. The publishers, L'Archipel, are small but they are pulling out all the stops to make me feel very welcome. Met the director, Jean-Daniel Belfond. A beautifully wrapped package from Christian Dior awaited me with a lovely scarf from them. More than I got from my publishers in Australia, or even in England. From them I received not even a carnation!

Dashed to the television studios through rush-hour traffic with Emmanuelle, the rather sweet French publicist. The journalist Daniella Lumbrossa was utterly charming and plugged the book seventeen times. This is so different from England and America where they seem to resent a celebrity coming on to sell their wares. As I said in my book, do journalists really think celebrities *like* to go and talk on TV just to talk on TV? Then back to the Ritz, do more television shows, from one television studio to the next and one interviewer to the next. All are respectful, charming.

Thursday, 7 November 1996 – Paris

Stella and I lunch at one of our favourite restaurants, Voltaire, and then managed to get some quality time at St Laurent before we went and did *Gala* magazine at the hotel. Met friends in the Ritz bar, where it's all happening. Doris Brynner asked me if I wanted to borrow anything from Valentino. I said, 'Yes, why not.' One of the most difficult things about these tours is that they expect you, or more precisely me, to always be in something new and different. That's too expensive for me.

Off to Le Doyen restaurant where Homero Machry [French publicist] is giving me a party for my book. *Tout* Paris seems to be there and I am engulfed by a sea of smiles, air kisses and paparazzi flashes as I come in wearing Nolan's ever popular black-and-white striped beaded jacket. Among those I'm very pleased to see are Wendy and Dino Fabbri, Jimmy Douglas, Nelson Seabra, Betty Catroux, Joan Juliet Buck, Diane de Beauvau-Craon who is fizzlingly effervescent and adores to hug one and run her fingers through one's hair. (This was done to me by David Hasselhoff at the Carousel Ball and it's not my favourite form of greeting, but at least it means they care.)

Many others are there, and at my table is São Schlumberger with Claude Roland [former adviser to the Mayor of Paris], whom I adore and who gives new meaning to the saying 'full of joie de vivre'. He also throws fabulous parties. He asked, 'How old is São?' I jokingly said: 'Pushing ninety.' At which point, she, who I thought had a touch of hearing disorder, looked over with a sharply narrowed eye. 'Shit, she heard,' I gasped. On my right was Alexis De Redé, who is the grand homme d'affaires of Paris. He has supposedly the most wonderful apartment in Paris and he assured me next time I was here he would adore to give a lunch for me. He was quite charming and we discussed Cappy

Badrutt, whom we both adored. The food was pretty naff. Having told Romero I was allergic, guess what the first course was? And garnished with mussels, no less. Had to ask for a salad which did not go down too well as it took them so long to bring it my plate had still not arrived while everyone else had nearly finished eating. Throughout dinner paparazzi circled like baby sharks.

At the crack of eleven, Homero grabbed me by the hand, and we went into a vast pulsating room full of Generation X, the beautiful people, pre the post-baby boomers. I don't know what the new name is but a lot of them looked more than freaky to me. The music was rather good, 1970s soul and rock, and we sat stiffly in a corner to be stared and pointed at by the crowd. After ten minutes of this and not getting a drink I went back into the main dining room to find that most people had left. Just as we were getting ready to leave, Jacqueline de Ribes, whose dress I wore two weeks ago, arrived in all her Valentino glory. ('She wore that the last time I saw her,' someone whispered to me.) 'Well, at his prices, I'm not surprised,' I said. 'She can't be always finding a new outfit.'

We try to leave as I'm exhausted, but Didier [Didier Leblanc, antiques dealer who also represented the Didier Aaron Galleries in Paris, and a good friend of JC] informs me that it is pulsating with people and paparazzi, so we've got to go out through the kitchen. Eventually we escape and go back to the Ritz with Stella, Didier and Didier's friend, Robert, where we discuss the evening's festivities and have a lot of giggles.

Friday, 8 November 1996

Not so full of giggles when I have to get up at eight to be ready for a *Téléjours* magazine shoot and interview. That goes well, but then when I go in for the most important interview with *Libération* newspaper, the photographer has cleverly set the scene so that I am supposed to be in the shower, peeping coyly out from behind the peach curtains. Since I'm wearing a red Chanel jacket and a tight black skirt and heels, I do not think this is a good idea. We retire outside while the less than charming photographer has to redo his lights. *Libération* only has an hour and a half to do the interview. When we return, the photographer offers me two choices of background: 1) the peach curtain, which is taken off the shower; and 2) the most hideous burgundy-purple mohair blanket I have ever seen. Neither goes well with pillar-box red Chanel. 'Why don't you use this beautiful room?' I say, looking at the exquisitely painted yellow-panelled faux-Louis Quinze. He shrugs disdainfully. 'Everybody who does this wants something different.' As a photographer he's about as innovative as tomato ketchup. I stare balefully into the camera, knowing these pictures will be shit.

One journalist is desperate to start. He seems very studious and anxious to do a good job, so I put him out of his misery and we go and do the interview in Stella's bedroom. Then to Brentano's for a signing of *La Gloire et Les Larmes* which goes pretty well. Jean-Daniel comes by to say he is interested in doing *Second Act* in French. That would be wonderful as I am less than pleased at the way it is going in England.

Arrive in London so tired I can barely speak, but go to see Tara at her flat. She is full of enthusiasm and excitement and new projects and bubbling on all levels. I feel like a limp old flannel.

Saturday, 9 November 1996 – London

Another bad night's sleep. I think I am seriously over-tired. Jet lag upon jet lag, plus my mind keeps on working on so many levels. The last thing I want to do is a signing at Selfridges, but that's what I do. Stella comes with one-year-old Amy, who is thrilled to be in the centre of the action. Quite a lot of people in the queue and Selfridges have done us proud. My most faithful fan, Sara, aged sixteen, who has 'loved me since she was three years old' is first in line as usual. Someone rather disdainfully refers to her as Eve Harrington.* I think we probably sign four hundred books. Then Santa Claus is going to come down to meet and greet. But a tiny hiccup occurs. Santa is stuck in the lift! Since this is my horror of horrors, I sympathise. Santa finally arrives – he gives me a teddy bear, I give him a book and we give the paparazzi what they want.

Dash to San Lorenzo to meet Philly Lawson and Katy. Girls' lunch – Stella and her daughter Amy too. Service as usual, totally appalling. The waiters are so arrogant. After asking for a drink and waiting fifteen minutes, I say to our waiter, 'We've ordered our drinks some time ago.' He looks at me disdainfully: 'This is a very busy restaurant.' You can say that again. Wave to Angharad Rees, who's at a table, and Janet de Botton and Princess Firyal, who are in a corner. Just as it gets slightly quieter and we are about to have a bit of conversation, in come Los Paraguayos, all four of them. They are now considerably older than when I first saw them in Acapulco some ten years ago, but their music is as wonderful as ever.

Monday, 11 November 1996 – London

My secretary comes over and we go through stacks of mail. I have clothes in every room for my forthcoming three months. New York, Los Angeles, Mammoth Lakes, Acapulco and New

---

* The ambitious young fan in *All About Eve*, who preys on her actress idol.

Zealand. Since I never pack light anyway, this means that I'm going to have to take every possible combination of clothes from bikinis to ski boots, and arrange it all carefully in different rooms with labels on the suitcases. Isabelle the concierge comes up to do the packing. Tonya arrives to put me through an hour of exercise, which I really need. Then dash to Harry's Bar to meet Stuart Wells for a quick business discussion. Harry's Bar is wonderful. I do love the food. Say hello to Nigel Dempster, who is unusually friendly. I wonder why?

Later, I go to the doctor to find out why I'm having such sleeping problems and get several prescriptions for sleeping pills. Then have a meeting about my forthcoming launch of skincare products called SilkSkin, which Bob, who was my make-up man on *Dynasty*, is launching. Carolyn Neville is a real hotshot and if I can believe anything she says, this is going to be very good. 'I truly believe you can't sell anything, a can of ketchup or a book or a lipstick without advertising behind it,' I say. She thoroughly agrees. I think this is one of the reasons why *Second Act* has not hit the bestseller list: it has had no reviews and ads, which I am admittedly bitter about, but life goes on.

Katy arrives looking beautiful and we go to meet Andre Van Graan and Robert Fry at Andre's offices on Harley Street to discuss various things. Then we are late for Una-Mary Parker's book launch party. Not only that, but the IRA had decided to play silly buggers again, so Marylebone High Street is closed and we have to go all round the houses to get to Una-Mary Parker's house. We arrive at eight thirty, which is when it is supposed to be over, and greet, naturally, the paps. Una is looking a little exhausted, understandably so. A few friends are still there: Angharad Rees, Nickolas Grace, David Wigg and his boyfriend Matt. He is great fun.

Tuesday, 12 November 1996

Met Jonathan Lloyd, who is going to be my potential new agent, at Harry's Bar. He took me up to Curtis Brown and I met the thirty-five employees, all of whom seemed enthusiastic. Amazing how enthusiastic everybody is at meetings.

Finished the final packing. To my horror, it's now fifteen pieces, but I am on quite a worldwide trip and a girl needs practically everything. Got tarted up and Biggins came over and had hysterics when he saw the luggage piled in the dining room. 'And you're going on air miles, too!' he shrieked. 'It's too camp.'

Katy arrived and we went to the Dominion in the pouring rain for the opening of *Scrooge*, Leslie Bricusse's new musical starring Tony Newley [Anthony Newley, actor, singer and songwriter and married to JC between 1963 and 1971], which I saw before in Birmingham four years ago with Theo Fennell. He was there with gorgeous Louise, and Roger Moore and Kristina, and Doug Hayward [renowned London tailor] sitting in front of us. We sat through two and a half hours of the same. I know Tony's potential and sadly he didn't reach it tonight. His voice seemed cracked and hoarse, and the stage was far too dimly lit. Leslie's lyrics are less than sparkling, as is the book. All in all, it was pretty disappointing, but I guess as Christmas fare that will do for the pundits.

Backstage to the usual melee of gushing fans, but at least not too many photographers. Tony and Tara had to give an interview to GMTV, which was slightly embarrassing as I did not want to upstage him, but I was put in the middle of the group. I ended the interview by saying, 'You look tired, Tony, why don't you take your clothes off?' This got a snicker, at least. Tara, who has become Miss Social Butterfly of London, looked great in her slinky dress and full-length fake fur coat. Katy also looked terrific. I don't think I'm prejudiced by saying this about my daughters. Managed to escape horrible and dreadfully sad goodbyes to Katy and Tara. I loathe goodbyes, but I couldn't face the party as I knew it would be hell.

Biggins and I dashed to The Ivy where we had a raucous evening. The consensus is that the show is not great, but will probably do well as it had $2 million of advance bookings. I hope it does well as I invested £5000 in it. Went into a slight fan frenzy when Lucian Freud came in. 'My God. He never goes out,' said Biggs. I consider him to be the third-greatest painter of the twentieth century, along with Picasso and Matisse.

My last night in London for at least two or three months. Naturally, couldn't sleep again. Got up, walked around, checked all baggage. I am a disgrace with too much luggage, I know it, but what can you do?

Wednesday, 13 November 1996

British Airways to New York in 'the coffin'. These recliners are fine when you go straight to sleep, which I did after four glasses of wine and a large port and watching Demi Moore's fabulous thighs and Burt Reynolds's ridiculous toupee in *Striptease*. I was awakened by a stewardess shaking me, which threw me. 'Don't touch me,' I snapped, alienating everybody around me. 'I don't like to be pushed awake.' It reminds me of the Blitz when it happened every night.

No car to meet me in New York – somebody got it wrong – but BA was wonderful, so I was piled into a massive limo along with my fifteen pieces of luggage and we sailed to the Plaza Athénée. Then I unpacked four of the cases, had a quick nap, then went to meet Peter Brown [New York-based English businessman and once assistant to the Beatles' manager, Brian Epstein] for a drinks party at his gorgeous apartment in Central Park. Then on to the Luxembourg Restaurant, which is a sort of bistro with rather good food.

Thursday, 14 November 1996 – New York

Spent the morning getting ready to do the *Geraldo Rivera Show*, which was a paean of praise to me. He made me sound like a mixture of Mother Teresa, Joan of Arc and our dear Queen Elizabeth. At one point, I almost felt teary as he was so effusive and so sweet. Of course, it's all true! Afterwards, my PR was effervescent about how amazingly positive the interview was. 'He can be so difficult, but he obviously adored you and what he said was beyond belief.' True. It was quite extraordinary.

I had a series of meetings in the bar at Plaza Athénée, one with my possible future agent, Russ Galen, Jonathan Lloyd's partner, who was extremely positive about me as a writer, and yet said that there was obviously an unofficial blacklist against me which I had to do something about. He thought the St Martin's Press deal was good, particularly with Sally Richardson. He was interesting and very blunt and I liked his ideas when he talked about the future of my career as a writer and not just what's going on now. Basically, we need damage control from the Random House fallout. We were joined by Don Zakarin, my lawyer, who explained details yet again, all the mishmash, Mickey Mouse stuff of the trial, and whether or not I should accept $1.1 million as against the potential $2.7 million that I could get. It's all unbelievably complicated, the bottom line being the least I will get is $500,000 or $600,000. It's still pretty good money, and I'm not greedy, but what should I do if I'm out of pocket?

Robert Trump arrived in a limo to pick me up, and we joined Blaine and went to Sirio's buzzing and trendy new restaurant, Le Cirque. We joined Andrew and Madeleine Lloyd Webber, who were in fine form. Naturally, the first thing Andrew said, as is his wont, was 'Why won't you take singing lessons? I want you to play in *The Merry Widow*.' He then started to hum, la la la la la, which I hummed along with him, his insistence. 'Isn't that fabulous,' he said to Madeleine. The whole thing was more than a little embarrassing, although I like being sucked into Andrew's enthusiasm for doing something with me. I think he's got the Hollywood chat down pat, however, as I don't see myself prancing around the stage in a black basque playing the Merry Widow.

Terrific evening and the food was great. Mucho discussion about a mutual friend. There ain't no love lost between her and Madeleine. 'I'm not talking to that woman,' she said crisply. For somebody so young (she's only in her mid-thirties), Madeleine is quite admirable. She has taken to understanding showbusiness with a vengeance, although it's probably horses she prefers. Blaine was looking very jeune fille in her simple Marc Jacobs pantsuit, and her hair in the Jennifer Aniston *Friends* style. I do not particularly think this suits most women, and I thought Blaine's hair was too fine for this style, but she is so adorable and charming.

Sherry Lansing came by the table to say hello and that she was calling Sue Mengers later to give me word on Jean-Claude's progress as he's got the big C. On my way out we were greeted by a man who I didn't recognise until he said, 'Joan, don't you recognise me? It's Peter Bren!' I was delighted to see him as he and Linda used to be two of my closest friends back in the sixties, no less! Went over to the table to greet her, and we promised to definitely get together the next time I'm in New York. I always promise to do this with people, but there are so many people to see, that one ends up not seeing anybody really, except the counter girls at Bloomingdale's, Bendel's and Saks!

Tuesday, 19 November 1996 – Los Angeles

Back again. Spent yesterday in a complete depression of jet lag, out of work, and what the hell am I doing here. The apartment is great, but I am feeling blue. Luckily, by this morning, it had passed, thanks to a good night's sleep. Did a shoot for the cover of *Beverly Hills 213*, the local give-away paper that is desirable for those who live and die in Beverly Hills. Then went to the Peninsula and did a little blurb for Oscar Levant's bio on the A&E network. Talked to Debbie Miller, who told me that Peter Marc Jacobson was in a complete decline over his separation from Fran Drescher. He seems unable to do anything with work and, therefore, our project is on hold. This seems to be typical of every project I ever discuss. How anybody ever gets anything to fruition is beyond me. Still, we will barrel on.

Lance Reynolds picked me up and we discussed again turning my novel *Prime Time* into a movie. He is always talking enthusiastically about what's going to happen to it. At this moment in time, I'm dubious about everything, but one's got to keep the faith. Went to the Academy for the premier of *Shine*, an Australian film that is absolutely brilliant with the most superb performances, particularly from Geoffrey Rush, who is astonishing as the flawed pianist. Went through the usual gamut of paparazzi. Why? When do these pictures ever appear? Said hello to Martin Landau. The party afterwards at Chasen's was a dreary affair. Chasen's, which I remember as being the most glamorous and scintillating of restaurants, is now a boring, cold, cavernous place, with several buffets of food, served on plastic plates and forks! Most of the patrons who came from the premiere were drearily, if not appallingly, dressed and there was little glamour to be seen.

I spoke to Geoffrey Rush, who seemed slightly dazed by all the attention. An Australian actor who has been in work all his life (he's in his forties), he's a friend of Lance's. 'Being in Hollywood is like a dream,' said Lance. 'Yeah, a nightmare,' I said. While we were talking to him, I got an impatient tap on the back from some pushy broad who I didn't recognise. It turned out to be Victoria Principal and her husband, the famous plastic surgeon, Dr Harry Glassman. (She insists she hasn't had anything done!) She was eager to say hello to Geoffrey Rush.

On a sad note, Jean-Claude Tramont went into hospital yesterday, but they were unable to operate. He had a biopsy and is in intensive care. Had several telephone calls with various people about this – my sister Jackie, Barbara Davis and Sherry Lansing; all of us are extremely concerned. Then Sue called me, her voice breaking, but wisecracking through it all. She said that he was bearing up and that if there was anybody he would like to see, it was me. 'He'd like to see a star, honey. He'd like you to come into the hospital. If we send a car for you, would you come?' 'Of course,' I said. Feel very philosophical about death and illness. One must appreciate every second, and I'm angry at myself that I get pissed off sometimes with my life, which is pretty goddamned good. So what if one doesn't have a TV series or a movie. Having one's health, one's loved ones, good friends, and the future of several idyllic months in the South of France to look forward to.

Talked to Jonathan Lloyd today and sent a fax to Ed Victor firing him, and appointing Jonathan as my agent for the St Martin's Press deal. It's time to change horses, though this is hardly mid-stream!

Wednesday, 20 November 1996

Spent all day doing photographs with Sacha for the portrait he's going to do of me. Then Gary Pudney came to dinner with Sacha and Erin, his girlfriend. My first dinner party at Sierra Towers – so ordered food in from the local Italian restaurant. It was absolutely great. Gary still besotted by Elizabeth Taylor's forthcoming sixty-fifth birthday celebration, which he is producing. He regaled us with anecdotes about her. Example: 'How am I going to do all of this on February the sixteenth without a husband?' she wailed. 'Oh, don't worry. It's three months away. By that time, you'll have one,' he assured her. Everyone finally left at twelve forty-five, not before Sacha said that the Patrick Nagels on my walls were 'mired in the eighties' and I had to get rid of them.

Thursday, 21 November 1996

Sacha came over for more pictures, then Lance picked me up and we went for lunch with Ehrich Van Lowe and Evan White, his agent. We talked about a potential sitcom starring me about a mother who doesn't want to let her son leave her. Here we go again! Ehrich was charming and a big mover and shaker in the show-running and producing world. He has a successful sitcom called *Homeboys from Outer Space*! I can't believe a show called that would be a hit, but, yes folks, it's true. Very positive meeting in which we agreed to meet again and then pitch to the agency. Had a call from Peter Marc Jacobson, who seems to have recovered from his separation from Fran Drescher and was again full of enthusiasm for our project, 'Diva'. We would like to pitch to Fox next week. Well, what can I do? One of these things must come off, surely? If Peter is going to pitch 'Diva' and Ehrich is going to pitch the mother–son combo, let's see if the best man wins.

Picked up by Dan Moss and whisked in the pouring rain to the Raffallo Club to meet Anne Archer and Terry Jastrow. The place was filled with cackling single women, behaving utterly appallingly and staring at Anne and me and making catty remarks. It's basically an upmarket knocking shop. Anne is very intelligent and we're on the same wavelength, particularly about women's issues and the difficulty of work for actresses. 'I haven't worked for over a year. All the older girl parts are going to Rene Russo,' Anne said without bitterness. She said it like it was, but the way it is is not good. Hollywood is a cruel, hard town for actresses, any way you slice it. And if you're over forty, fergeddaboutit!

Friday, 22 November 1996

Got up at the crack to go to KTLA Live, where I pitched a charity for brain-damaged and handicapped children. It's a very worthy cause indeed. However, it is so hard to get money for small charities like this which are not trendy or supported by bigwigs like David Geffen and Elizabeth Taylor (who support AIDS) or the Marvin Davises (supporting children's diabetes). Nobody realises the number of handicapped children, both from birth and from accidents, and how much help they need. Did the best I could.

Lunched at Le Dome with Wendy Stark, David Niven Jr, Eddie Collins. One of those great English-type lunches in which we all smoked and drank without feeling like a pariah, which is what usually happens. Charles Benson arrived late and bumbling, and we planned an elaborate gossip story that we would make up during lunch to see how long it would be before he managed to get the tidbit in a column. Luisa Moore came by, with her son Geoffrey, as did Natasha Fraser and Ellen DeGeneres. Sitting in a corner was a woman with the most terrible face job I've ever seen. She shall be nameless, but she was married to a very famous actor and is a real estate agent. She had silicone implants in her cheeks some two decades ago. These slipped down her face in some unfortunate manner and she has since had thirty – yes count 'em, thirty plastic surgeries to try and correct this. She looks like Dracula's grandmother, and is the epitome of Hollywood's quest for beauty gone wrong. If I looked like that, I think I would move to Afghanistan and take the veil.

The lunch went on and on. As Niven said, 'It's one of those lunches.' Jokes galore, scurrilous and politically incorrect, which I love. Went home to watch myself on *Geraldo* to find that it had been pre-empted by the O.J. Simpson trial. Will we ever hear the end of this ghastly murder? The flat was in an uproar. The bed hadn't been made. There was a man showing Judy how to fix the TV. All in all, it was not a sanctuary. Got several faxes from various people. Ed Victor had accepted me firing him graciously and so I am now with Jonathan Lloyd. Got a call from Betty Miller at my fabulous agency. NOT. She informed me that although she had been in talks with CBS, they were not prepared to go forward with me 'on anything particularly right now', even though *The Nanny* had great ratings and even though they 'loved me' and thought I was 'part of the family'. What a load of utter crap, but one must accept this if one is going to live in Tinseltown and try to make a project work. 'The trouble is,' said Debbie, 'I think CBS still visualises you too strongly as Alexis.' This is really shattering and horrible news. 'How long must it take before a character that you did is forgotten?' I asked bitterly. It was so frustrating that I went home and straight to sleep.

Leonard Gershe picked me up and we went to Billy and

Audrey Wilder's for dinner. As usual, she was the epitome of chic. How can a woman make just a white blouse and black trousers look chic? How does Audrey do it? As well as smoking and drinking like a trouper. Their apartment was, as usual, beautifully designed and decorated. Other guests were Barbara and Richard Cohen. She used to be married to Cary Grant, is very English, very nice, very proper, and I think probably a bit of a tartar under all the sweetness and light. He used to go with Linda Evans when we were making *Dynasty*, and was a great pal of Jackie's. Linda was in charge of all the seating of guests for the Thursday night screenings. Over a period of five years I was only ever invited to one of them! Does this say something about the Collins–Evans relationship?

Audrey served the most delicious tartare I've ever eaten, large reddish-pink caviar eggs covered with sour cream and topped with beluga. With this, she served lashings of vodka. Needless to say, I had several. The conversation got on to the Davises and the forthcoming wedding of Dana. 'We are not going,' said Audrey. 'First of all, I've given so much to her charities and we never get invited to any of their parties. Besides which, why should I spend five hundred bucks buying a present for a dame I hardly know.' Audrey is so wonderful because she doesn't give a damn about what she says and she says it straight!

The Wilders are old Hollywood royalty, of which there are few left. I can really only think of the Pecks as another couple who epitomise the golden age of politeness and glamour, talent and great living. James Stewart has apparently become a recluse. Sinatra is not in good shape, although everybody is trying to pretend he is fine. And with the exception of Lou and Edie Wasserman, the rest of them are long gone. I guess Brad Pitt, Keanu Reeves and Johnny Depp are the new Hollywood royalty. Fat chance.

Saturday, 23 November 1996

Jeffrey and I went into Beverly Hills. It was a beautiful day. The tourists were out in force in their baggy shorts and dirty sneakers and T-shirts. Some of them were snapping and Jeffrey had to stop me being photographed. Went into Tiffany's to look for Christmas cards; people were milling around and sucking soft drinks, dressed as if for the beach. I know I'm horribly old-fashioned, but I find it an affront. Didn't like the cards there, so went to Francis Orr and found a perfectly adorable Christmas card featuring three palm trees in different colours. Lunch at Drai's Café. Victor Drai seated us. He's dyed his hair blond, but to me it looked completely grey. Then Jeff and I went to Century City to try to get in to see the new Streisand flick, *The Mirror Has Two Faces*. To our dismay, it was sold out for both the four and five o'clock screenings. She's a popular gal.

A quiet weekend, mostly spent with Judy and Jeffrey seeing several movies, and shopping. Saturday night, went to the Gardenia restaurant with Wendy Stark and John Morrissey, and Michelle Phillips and her partner, Geoff Tozer, and saw the Linda Purl thing. Quite good, but nothing to write home about.

Monday, 25 November 1996

Received a message from the British Consul General, Mr Merrick Baker-Bates, that he wanted to talk to me. He had a message for me from John Major. How exciting, I thought, figuring that Major wanted to give me the gist of the speech I'm making on the thirteenth with the Anglo-American group.

Instead, Mr Merrick Baker-Bates enquired: 'Mr Major would like to know how you would feel about accepting an OBE – Order of the British Empire.' My mouth dropped open. I mean, this does not exactly happen to a girl every day. I was completely thrilled and said, 'Well, of course, I would be delighted to accept.' I mean, who wouldn't? It's a wonderful honour and, considering that I'm not having the greatest success with my career right now, it gave me a very optimistic feeling. When I told Judy we both jumped up and down like teenagers and got goose pimples. Must keep this a deep, dark secret, however, as news won't be coming out until the New Year's Honours List.

Yvonne came over and we moved pictures around, taking away the Patrick Nagels and replacing them with my railway posters, and then organising for various trees and shrubs to be moved.

Dined with Jackie and her fiancé, Frank Calcagnini, at the Davises with the charming couple Anne and Arnold Kopelson. He is one of the most important producers in town, having produced *Platoon*, *Outbreak*, *The Fugitive* and many other huge commercial films. He asked me who my agent was. When I told him Metropolitan, he sneered: 'I don't think Metropolitan could actually start a piss-up in a brewery.' He told me that he would soon be going to Fox and had a great deal there for television. He said he would be interested in working! I told him that I'd been talking to a few studios but had not had too much feedback. He looked at me in amazement. 'But you're Joan Collins,' he said, 'a huge television star. You should be able to get anything you wanted from the network.' Hah, I thought. How little he understands. He wants me to call him, and I shall follow up on this. Obviously, I've got to start becoming a bit of a hustler. Which I hate doing.

Tuesday, 26 November 1996

The winds have become ridiculously strong. Woke up, yet again, in the middle of the night and had to take a pill. For somebody who is anti-drug and anti-pill, this is becoming ridiculous, but I do feel that good sleep is essential. Barbara and David Niven Jr came to pick me up, went into the bedroom and heard the horrible, terrifying creaking in the walls. 'I've never heard anything like it,' said Niven. 'It's disgusting. How can you sleep?' 'I can't,' I said simply. 'It's a nightmare.' 'I'll send you something over,' said Barbara soothingly. 'Something that will make you sleep. I can even sleep when Niven is snoring with this.' We went to La Cielo, an open-air restaurant, to meet Charles Benson and Allan Carr. The wind was howling like an absolute banshee, but Niven insisted on sitting outside so that we could smoke. Being a smoking pariah means you take your life in your hands, for not only were all the tall heating fixtures swaying, but halfway through dinner, with an almighty crash, the window caved in behind Allan and a huge slab of glass, about two foot by one foot, suddenly fell and almost sliced his shoulder in half. He looked suitably stunned and we were glad to report it was only Plexiglas, but we hastily moved inside. Charles Benson, who is supposed to be a great English wit, tried to regale us with some Fergie stories from London, but they didn't really make up for the terrifying winds. That night, it was even windier than usual.

Lunched with Alan Nevins [JC's literary agent] at Drai's Café. We gossiped about the publishing business and then he said how shocked and horrified he was that I was only getting a $150,000 advance from St Martin's Press for my autobiography.

'I went in to see Judith Regan during the height of your court case and she said, "You're Joan Collins' agent. I'll give you $750,000 for her autobiography and the book,"' he told me.

'Really?'

'Yes,' he said, 'and I told you, and you said you were going to tell Ed Victor.'

'I do remember,' I said vaguely, 'but I was dealing with so many telephone calls and I was in such a state with the court case, so maybe I didn't tell Ed.'

'It's utterly ridiculous that you are getting so little money,' huffed Alan.

It seems to me people are always trying to wind me up about what I *should* have done or what *could* have been. That's not the way to live one's life, but I do think Alan has a point. Ed Victor was not a good move; even though he's probably a good agent for other people, he wasn't for me.

Thanksgiving Day, 28 November 1996

The most important day in the American calendar, holiday-wise. Jeffrey and I worked out in the gym in the morning. An ancient geriatric, one of the many who live in this building, came and did three of the tiniest arm push-ups I've ever seen, then left! Jeffrey and I got hysterical as we were working our guts out.

Went to David and Barbara Niven's for a drink; they were having what they called 'the orphans'. Most people I didn't know, but it was, as ever, fun to see David and Barbara. I told them that I had really appreciated the sound machine she had sent me to drown out the dreadful sound of the wind. (In actual fact, I had put the sound of the ocean on and had frightful dreams all night about octopuses.)

Nolan picked me up and we went to Drai's Café, again. Our new favourite place. We drank vodka, the only civilised drink in this town, since the white wine is usually pretty filthy. Basically, he said that he could not believe that I had not worked acting-wise for fourteen months.

'It's true,' I said. 'I just talked to Robert Wagner on the tele-phone, and he couldn't believe it, either.'

'But you're such a big star,' said Nolan, 'you're huge.'

'I'm sick of hearing it,' I said. 'It doesn't mean a damned thing any more. The studios only want some twenty-year-old that hasn't done anything. It doesn't matter that there are hundreds, or maybe thousands or maybe hundreds of thousands of people who would like to see me on their television screen. The networks ain't buying me.'

Nolan was sympathetic, but I told him not to bother. 'The main thing,' I said, 'is one's quality of life.'

Basically, I am very happy, though I really wish I was in the South of France or in London. I don't really like the lifestyle in Los Angeles, and I hate the fucking weather. It's either raining, or it's too hot, or we have these ridiculous winds, and there's always the threat of an earthquake. Meanwhile, what am I doing knocking my head against a brick wall with producers, few of whom even remember me in any case? It's true, I don't really feel at home in Hollywood. Even though I have friends, it's not my scene. I belong in Europe, and I really don't care if I'm not going to get another gig. When I see the utter shit that is on television and the dull personalities and performers that are on the screen, I just feel, what is the point? If it wasn't for the money, I'd get the hell out.

Tracked Roger Moore down on his mobile in Montreux in Switzerland, where he was buying shoes. 'Call me back,' I said. 'No, darling, it's OK. Let's talk here,' he said. I don't like talking business unless it's a business situation, but we discussed doing *Love Letters* together from March to May next year. Roger doesn't really seem to want to do it, unless he gets $75,000 per week – wow! When I talked to Robert Wagner, he would not tell me how much he and Jill had got, but Charles Duggan said they had a guarantee of $25,000 to $30,000 and they made up the rest on a percentage of the gross. This seems pretty fair. After all, it's only for five or six weeks, and I need the money even if Roger doesn't. I suggested to Charles maybe we use George Hamilton, and he thought that was a possibility.

Why are actors so driven? What drives us? Is it money? Is it success? Is it security? None of those things are guaranteed. There goes that noise again! I simply cannot believe the horrifying sound effects in this apartment building. It is slowly driving me mad. If I throw myself off the balcony, maybe people will understand. I feel like I'm in a scene from *Mutiny on the Bounty* in Trevor Howard's stateroom. 'When will it end, oh Lord? When will it end?' All I want is to be in my house in the South of France. It doesn't matter how much the wind blows there. The fucking house doesn't move like it's on rollers.

There is no security in Los Angeles. Not with work, not with money not with weather. Any minute, I feel an earthquake could occur, or there could be a blackout, or the TV could fuse. I guess that's why I can't sleep, because I don't feel at peace. In my flat in London, I feel totally relaxed and at peace and can sleep for eight hours easily. Here, I can't, and it's dragging me into the depths. I try to ignore it, but it doesn't work.

Friday, 29 November 1996

Had dinner with Nolan at Drai's Café. He was full of gossip. One of the most interesting things he said was that Aaron Spelling had been pitching a series called 'Brentwood' to the network, and they are adamant that they don't want anybody over the age of thirty-five in it! What about the fact that one of the main women has to be an expert in real estate, having been in the business for twenty years! 'They don't care,' said Nolan. 'They just want twinkies and teenagers and young things – that's what it's all about today. Demographics, demographics, demographics.'

JOAN COLLINS

Talked to R.J. Wagner about *Love Letters*, which he has been doing on tour with his wife, Jill St John. He had a ball doing it. I told him that Roger Moore wanted a considerable amount of money, which could possibly throw the deal. R.J. said that the deal should be constructed according to the size of the theatre and whether or not it's on subscription, etc. I agree with him. I spoke to Roger, tracked him down to a restaurant in Montreux on his mobile. He's still not interested unless he gets $75,000 per week. 'Well, it's hardly worth it, is it, Joanie!' he said.

'I don't agree, actually. I think that we should do it for less and a percentage, like R.J. did.'

R.J. was very positive and talked about the vagaries of the profession, particularly the shittiness of many agents. He seems to be very together and certainly happy in his marriage. 'I'm glad I didn't do *Applause* with Stefanie Powers. It closed out of town as it was a terrible production,' he confided.

Saturday, 30 November 1996

Went with Jeffrey and Erin to see *101 Dalmatians* at the Academy. God, what a piece of shit! Without too many sour grapes or bitterness, I thought Glenn Close was perfectly awful as Cruella de Vil. I really wanted to play this role, and would have done anything, well almost, to get it. She plays it totally without humour and without any kind of vulnerability. All in all, it was the yawn of the year, and I'll be amazed if it makes anybody over the age of nine want to go and see it.

Went to L'Orangerie with Peter Marc Jacobson. He is still suffering from his break-up with Fran, and they are in therapy together. He is very sweet, very sensitive. He was quite impressed when Betsy Bloomingdale arrived with Nancy Reagan and they both came over to the table to say hello. His life is in turmoil,

90

so it doesn't look as though 'Diva' is going to be green-lit imme-diately. However, one interesting bit of news was that he is in a development deal with TriStar to do a half-hour sitcom with Joanna Lumley called 'The Godmother'. This will be the first time she would work outside England, something I had thought she didn't want to do. 'The Godmother' sounds suspiciously like 'Aunt We All', which I gave to TriStar some weeks ago for me. Don't want to be a cynical old crab, but I called Lance to find out if he thought that this might be the case, and he said I should do some super-sleuthing tomorrow.

Peter was very positive about me. He said how beautiful I was, etc. etc., how great I looked, blah-blah. And he did make some very interesting suggestions: a) he thought I should change my hair, as my short, dark hair is so much associated with Alexis. He suggested going sort of a deep red, as producers would then see me in a different light.

'That's probably why they don't want to develop something for you, because you look the same as you did in *Dynasty*.'

'Maybe it's a good idea. I'm fed up with the way I look, anyway,' I said.

Then, b), he said he thought I should go on the *Howard Stern Show*. I've always wanted to do that. I think he's rather brilliant. I thought I'd say as my opening line, 'I've always wanted to know whether your dick is as small as you always brag about.' Peter seems to think that getting a younger, hipper audience is the answer. Answer? I really don't know what the question is. Do I really want to get down and dirty, trading scatological jokes with Howard Stern? What do I really want to do? I would like to just live a happy life, and I don't think that doing an American sitcom is going to make me that happy. What is the answer? Money! And with my kids and lifestyle, I need plenty of it.

December 1996

Talked to Stella Wilson in London earlier today. She sounded utterly miserable because her heat has gone off. There are many advantages to being in California, and thank God that damned Santa Ana wind has stopped. Also, thank God for American Movie Classics and Turner Classic Movies on TV. I'm discovering all over again Barbara Stanwyck, Irene Dunne, Brian Aherne and Bing Crosby. They don't make stars like that any more.

White Rabbit Day. Met with Ehrich Van Lowe and his assistant, Robin, and Lance at Ehrich's house in Brentwood. There, we hashed out the plot of the potential sitcom for me, 'Mother and Son'. I came up with some great ideas and now they want to pitch it to Peter Roth at Fox. It sounds like a great idea, but there are a lot of great ideas in Hollywood!

Sunday, 1 December 1996

Went with Jeffrey to the wedding reception of Ashley Hamilton and Angie Everhart at the Beverly Regent Hotel. Ashley is George Hamilton and Alana's son, and she is an ex-girlfriend of Sylvester Stallone. I didn't know most of the people there; they seemed to be relations or friends of the bride and groom, who did not appear until sometime later as they were busy with paparazzi! We didn't know whether it was dinner, but it was in the large and gloomy ballroom with the music so loud one could not hear oneself speak. Sat with Jackie and Frank and the Schlatters. The only other people there we knew were the Sinatra clan: Tina, Nancy and Nancy Sr. The bride and groom danced together on the dance floor. She put her hands on his bottom and squeezed it, and he was chewing gum. Charming. They did not come around the tables to greet their guests, nor was there any kind of a reception line, so we never actually said hello. Went over to Jackie's house for a drink and got the grand tour. God. It is so huge. I would hate to stay in a house this gargantuan.

Monday, 2 December 1996

Had one of those wonderful British lunches given by Charles Benson at Le Dome with Wendy Stark, Niven, Stefanie Powers, and Lynn outrageous and gossipy. Charles had bought the Fergie book by Allan Starkie in which he talks about her sex life, and I gave a few assorted readings! Went with Lance to the premiere of *The People vs. Larry Flynt* at Mann Village Theatre. Although it was supposed to be a low-key affair, there were a zillion paparazzi, all of whom wanted to get a picture of me and Lance together. There had been a photograph of us in the *Enquirer*, so I guess they think we're an item!! The film was excellent. Woody Harrelson was terrific, and the girl, Courtney Love, utterly mind-boggling as a drug addict. Went across the road to Mario's for the off-premiere party, which was about as festive as a wet weekend in Wickham. Sat in a booth with Lance, and we were joined by George Christy and Alan Nevins.

Had some appalling pasta and said hello to Roseanne Barr, who looks totally unrecognisable. She has had an enormous amount of plastic surgery, I think, including new silicone cheekbones. She now thinks she looks like Elizabeth Taylor twenty years ago, and strangely enough, she does!

Tuesday, 3 December 1996

Jeffrey calls and says all the tabloids have been on to him about me and Lance being an item. What a joke! There's also another story about me having a romance with Claude Roland!!! Since

Claude Roland is gayer than laughter, it seems a little strange, and the photograph in the paper is of me and Alexis de Redé, who is pushing seventy-five. I am amazed how the tabloids make up these ludicrous, totally outrageous stories.

Lunched at Drai's Café with Betsy Bloomingdale. Also present were Nancy Reagan and Carol Price, wife of the ex-American ambassador to St James. A very sophisticated ladies' lunch in which everybody was interesting, cordial and well mannered. Betsy is so adorable and bubbly, and Mrs Reagan is very sweet. She seems a little subdued, but I guess that's because Ronnie is not well. Rumour has it he's got Alzheimer's, which is really tragic. I thought he was an excellent president.

Met Jeffrey and went to a meeting with Tom Chasin at his office. He is my potential new agent, and I immediately took to him. After an hour's meeting, Jeffrey and I decided that I can't possibly do worse than Metropolitan, whom I am with, so I immediately fired off a letter of dismissal to them. I have been trying to reach agent Debbie Miller for several days to no avail. Well, that's done then. Off with the old, and on with the new. That's two agents I've fired in as many weeks. Jeffrey and I went into David Webb and borrowed a sensational pearl and emerald necklace for the Davis nuptials this weekend.

Had early dinner with Robert Wagner and Jill St John at Spago. R.J. is one of my oldest friends in this town, and still one of the nicest and most genuine of men. Jill came up with a great idea for a sitcom for Suzanne Pleshette, herself, and me. Why not? The more the merrier. A really fun evening. Chevy Chase came by to say hello. He was very subdued, in a business suit with white shirt and tie, quite unlike his zany television image.

Wednesday, 4 December 1996

Took Billy and Audrey Wilder, the Wassermans and Leonard Gershe to Le Dome. A wonderful evening. Billy in sparkling form and Audrey was so adorable and gave Edie and me each a Chanel camellia. How chic.

Saturday, 7 December 1996

After lunch at Drai's Café with Lance and Leonard Gershe – which was so sweet because Lance is a huge fan of Leonard's work and Leonard was suitably modest – I got ready for the wedding of the year. Jeffrey and I arrived early at the parents' giant mansion. There were sixteen bridesmaids and eight men of honour. The ceremony seemed to go on forever, but what can one say about a wedding? And we reminisced about Leonard teaching me to ride. Movie stars there included Gregory Peck, Don Rickles (is he really a star?), Louis Jourdan and various others. Jeffrey and I jived and jitterbugged, and ate caviar, but the food didn't come until about a quarter to eleven, and we were starving.

Sunday, 8 December 1996

Jackie had a wonderful Christmas party at her house with the usual suspects. Sat between George Hamilton and Fernando something, who were very into their health, as everybody is in this town. Jackie and Frank seem besotted. I'm so happy for her.

Monday, 9 December 1996

It poured with rain. Nothing is more depressing than Los Angeles when it rains. Jeffrey and I had brunch with Merrick

95

Baker-Bates at the Four Seasons, and he discussed the ins and outs of my forthcoming OBE and also the speech I have to give on Saturday. In the afternoon, had another meeting with Jeffrey, Max Rosenberg and Mark Paresio at Metropolitan re 'Georgetown'. Max Rosenberg is about 109 and I did a film with him called *Tales from the Crypt* way back when. He makes Billy Wilder look like an adolescent. There is no way we could go to a network with his ideas. They all thought it was a great idea, me playing the Pamela Harriman character, but there are tons of good ideas in this town. Even though I've left Metropolitan, Mark Paresio still seems hot on this idea. Meeting at five o'clock with Janice French, whom I was introduced to by Ann Turkel, who said that she is a hotshot in financing stuff. She was very interested in doing a TV show of *Prime Time* and seems to think she can get things done. I like these Hollywood women who talk fast and move quickly. Let's hope she can.

Had dinner in Jeffrey's flat with Diahann Carroll, who had just flown in from Vancouver where she's playing an exhausted Norma Desmond in *Sunset Boulevard*. She seems really upset because of her upcoming divorce from Vic Damone and having problems with the producers. We listened to her tales of woe. She has also broken out with some kind of skin condition, eczema. I told her I had the same thing when I was going through stress with Random House. (When aren't I?)

Tuesday, 10 December 1996

Lunch with Nolan and Yvette Mimieux at Drai's Café. Lots of gossip and he was moaning about Barbara Davis not having paid him yet for his two dresses, when in she comes! Yvette was winding him up: 'Ask Barbara about the dresses, ask her how she likes the dresses.' He didn't rise to the bait – he's far too nice.

Katy arrived from London. It was so great to see her, even though she was exhausted. She seemed in good form and was looking great. Even though she hadn't slept for forty hours, so she said, she still felt like going to Spago, so the two of us went in the pouring rain. But it was great fun.

Wednesday, 11 December 1996

My lawyer, Don Zakarin, called in the morning. My lawsuit is definitely settled! Random House has agreed to pay me $1.2 million. That ain't chicken liver, by any means, and I cannot believe it's actually all been settled. It has been four years of hell. It's cost me over half of that amount in legal fees and paying for me and other people to fly in and testify. Big celebrations all around.

Tonight is my Xmas party. The weather is pretty bad. Men came to put up plastic covering outside on the patio. Judy and I spent the day tweaking the house, putting up lilies and poinsettias and all manner of decoration. Don't know how fifty people will fit in this apartment, but I'm going to give it a good try. The Davises came quite early. He sat centre stage, with his bodyguard almost blocking the way. Their handmaidens gathered around Jackie and Jolene. Wendy Stark and John came, as did Lance, and Nolan Miller came with Candy Spelling. She was wearing the most extraordinary, beautifully cut, and large pear-shaped ring I've ever seen – really, really something spectacular. She was in jolly mood. Lennie Gershe seemed a little out of it; I don't think he's a party person. Stefanie Powers stopped by with her mother, who had a diamond stud in her nose!

Everybody had a great time. Alana, Yvette Mimieux, George Hamilton, Ian and Doris La Frenais and Arnie Kopelson stayed up unusually late for a Hollywood party. I must say I thought it went really well.

Thursday, 12 December 1996

Katy went out with some friends, so had lunch at Yvette's with Jolene Schlatter, Evie, and a few other girls. Yvette has a great life. Her husband is incredibly rich and she has got the most beautiful house and really knows how to enjoy her money. Went with Jackie to Channel 5 to do Scoop TV. Wasn't too keen on doing it, but Jeffrey says it's great 'exposure' – his favourite word. The Christmas traffic is appalling. Went with Jackie to the Four Seasons for an absolutely ghastly gathering for Melanie Griffith and her charity. A complete crush of hags, facelifts and ancient old men in flashy suits. Did a quick photo shoot with Melanie, who was rather adorable, and sat with Loni Anderson, who looked like a Barbie doll with much cleavage and a tight velvet suit. Brenda Vacarro told me she was annoyed that she wasn't invited to my party. Well, since I haven't ever been invited to one of hers, I don't get it.

Friday, 13 December 1996

Went to the Chamber of Commerce Annual Christmas Anglo-American Lunch at the Beverly Hilton. Lots of British expats who have lost the English art of restraint and seemed to really like to paw and hug one and put their faces very close to one's own. Was nervous about making the speech but had spent the morning working on it so, once I got down to it, I was able to give it my all.

Judy and I did some Rodeo Drive shopping. In the evening, Katy and I got dressed up in our Christmas gear and went to Paulene and Mark Burns' party, an excellent gathering. Sacha was there, and everyone was admiring the portrait Sacha had done of Mark. 'Remember when you and I were naked on the swing in *The Stud*?' asked Mark lecherously. 'Not my favourite moment,' I told him. 'I loved it,' he giggled.

Saturday, 14 December 1996

Brunch with Ann Turkel, Lance, Jeffrey and a woman called Janice French, who was very interested in doing *Prime Time* as a movie. Lance has told me that they thought the Movie Channel, and possibly ABC, have passed on Ehrich's idea. I believe that the networks are simply not interested in preparing shows for anyone over the age of thirty. It's a bite-the-bullet situation, but the sooner I accept it, the better, and I can get the hell out of Dodge City!

Katy didn't want to come to David Niven's party, so I went with Lance. The usual suspects, and a lot of people that one really didn't know and really didn't want to. Left at ten o'clock with Lance, the Schlatters, Tina Sinatra and Suzanne de Passe. Everyone came back to my apartment, drank vodka and gossiped. We are now calling the Sierra Towers the Fawlty Towers!

Sunday, 15 December 1996

Left early to pick up Max and Judy and travel up to Mammoth Lakes. Sacha joined us and we went in convoy, stopping several times for potty breaks and food breaks. Then Judy made a fine pork roast with crackling. At the end of the night, I felt I had eaten 5000 calories!

Monday, 16 December 1996 – Mammoth Lakes

Everyone went skiing. I stayed in the chalet, which looked really pretty, and made telephone calls and started to write *Prime Time*, my new novel about four actresses. I'm feeling rather depressed. Don't know whether it's this time of year, or whether it's all the rejection that I'm getting. Called Sue St Johns in London and told her to expect me back in England in February! She was thrilled, as am I. I'm much too European to enjoy being in Los Angeles when I'm not working. It would be great to work, but if I'm not – I'm not, and I'll just have to accept it.

Took everyone to a very good restaurant called Nevado's, then woke up in the middle of the night with frightful pains in my stomach. Had them last night, too. It's like the pain that I had from the ulcer that I was getting during the court case. Max says not to worry because it's just the altitude!

Sunday, 22 December 1996

Last five days have been a blur. I've had the most shocking cold I've ever had. Absolutely out of it, coughing and sneezing – I have gone through twenty boxes of Kleenex. Thank God for cable TV. Felt terrible that I couldn't go out and do things with Katy. Did go and take a meeting at CBS on Friday with Peter Golden, who is some head of talent there, but I feel so cynical about the whole thing now that I didn't even bother to look particularly good. That was probably a good thing.

Jeffrey Lane, who loves glamour, looked askance when he saw my hair hanging down and minimal make-up, but I told him, 'This is the way they like you to look in Hollywood. Everybody knows that I can look glamorous and now let them see me like this. Maybe then they'll think I can act as someone other than Alexis Carrington.'

Monday, 23 December 1996

I called Barbara Davis because I thought I was getting pneumonia and she put me in touch with Dr Cantor. Managed to persuade Sacha to pick up the antibiotics, which I took immediately. Today I feel a hundred per cent better. Linda Dickson came and gave me reflexology on my feet again. I'm still pretty weak. It's a ghastly day, pouring with rain. No wonder everybody's sick in California, it's either feast or famine, either boiling or freezing. Onward to Christmas.

Christmas Eve 1996

Went with Katy to a huge party at Aaron Spelling's. Bumped into Peter Roth, the head honcho at Fox. I had two meetings with him a year or so ago when he seemed very enthusiastic about doing something with me. However, according to Lance two weeks ago, his people out and out rejected Ehrich's sitcom that we had been planning about the mother and son. Anyway he was terribly attentive and complimentary, saying how gorgeous I am and how he always thought I was beautiful when I came to the office but that I look better than ever, blah-blah-blah. He then said that they had a project for me that he had been talking about with Aaron and he told me it was called 'Brentwood'!!! This was the project that I heard last week was only going with twenty-five-year-olds. 'Don't say anything to Aaron,' says Peter. 'Wait until he tells you.' Half an hour later Aaron takes me aside and starts to tell me his idea for this character. It all sounds interesting but I'm not going to get my knickers in the tiniest bit of a twist about it. I told Aaron that I was close to closing my deal to do *Love Letters* on tour and he looked slightly panicky. 'How soon do you have to tell them whether you're going to do it or not?' he asked. I said probably about the first or second week in January. 'Stall until the last minute,' he said. I like Aaron but one cannot take anything he says seriously.

Neither can one take anything any television executives say seriously. They are as fickle as amoeba, constantly changing and moving with the tide. Chatted with Tori Spelling and Katy commented that her tits looked extremely fake, which they do. The Spelling house was so gorgeously decorated that it seemed strange the food was just chicken sandwiches and cold cuts from Nate 'n' Al's. Can't they afford a chef?

Afterwards went to Stefanie Power's party and bumped into David Niven, Judy Quine and darling Sydney Guilaroff, the famous hairdresser from MGM. He was very sweet, although he is nearly blind. He even did Garbo. We reminisced about *The Opposite Sex*, when I sat in the hair and make-up room with Liz Taylor, Grace Kelly and Ava Gardner. I was so shy I couldn't speak.

Christmas Day 1996

Went to Jackie's, where there was a real Christmas feeling since everybody was there, from Jackie's grandchildren (aged three months and three years), up to Jackie's possible future stepmother and aunt (Frank's relations). In between people I didn't know, glad to see that the Bricusses were there, as was David Niven Jr and Barbara. It was very enjoyable; family and Christmas-ish. Watched the new Woody Allen film, which Jackie and I both hated.

Friday, 27 December 1996

Did a little shopping at a men's shop, then came home to the dreadfully sad news on my answering machine that Jean-Claude

Tramont had died. Sue Mengers had left the message and she sounded dreadful. I was terribly, terribly upset. It was only seventeen weeks ago that he was in the South of France, frolicking in the pool, playing poker, full of life and jokes. We just adored him, so it's a terrible blow. Went in the pouring rain with Jeffrey to a party at Ian and Doris La Frenais's place. A lot of reasonably interesting people there, like Kiefer Sutherland, Helmut Newton and his wife June, Dani Janssen, Wendy Stark and John Morrissey. The food was good and it was great seeing Ian, who's always fun and cheered me up.

Saturday, 28 December 1996

Nikki Haskell gave a do in my honour. A scintillating group, very animated, lots of fun – Jackie Bisset, Tony Curtis, Angie Dickinson, Allan Carr, Jack Scalia, Connie Stevens, Suzanne Pleshette, the Bricusses and the John Gavins, Sacha and all the usual suspects. Tony Curtis was very funny and was telling all of his outrageous stories. He was with the definitive starlet, huge tits and ass in a tight strapless white dress! Told Jackie Bisset about Jean-Claude's death and she was so upset she burst into tears.

Sunday, 29 December 1996

Had dinner at Trader Vic's with the Bricusses. Have never known a restaurant go off more. The service is utterly appalling and my Indonesian lamb roast, usually so delicious, was frightful. Even the drinks, their famous cocktails, were horrible. Leslie was slightly miffed because he had wanted to go to Spago.

Monday, 30 December 1996

Nolan came over for dinner and he said that he'd had a call from Jonathan Levin, the head money honcho at Aaron Spelling, who said they were very interested in me for 'Brentwood', now known as *Pacific Palisades*. He wanted to reach my agent. Nolan told him, 'I know she's got a conflict of interest with the Roger Moore *Love Letters* situation.' He said, 'Aaron is still very excited about having you in it.' Naturally the dates are totally conflicting. Don't know quite what to do. I guess I'll have to play it by ear until I can talk to my agent. It's absolutely typical in this business, either feast or famine. On the other hand, I spoke to Charles Duggan and Roger has NOT definitely committed until he can get the money he wants. Don't know what to do. Oh Lord, oh Lord.

New Year's Eve 1996

Had a meeting with Bob Sidell about our line of cosmetics and then another meeting with Eddie Sanderson about the photographs he'd taken of me and Katy the other day for *Hello!* Went shopping with Judy to get food for tonight, and tweaked the apartment. The barman, Richard, came and a select group arrived for New Year's Eve drinks. The usual suspects: Judy and Max, Jeffrey and the Bricusses, Sacha and Erin, Wendy Stark with her husband John, and Morgan Mason without his wife Belinda Carlisle. Robin arrived from London. I thought the flat looked rather good but Robin thinks it's hideous. 'It's back to the mid-eighties, your *Dynasty* days, dear,' he says, the ultimate taste tyrant. He's getting quite boring.

1997

Sunday, 12 January 1997

A lot has happened on the Aaron Spelling front. Dined with Aaron and Nolan Miller, Candy Spelling and Joanna Carson [ex-wife of television host Johnny Carson] at Spago. Aaron said that he wanted me very much to be in *Pacific Palisades* ('Brentwood') now and that my agent Tom Chasin was an idiot. He said I must fire my agent and go to CAA. Instead of giving me forty thousand an episode he would give me forty-five! I said, 'OK, why not!' Fuck loyalty. Aaron was terribly excited and made this toast: 'My baby's back with me again.' I think he was a little drunk, but nevertheless he can be very sweet. But I also think that money's the only thing that matters to people in La-La-Land.

Aaron has also agreed to have Nolan design my clothes. It was all very friendly and nice and wonderful, and there were lots of toasts to future projects. Aaron seemed annoyed that I hadn't called him about negotiations, but I said I didn't want to bother him.

Monday, 13 January 1997

Left for Acapulco to stay with Leslie and Evie, feeling terrific about everything.

'This is what you came here for, JC,' said Leslie. 'To get a series, and now you've got one with Aaron, even though it's only three episodes.' Today the goalposts have been moved a bit. Gary Concoff, whom I have instructed to be my agent instead of Tom Chasin, now informs me that when Jonathan Levin was told Aaron had agreed to the 'forty-five thou' an episode, he said, 'Absolutely not, I only agreed on forty.' I'm completely stunned by this turnaround since Aaron did say he would pay forty-five in front of the whole group at Spago. That's Hollywood, folks. Anyway, they want me to do another scene for ten thousand dollars, bringing it up to ninety, so I guess I'll bite the bullet, although I'm quite shattered by the fact Aaron can lie so blatantly. Jonathan Levin makes me uncomfortable, like most money men. Only time will tell if he is to be trusted.

Friday, 24 January 1997

Went to Miami to stay at the Biltmore Hotel in Coral Gables with Jeffrey and his new friend for a Marine Optical cocktail party. It was quite successful and I met all of the people who had turned my eyeglasses into the most successful Celebrity Eyewear in the world! Hey Hey Hey! Had a jolly evening and ended up doing the 'macarena' with a wild band. We all danced together and it was back to the seventies, folks.

Then went to New York with Jeffrey, his new friend, and a mover and shaker called Aaron Tonken. I'd met him before at the Melanie Griffith party. He said, 'I want to give you lots of presents!' I didn't say no. He's gayer than laughter, and fun.

Saturday, 25 January 1997

True to his word, Aaron Tonken whisked Jeffrey and me off to Cartier, where he bought me a beautiful diamond-studded ring worth a few bucks. Then to a new fabulous boutique on Madison called Etro, where Aaron said I could get outfits for Katy, Tara and Sacha – which I, the good mother, duly did. I whisked through the store at top speed, grabbing the most beautiful red suit, black suit, white jacket, silk blouse, and suede skirt. After plundering like crazy (Aaron said he'd never seen anybody shop so fast), I realised I needed another suitcase, so they took me to the top floor where gorgeous Italian luggage in dark Paisley leather was displayed. I found a suitcase and a duffel bag, then spotted some wonderful cushions, ashtrays and accessories for the apartment. Got those too! Talk about greedy!

Bumped into Gert-Rudolf ('Muck') Flick, a scion like his younger brother Friedrich Christian ('Mick') of the Flick family of German industrialists. Tall, good-looking and very sure of himself. He asked me out and I said maybe!

Dinner that night at Mr Chow. Beforehand had drinks with Nancy Holmes and Randy Jones. Suzy Menkes, the columnist for *Women's Wear Daily*, held court. She is an amazing-looking Lady of 'uncertain age', with the most enormous social power in New York. If she likes you, you're in, if she doesn't, forget it. Dinner was great fun. Rupert Everett, who looks wonderful, kept everyone in stitches, and it's always good to see Blaine and Robert Trump.

Sunday, 26 January 1997

Lunch at the Four Seasons with Tom Dunne, the CEO of St Martin's Press, who are publishing my autobiography, *Second Act*, in America. He told me they wanted me to put more stuff in about my sister, as 'she's hardly in the book'. Well, that won't be difficult.

Jeffrey and I went to Muck Flick's apartment for drinks. Lo and behold, when we went into his library every bookshelf was filled only with copies of *Second Act*. There must have been at least a thousand. I was very flattered, and slightly embarrassed. I signed a couple of copies. Then Muck asked me if he could throw a dinner party for me in London to celebrate receiving my OBE, as he's a fan. I said yes, and he told me to put together a guest-list of twenty people. Sounds great.

Monday, 27 January 1997

Lunched with my lawyer Tom Hutton at 21 and we talked about my deal with California Cosmetics, for which I'm shooting photographs next week. Told him that I would love to have my own line of clothes. He's a really great lawyer (according to Nolan) and if he can get me a good deal, he will. I hope I'm finally surrounding myself with some good people. Jonathan Lloyd certainly is on the ball in London, Don Zakarin worked out the Random House situation, and all in all I hope that CAA are going to be good for me. One can but hope.

With the bitter triumvirate of Ed Victor, Michael Viner and Ken Burrows so involved in my life for the past three years I have not reaped good results. They were of course all joined at the hip. Jeffrey told me that Viner was probably going to jail. Good. I haven't seen a single financial accounting of my book [*My Friends' Secrets*] since he published it three years ago. Everyone says that he is a crook.

Flew back to LA. Katy arrived and it was great to see her.

Wednesday, 29 January 1997

A meeting at Aaron Spelling's palatial offices where Jonathan Levin – all smiles and, as they say in *My Fair Lady*, 'oozing charm from every pore, he oiled his way around the floor' – made nice to me. Also there were the writers Diane Messina and Jim Stanley, along with Steven Tann (Vice President of Programming) and Jim Conway (Executive Vice President of Spelling Television). Sat there trying to be intelligent about a role that I really know nothing about. They've decided to call her Christina. I've suggested Zelda or Valentina, but they wanted something more 'royal'. The actress who was to play my daughter is now no longer on board and they still haven't cast her, although they are supposed to start shooting in three weeks. How Hollywood.

Thursday, 30 January 1997

Dinner with Sacha and Katy at Hamburger Hamlet. We're all in a fever pitch of excitement about Sacha's first exhibition tomorrow at the Chateau Marmont. Sharon Stone is supposed to come, as are a host of other celebrities. We won't hold our breath!

Friday, 31 January 1997

Arrived at the Chateau Marmont at five o'clock to do some photographs with Sacha. Pose in front of my portrait, which I think is wonderful. It's Sacha's first horizontal painting and it is an excellent likeness. Much better than his last one. A lot of media attention, but while I was talking to them, Sharon Stone walked in, saw me doing the interview, saw Sacha who was on his way out front to talk to the press, and then, inexplicably, she turned on her heel and left through the kitchen. Maybe she thought the crowd was too small. It was only 6.15, after all. However, the exhibition was fabulously successful. Betsy Bloomingdale came as did Dominick Dunne, Wendy Stark and Roddy McDowall, Helmut and June Newton, Billy and Audrey Wilder (Billy is one of Sacha's biggest supporters), Leonard Gershe, Samantha Eggar, Stefanie Powers, Katie Wagner, Pauline Morton, Judy Quine. So many people said how proud I should be of my son, and indeed I was. Over 450 people came and it lasted four hours and was a raging success.

Many of us ended up at the Chateau Marmont café next door, where Dominick Dunne held forth to Sacha, Katy, Wendy Stark, George Schlatter, the Bryers and me about the shocking situation with the O.J. Simpson civil trial. Then Oliver Stone arrived and Sacha took him back to the exhibition, where Oliver bought Sacha's painting of Beethoven's death. The next day Katy and I were so exhausted we just tottered around and went to lunch at Le Dome with Judy, excitedly discussing everything.

Sunday, 2 February 1997

Did a spread for *Hello!* with Eddie. I agreed to do this after I axed Viviane Ventura, who had wangled her way in. Even though I've not spoken to this woman for three years she is still trying to manipulate me with this magazine. Finally I had to send a fax to the lawyers at *Hello!* last week saying that in no way, shape or form did Ms Ventura represent me or any of my family.

Went with Katy and Jeffrey to a screening at Carole Little's house of a French art film with Catherine Deneuve. The Goldbergs were there, Leonard and the lovely Wendy. She still does that terribly un-chic thing of imitating one's English accent. I guess you can take the girl out of Pomona but you can't take Pomona out of the girl.

Monday, 3 February 1997

Did a video shoot and photographs for my cosmetics, SilkSkin, with Bob Sidell. Had dinner with Doug Cramer, the Morrisseys and Sacha. Doug is a big art aficionado and was at Sacha's exhibition.

The last few days were a whirl of Katy leaving for London, Judy packing for Vegas, fitting in interviews, manicures, pedicures, facials, deciding on photographs, picking up furniture, farewell drinks and finally a goodbye dinner for Judy and Max – they are leaving to live in Las Vegas – at the Hotel Bel-Air given by Frank Bowling. Went with Jeffrey and it was quite fun with great red wine.

Saturday, 8 February 1997

The last three weeks have been a total whirl. True to his word, Aaron Spelling called and told me to contact Steve Tellez from CAA. Which I duly did. CAA is the top agency in town and I had been told previously they were not interested in little old me. However, a word from Aaron and suddenly things change. Steve seems a nice enough man in his early forties. He didn't make any flowery promises, for a change, but seemed confident and happy that I was going with them. We shall see. At least I've got the *Pacific Palisades* series, albeit only three episodes, and Aaron has finally agreed for Nolan to do my clothes. He actually said that he told Nolan he could do it as long as he wouldn't charge too much! That's very good news. Meanwhile the endless negotiations go on between Charles Duggan and Gary Concoff, about whether or not we can slide *Love Letters* in.

New Zealand is beautiful. Arrived with Stella in Auckland at 6 a.m. Drove to the Cambridge Stud Farm, home of Sir Tristram, who is apparently the greatest stud stallion ever, having sired over one hundred very important horses. Our host was Patrick Hogan, the owner, who had apparently been trying to get me to come to the race meeting tomorrow for over fifteen years! Spent the afternoon sunbathing and just relaxing. It's the first time I've relaxed since Acapulco and I'm pretty tired, with a hell of a few days coming up. Huka Lodge is simply divine and I think I will be very happy here.

I've never had such good press as I've had in New Zealand. They keep telling me how beautiful and glamorous I am, what a flawless peaches-and-cream complexion and svelte figure I have. Oh Lord! Added to this they are charm and courtesy incarnate, and it's a wonder my head isn't getting too big for my body.

12–15 February 1997 – New Zealand

Wednesday: at the rather fabulous Centra Hotel in Auckland, I signed copies of *Second Act* for a huge number of eager fans. That evening there was a gala fundraising evening for the Variety Club and I did my usual 'Hello, how are you?' and met millions of people, shaking hands everywhere. Then . . . on stage with David Hartnell, who is known as Mr Hollywood, and I talked about my life and career. I find this all rather difficult to do, but when I saw the two seriously handicapped children in their wheelchairs and I was able to give them the keys to a Sunshine coach for which this charity has raised the money, it was all worthwhile.

Thursday: went from Auckland to Wellington, where there was yet another evening for Joan Collins at the Plaza International. This time it was a fundraising evening for UNICEF. Met two very nice chaps call Zane and Richard who are arranging the whole thing. It was practically the same as last night except no dinner, and again the book-signing. I'm always amazed at these women who look absolutely nothing like me, except that they have jet black hair and wear a lot of lipstick, who come up to me and say that they are always being mistaken for me.

Left Wellington for Christchurch. There met Mr X, the organiser for the cancer charities, who turned out to be a nightmare. There was a whole bunch of nonsense in the papers about 'Joan wants to meet a sheep farmer while she's in New Zealand.' So they contacted this man who was immediately inundated with reporters who were trying to make up some sort of romance out of this. When I told Mr X at our meeting that I didn't want to have any photographs taken with this sheep farmer, he got on his high horse and snapped, 'He's doing more for the charity than you are. His wife died of cancer and he's written this beautiful book of poems from which we're going to make a hundred thousand dollars.'

'Great,' I said. 'I just don't want to be photographed while I'm eating.'

'Right.' Sounding aggravated, he punched in a number on his mobile and said, 'Dick, tell the press that Miss Collins doesn't want them there.'

'No, no, no,' said someone in a panic. 'She doesn't mean that. She just doesn't want to be photographed while she's eating.'

I was so irate I stormed outside to have a cigarette with my trusty bodyguard, John Fraser. Mr X is obviously a total moron. I was then informed that I was going to be brought into the auditorium a) by a fanfare of trumpets, b) escorted by several members of the New Zealand army and c) in a Rolls-Royce. The whole thing was cringe-makingly embarrassing but, like a good little girl, I did it. Then sat between the sheep farmer and a nice local DJ. The sheep farmer was charming even though he'd actually never heard of me! Then when I came on the stage I was on a sort of moving chair that made its way downstage with huge puffs of fake smoke issuing from all around and, naturally, the *Dynasty* theme playing. Luckily the interview was OK.

Escaped with Stella and Chris and we went immediately to the Christchurch Casino where we played blackjack for two or three hours, which was great fun although I lost a bit.

Saturday: walked around Christchurch, dreading the endlessly long trip back home.

Sunday, 16 February 1997

Stella and I began our nightmare trip. Three and a half hours from Christchurch to Sydney, then three hours at Sydney airport. We wandered around and I bought an Australian hat and read a magazine. Thirteen and a half hours from Sydney to Los Angeles. Since the plane was going to be an hour late to London, I had the brilliant idea of ordering a car and going to Sierra Towers for a shower. Naturally the stupid car wasn't there and it was boiling hot, so we jumped in a taxi, who took us the wrong way. The apartment looked good and we showered, fiddled around, changed and then it was back to the airport, back on Air New Zealand to London. This time only eleven and a half hours. By the time I arrived I was feeling pretty wrung out, to say the least. I spent the next two days taking it very easy indeed.

Tuesday, 18 February 1997

Katy and I leave for Paris, where we are met by Tara and her new fiancé, Michael Adam. She is a changed girl, so excited and so happy about getting married. I'm excited and happy about it too, as I was wondering if it was ever going to happen. 'You've kissed a lot of frogs, darling, and now you're marrying one,' I tell her jocularly. 'So have you, Mum!' she retorts.

We stay at a new hotel called Costes, which is elegant but dark, super trendy with faces that you vaguely recognise milling around in the lobby. I must say I miss the Ritz. Tony Newley is here with Grace, his mum, Gina Fratini his girlfriend, and Shelby, his daughter – the whole family in fact. Traffic is appalling in Paris and Michael and Tara sanguinely inform me that there are constant terrorist bombs going off all over the city, particularly in the Metro. 'Great. Are you going on the Metro?' I ask. 'Oh, yes,' they shrug.

To the Buddha Bar for lunch, where we meet Michael's parents, my future in-laws, Joselin and George Adam. They seem charming, but I can see that I'm going to have to polish up my French. The lunch is very good, even Tony didn't have any complaints. We sample a lot of the dishes for the wedding, and meet three florists, all with their own ideas.

That night in the hotel I give a big engagement party and it is so sweet and so charming. I've never seen Tara so happy or so pretty. Joselin and George give her a beautiful sapphire and diamond bracelet from Cartier and Michael gives her a diamond and gold ring from Mauboussin. I'm very teary-eyed I must admit, and so is Tony.

Wednesday, 19 February 1997

I take Tara, Shelby, and Tara's friend Lisa to lunch at Stresa, then we go shopping all over Paris to find a wedding dress. We end up at Jean Paul Gaultier, where Tara has an appointment. She tries on many things and we see his video, which is great, and I think the clothes are right for us.

I think I like being a prospective mother-in-law, although I

won't be able to get involved in so many of the preparations because of having to go back to LA. That night I have dinner with
Tara and Michael at a Vietnamese restaurant. I'm so exhausted
that I find myself nodding off during the dinner. Not a bella
figura.

Friday, 28 February 1997

Arrive back after eight days in Destino feeling completely reju-
venated. Lunch with Muck Flick at Harry's Bar. He still wants
to give a party for me on 11 March to celebrate my OBE, but he
wants to uninvite Adrian Gill and his girlfriend Nicola Formby.
This is because Adrian, who is the *Sunday Times* restaurant critic
under the name A.A. Gill, has written a very unflattering piece
about Anouska Weinberg, or Hempel as she was known: 'She's
a 1960s model, actress, whatever, frock maker and innkeeper, and
a knight's wife who has pushed and elbowed her way into the
A–Z without even having the decency to wait until she's dead. If
you can think of a more embarrassing and crass piece of nouveau
riche, arriviste social climbing, I can't.' I was vaguely aware of the
article when I was in LA, but since I have ghastly things written
about me all the time didn't take much notice. However, Muck
seems to think this is a cause célèbre, and even though Adrian
and Nicola have been invited, he wants to disinvite them. I tell
him I don't know how I could possibly do that, it's the rudest
thing.

   During lunch, Donatella Flick, the fiery Italian soon-to-be
ex-wife of Muck, arrives and gives me *le froideur* greeting of all
time. Muck gives her a cheery greeting but she is not happy as
she joins Kooky Fallah. Across the room are Marguerite Littman,
Princess Diana and Christopher Balfour, the CEO of Christie's,
obviously discussing the princess's forthcoming sale of frocks to

Christie's. When Donatella gets up to leave she ignores us, goes over to the princess, drops a deep curtsy and chats with them. After she's gone, the princess looks over and waves at me and makes a funny face. Later, as she's leaving, she comes over and says, 'That's one of the most amusing lunches I've had in a long time.' I compliment her on how lovely she looks and she's so modest. I ask if I can send her my beauty book and she seems pleased.

Sunday, 2 March 1997

Receive a call from Muck Flick, sounding Germanic and military. He says that he has sorted out Gill and disinvited him. I am utterly appalled. 'How can you do this? Wouldn't it be better for Anouska not to come if it's going to be so embarrassing for her?' Muck seems to think not. We call Adrian, and Paul Raben, Adrian's best friend, profusely apologising. Adrian thinks it's all a hoot and doesn't take much notice, but I am mortified. What an outrageous thing to do. Muck has been planning this party for three weeks and it sounded like it was going to be a blast, although he's invited many more of his friends than mine. C'est la vie. I think I'll disinvite myself.

Went to the party at Greville House after the premiere of *The English Patient*. I've seen it twice already and couldn't stomach it again. Sat at Lily Mahtani's table with John Bowes-Lyon, the Fennells and Duncan McLaren. Sat next to Bosie, who was quite put out that he had done the *placements* so that I was facing the room with my back to the wall but instead I'm sitting with my back to the room, facing the wall. 'Someone changed them,' he muttered. Can't really see too many people, although we bump into Francesca Annis on the stairs, looking rather pleased with herself as she has just snared Ralph Fiennes. The director John

Boorman is terribly amusing and fascinated that I'm going to do a series. He's recently finished a series with Raquel Welch, and says it was very difficult for him to work with her. Many friends come over, including Bianca Jagger; we have our usual chat about why we hardly ever see each other. This could be because she lives in New York and I live in London, LA or on a plane. A good time was had by all.

Monday, 3 March 1997

Into second gear now, seriously investigating the clothes situation for my OBE investiture on 11 March. David Emanuel and Co. come over with very pretty lilac fabric and we discuss the suit. I tell him I will have lost seven or eight pounds by next Monday but he is doubtful. 'You don't know what I can do when I put my mind to it,' I say. Dash over to Philip Somerville to discuss the hat.

Tuesday, 4 March 1997

Lunch with Stella at San Lorenzo to discuss various things. Then we go out into Beauchamp Place to Isabell Kristensen Couture to see if I can find a dress for Muck's party, followed by three or four paparazzi snapping mindlessly away. When I ignore them they say in their charming way, 'Oh come on Joan, give us a smile, you know you love it.' What makes them think I love it? Who loves trying to do a bit of shopping and being photographed all the time?

Next it's The Ivy to do my *placements* for the luncheon party I'm giving after the OBE ceremony next week. Then another fitting with David Emanuel for my suit.

Thursday, 6 March 1997

I've had several conversations throughout the last few days with Philippa, Muck Flick's secretary, about his evening party. He certainly is behaving extremely strangely. As I am talking to various builders about trying to put in a new bathroom and kitchen, a fax arrives from Philippa saying, *Mr Flick would like to have John Reid's telephone number so that he can disinvite him and his friend Dr Thompson.* Utterly appalled, I call Muck, only to be told he is unavailable.

Philippa says that Muck had thought that, since Elton John was not coming, neither should John Reid. 'How can he disinvite two of the people on the list that I actually know?' I ask. 'After all, isn't it supposed to be a party for me?'

Philippa seems sympathetic but she's obviously a girl who doesn't want to lose her job. 'If John Reid is disinvited then Robin won't go – and I probably won't go either,' I said, and then told her that I would not give her John Reid's telephone number because I thought it was too unutterably rude. Half an hour later another fax from Philippa: Mr Flick says that if he doesn't have John Reid's telephone number by five o'clock he will 'pull the trigger'. I don't know what he means. *We have ways of making you talk?*

I call Philippa and tell her how appalled I am by all this, and that I can no longer handle it. If he wants to 'pull the trigger', whatever that means, go ahead. I'm disgusted by his behaviour. Within half an hour another fax, this time from Muck: *Dear Joan, here's the situation. Robin Hurlstone, John Reid and his friend, Sue St Johns, Stella Wilson, Paul Raben, Roger Moore, Kristina Tholstrup and yourself are disinvited. Best regards, Muck.*

To say that I am stunned is putting it mildly. I'm extremely upset, but I have to go out to meet Amanda and look at bathtubs.

While I'm out, John Reid speaks to Christopher Biggins, who has spoken to Louise Fennell, and by the time I get back it's a done deal. John Reid is going to give the party on the Flick night. The Fennells say they have never heard such disgusting social behaviour and are cancelling going to Muck's, as does Christopher Biggins. All in all, a hell of a day – and now I know why we went to war against Germany. Oooh!

Friday, 7 March 1997

Am getting very excited about the OBE. Receive a flurry of phone calls from everybody who has heard about the party cancellation. All of my friends called Muck or wrote and disinvited themselves. Andrew and Madeleine Lloyd Webber, Tim and Virginia Bell, Charles and Pandora Delevingne, Duncan McLaren. I called Marguerite Littman and told her and she said she'd never heard anything so disgusting and she was not going to go either. Called Roger Moore and told him about the Anouska Hempel/A.A. Gill situation and asked him if he still wanted to come over, as it was now only going to be a party for twenty rather than forty. He said, 'I don't want to see f—ing Muck Flick, I want to see you and congratulate you.'

I talk to John Reid, who is rather excited now about having this party. I order a dozen T-shirts with 'The Uninvited – 12 March 1997' printed on them to give to my guests.

That night I play poker at Paul Raben's. Win a bit. That's good.

Saturday, 8 March 1997

Adam Bricusse came over at five o'clock and started cooking a fine Maltese leg of lamb I'd ordered from Allens of Mount Street. Adam and Sacha went to work in the kitchen, slicing and scraping and doing their army kitchen chores. Adam put about ninety cloves of garlic in the lamb. Katy and her new boyfriend, Paul Robinson, and Tara and Michael arrived and we had a wonderful family evening and Adam's food was delicious.

Sunday, 9 March 1997

Today is Mother's Day in England. Katy and Tara brought me lovely flowers last night, and Sacha and Erin bring me lilies today. I take Sacha to Moss Brothers in Regent Street to order his morning suit for next week. He looks completely dashing and I'm very proud of him. Then off to Daphne's for lunch. In the evening Lily Mahtani picks me up and we go to The Ivy's upstairs restaurant for a party for John Major given by Tim Rice. Lots of showbiz Tory supporters there: Barbara Windsor, Lorraine Chase, Frederick Forsyth. We all mill around doing our cocktail party talk. Mr Major is over an hour late. After talking to the Lloyd Webbers and Virginia Bell, Lily and I have to go because we're meeting friends at the Caprice. Then Hywel, Mr Major's right-hand man, begs me to stay. 'John will be so disappointed. He was so looking forward to seeing you,' he says. Why, I wonder. 'What advice can you give to Mr Major?' asks Hywel. 'Well, the first thing I think he should do is get smaller glasses,' I say. 'Those glasses are very seventies and overpower his face.' 'Why don't you tell him?' says Hywel eagerly. 'Maybe I will,' I say. A flurry of activity and our prime minister himself is in our midst. Tim Bell drags me over to meet and greet. Mr Major is utterly charming. It's a pity that charm, niceness and a certain kind of sex appeal doesn't come through to the voters. I don't think he's got much of a hope in the coming election. Boldly I ask, 'Mr Major, may I make a suggestion?' 'Of course,' he says. 'Why don't you get smaller glasses? You are so attractive

I think that you would look far better with a smaller pair.' He grins and says, 'I'll think about it.' Snap, snap, go the snappers and then Lily and I head off to the Caprice.

Monday, 10 March 1997

Early telephone call from Sue St Johns, who has arrived from California for my big day. I am really thrilled that I have such good friends who will make this big trip. Final fitting at David Emanuel's for the suit and the Philip Somerville hat. They both look great. I've lost seven pounds by dint of practically eating nothing and look pretty good. Have a day of maintenance, manicure, etc., then at seven Duncan McLaren comes over to look at the picture that Sacha has painted of him.

Tuesday, 11 March 1997

Woke up full of excitement. Stella came over and we took a million pics with Sacha and Erin.

Stage fright! These words strike terror into the heart of most performers. On this glorious spring morning as I passed through the historic portals of Buckingham Palace with Sacha, that familiar feeling started. My mouth was suddenly dry and butterflies were playing tag in my stomach, even though I was thrilled to bits. Several hundred British subjects are awarded the title of Officer of the Order of the British Empire every year and it is an accolade which only a few in my profession receive.

My son would be accompanying me to the palace. I had asked Robin but he'd sneered, 'I'm not going to Buck House with you just to get a silly little OBE. Maybe if it were a damehood then I'd accompany you.' I was speechless.

Sacha looked resplendent in his morning coat, and my ladylike lilac suit and rather large hat worked. We were not the only people thus attired. One hundred and forty of today's honourees, including a handful of knights, were gathering nervously inside the palace gates, watched by well-wishers outside, eager faces pushed between the railings. We walked up red-carpeted steps to the entrance hall. Erin, Stella, Sacha and I were separated, then I was ushered past solemn Beefeaters in their dazzling red-and-gold uniforms up more stairs towards the portrait gallery. Just before I went in, a fellow performer hugged me. 'Hello, luv, how're you doing? Are you nervous?' said Paul McCartney, there to receive his well-deserved knighthood. 'I'm scared stiff, are you?' I asked. 'Terrified.' He grinned his mischievous grin, so familiar to millions of fans throughout the world. 'Absolutely terrified. Silly, isn't it?' We chatted for a minute, then were separated by an equerry and I walked into the long pink gallery hung with magnificent paintings. The men in morning coats and the women in hats talked together excitedly, for we had known about this day for three months but now it had arrived we were tense. Finally, summoned in batches of twenty outside the great ballroom, we stood in line and with much neck-craning managed to see the Queen. Stately in royal blue and pearls, she was pinning a medal on each recipient while a five-piece band played show tunes.

It was almost my turn. My mouth was the Gobi Desert now, my knees knocking. Everything seemed effortlessly simple, yet the pomp and circumstance that pervaded the proceedings were redolent of an age of grandeur. 'Are you all right?' asked the kindly equerry who stood beside me. 'I'm petrified,' I whispered. He looked amazed. 'You?' he said. 'I'd never have believed it.' Then I was announced and, as instructed, I strode confidently into the ballroom, turned to the Queen, performed a deep curtsy, which I managed to do without falling flat on my face, took six paces forward, approached the dais and stood before my monarch.

'I'm very, very happy to be giving this to you,' the Queen said as she busied herself with pinning on my medal. 'Thank you, Your Majesty,' I said, my nervousness evaporating. She spoke for the allotted few seconds then held out her hand. I shook it, walked five paces backwards, curtsied again and marched out, mission accomplished. I joined my fellow recipients and we watched the rest of the proceedings from the back of the historic ballroom, commenting on the Queen's graciousness and how difficult it must be to shake hands so many times without getting crushed fingers.

The cream-and-gold ballroom hung with scarlet drapes was vast, yet the five hundred people fitted in easily. I felt an enormous surge of patriotism and pride, and sneaked a look at my badge – a gold cross on a coral silk bow, pretty as well as prestigious. When the ceremony ended there was a tremendous feeling of jubilation as everyone filed out clutching red leather boxes containing the precious medals.

Outside in the spring sunshine the press descended and I happily answered their questions and posed with Sacha. Erin and Stella were extremely excited by all the pomp inside. 'It's the most exciting day I've ever had,' said Stella. We got in Steve's car and raced to The Ivy, where some of my closest friends and family let out a big cheer as Sacha and I walked in. Virginia and Tim Bell, Louise and Theo Fennell, Peter Charlesworth, Johnny Gold, Patrick Donovan, John Bowes-Lyon, Sir Basil Feldman, Lance Reynolds (who'd flown in from Los Angeles), Jonathan Lloyd, my brother Bill and Hazel [his wife], Carole Bamford [friend of JC, and founder of the Daylesford Organic Farmshop chain], Tony Newley and Gina Fratini, Sue St Johns, Una-Mary Parker, Doug Hayward, Adam Bricusse, Charles and Pandora Delevingne, Lily Mahtani and of course my daughters Katy and Tara, and her fiancé Michael – even Robin deigned to attend.

The lunch was one of the best I have ever had. Not just because the food and the wine were excellent but the ambience was absolutely wonderful. Tim Bell made the most touching speech. It was really great.

Everybody was in sparkling form; jokes flew, quips and badinage (none of which I can remember), and we eventually finished lunch, a hard-core group of us, at a quarter to six! Tottered home totally flaked out. Got a call from Donatella Flick, who'd obviously heard the news about the Muck Flick uninvitings. I told her, 'Darling, you deserve a copy of my OBE for what you put up with from that man.' I assured her I would never speak to him again, which I won't.

Wednesday, 12 March 1997

Had a quick lunch with Sue at San Lorenzo. She said that yesterday's lunch was the best she'd ever had. At eight o'clock I went to John Reid's in full black-tie regalia. Roger Moore and Kristina arrived first, always on time. They'd just flown in from Switzerland. Adrian and Nicola (the original uninvited) were there, along with the Bells, the Delevingnes, Paul Raben, Sue, Stella, Duncan McLaren and Robin. Afterwards Patrick and Lance came. The dinner, which started with caviar and blinis, then duck and then a rather delicious pud, was excellent. Several speeches were made, then Roger got up and hysterically read out the 'Collected Works of Muck Flick'. He did a lot of this with a German accent which had us literally hugging our sides with laughter. I'm so sad that I didn't do *Love Letters* with Roger; it would have been great. John Reid, however, said, 'Any time you two want to do *Love Letters*, I want to produce it.'

Andrew Lloyd Webber started playing the piano. As usual he asked me, 'Why didn't you play Norma Desmond?' As usual

I told him that I couldn't sing well enough. He then started playing fifties, sixties and seventies show tunes and I sang along with him, as did Theo and Louise. Had the most wonderful time and tottered home around the two o'clock mark.

Thursday, 13 March 1997

Stella and I flew to Cologne for a German TV show and met the host. Because of Muck Flick, I'm tentative about Germans at the moment. She assured me this was a very serious programme for which she wanted to show the 'real Joan Collins' and not the Alexis that everybody confuses me with. We talked at length about how serious it was going to be and I thought about what stories I could tell to illustrate my seriousness as a human being. I waited around for hours then finally went on camera at a quarter to midnight, having been introduced by her as 'The Denver Beast, a man-eater, who has had four husbands and many lovers and is a woman that people are terrified of.' Ha ha ha. Went on and the first question she asked me was: 'Do you think men should wear underwear?' I pondered the seriousness of this question before answering. Several questions of the same mode came up, for example: 'Do you think the Queen has a hard time with all her relations?' I was wondering when the serious questions were going to be asked, when she stuck out her hand and said: 'Thank you very much for coming.' To my astonishment, after seven minutes the show was over. Stella rushed down, her eyes wide in amazed shock. 'I don't believe it,' she said. 'How could it go so fast? You were supposed to do twenty minutes.' 'Never mind,' I said. 'Money for old rope.'

Friday, 14 March 1997

Returned to London, dashed around and went to meet Jean Diamond at London Management. They all seem really nice and I'm seriously thinking of going there, but I have a bit of a problem because of my loyalty to PC. Left to do the *Clive James Show*, which is a completely different kettle of fish from last night's debacle. Clive was charming, interesting and funny, and I tried to match him in those departments. He asked the questions that everybody seems to like from my book.

Had dinner with Adrian Gill and Nicola Formby at Nobu, the Japanese restaurant at the Metropolitan Hotel that's the new hot spot in London. We discussed the Muck Flick situation and sat for three hours as course after course after course arrived, each one more delicious than the last. Everyone assured me nothing was fattening, but everything is fattening. Paula Yates, balancing a gorgeous baby on one hip, came over to say hello, and to tell Adrian that he was the only person who had ever written anything nice about her, 'So can I give you a blow job?' she said boldly. Even Adrian looked surprised. I can see Paula's charm and why she managed to wrest Michael Hutchence away from Helena Christensen. She's sassy, sexy, and speaks her mind. I can also see why she's hated. We asked why the baby was out so late. 'Oh, I take Heavenly Hiraani [the baby's name] with me everywhere,' she said. 'I have to. I breastfeed her every half an hour.' Nicola and I looked at each other, somewhat stunned. 'Every half an hour?' I said. 'How long is this going to go on for?' 'Well, the last one I breastfed until she was three years old,' she said. 'In fact I met Warren Beatty at a party and I was talking to him when Pixie came in, undid my dress and started having a swig. Warren looked quite nonplussed, raised his eyebrows and walked away.' She laughed and we laughed back. She was quite endearing.

Sunday, 16 March 1997

Lunch at the Delevingnes, where I played with my godchildren: Cara Delevingne, who is four, and Coco Fennell, who's seven. Both children are adorable and it was a very jolly family day. Played poker at Cathy Sloan's. Lost three hundred pounds. *Quelle horreur!*

Friday, 21 March 1997

Had to go to the American Embassy to get my US work visa as one of Aaron Spelling's minions had just left it sitting on their desk for two weeks! At seven o'clock Jean Paul Gaultier and his assistant, along with Tara and Michael, came over to discuss the wedding dresses. Jean Paul is completely different from the way I had imagined him. Even though he wears three earrings in one ear and two in the other and cropped hair dyed yellow, he is utterly charming and loves a gossip. We talked about Madonna and her baby and movies for an hour. Then when Sue St Johns arrived, Jean Paul leapt into action and produced the dresses that we had seen in Paris. Tara and I tried them on and we planned colours, fabrics and lengths. Sue was terribly impressed by the fact that he does very simple clothes as well as avant-garde. I think that Tara is going to be a gorgeous bride.

'He's my new best friend,' said Sue about Jean Paul. 'He's wonderful.'

Indeed he is, and I only hope when the bill comes for the clothes that we will still think he is wonderful!

Saturday, 22 March 1997

David Emanuel comes over to deliver my *point d'esprit* dress for Tara's wedding-night party. Finally, after four fittings, it looks terrific. Tara and Michael and I discuss the wedding preparations for two hours. 'It's going to be the wedding of the year in Paris,' says Tara. She is incredibly enthusiastic and I just hope that it all goes as well as she hopes it will. Whatever, I'm excited to be the mother of the bride – and my first-born at that.

Sunday, 23 March 1997

Flew Air New Zealand to Los Angeles. Ten hours, pretty uneventful, good food, and the luggage came through extremely fast – a major plus. I ate and drank too much and slept. The apartment looked unlived in and I was fiddling about with it and unpacking when Jeffrey called and said I should watch the Judy Garland biography programme, which was fabulous. God, what a life. Poor woman, when she died at forty-seven she looked more like seventy-seven.

Monday, 24 March 1997

To Nolan for a fitting for the dress I'll wear to the *Vanity Fair* Oscar party. Worked out in the gym and found out that I had not lost any weight, so I'm cross with myself. Nolan and I arrived at the *Vanity Fair* party at Morton's in broad daylight at quarter to six. The usual soundbite crews and paparazzi were there in spades. Oscar night really is the night when Hollywood comes into its own and at the party there was no shortage of familiar faces, even though it was short on stars. Greeted Lynn Wyatt; Denise Minelli was there with Willy Brown, Mayor of

San Francisco, Wendy Goldberg and Graydon Carter and lots of movie businesspeople. Sat next to Dominick Dunne, which is always fun as he is a true film buff. He and I spent much of the time trying to get the waiters out of our eyeline and people like Ryan O'Neal and Tony Curtis to stop standing in front of the TV screens. It's totally different from Swifty's party at Spago where everyone was really on their best behaviour and wouldn't dare to chat when the nominations are announced. Shirley Mac-Laine and date, who were supposed to be at our table, didn't show up, so Kirk Kerkorian and his wife, and Fay and Frank Mancuso were at our table. Also there were the Schlatters, the Poitiers, the Davises and sister Jackie, who came over and was very friendly. She congratulated me on the OBE and said that she'd heard that my lunch at The Ivy was fun. I told her I was sorry she hadn't flown over, but she was working on a new book.

During the commercial breaks, I did some tentative table-hopping. Wendy Stark was with Ryan O'Neal, who's separated from Farrah Fawcett. Or rather, Ryan was at her table chatting up Bianca Jagger. Alana Stewart Hamilton came over; she'd heard that I was mad at her for not coming to Sacha's show, and apologised, saying that she hadn't been invited. We kissed and made up. Tony Curtis was there with his amazing girlfriend, Jill, the definitive starlet with a huge bust and bottom and the tightest white skin-tight trousers and halter-top I've ever seen. Tony wears a huge medal all the time. I asked him what it was and he said that it's some sort of Viennese honour. 'Why don't you wear yours?' he asked. 'Well, that's not exactly done,' I answered.

Everyone was disappointed that Lauren Bacall did not win Best Supporting Actress, and the camera kept lingering on her when the nominations were announced as her eyes seemed to fill with tears – I thought it was most unfair, even though I didn't think her performance was worth it. *The English Patient* seemed to get a hell of a lot of awards, although I was surprised that Kristin Scott Thomas didn't pull off Best Actress. I was thrilled for Geoffrey Rush in *Shine*. Having been to the premiere four months ago of this film I'd never heard of, it was wonderful to see it so acknowledged. Towards the end of the ceremony, which was unbelievably long, the whole of the room was talking and the waiters started removing the flowers and the candles and glasses from the table. 'Swifty would turn in his grave,' I said. Old Hollywood was not represented at all in terms of either directors or stars. There were no Billy Wilders, Gregory Pecks, Kirk Douglases. I suppose the oldest person there would have been Al Ruddy, producer of *The Godfather*.

Ellen DeGeneres, who has a sitcom called *Ellen* and is extremely famous in the US, dropped by our table. Dominick asked her if it was true she was 'coming out' in her show, as there have been hints that she is a lesbian – which in real life she is. She said yes and they expected to get tremendous ratings as it's an hour-long special, and they have Demi Moore and Oprah Winfrey on, among others. When she told me the date I got slightly nervous, as it is the same date that my first episode in *Pacific Palisades* will be airing. Typical. I'm going to call Aaron Spelling tomorrow to see if it's true.

Jeffrey and I hotfooted it to Dani Janssen's penthouse in Century City where the crème de la crème and really good (supposedly) would be dining. Chatted with Jack Nicholson, who seems to have lost his wolfish sex appeal – or maybe he just wasn't taking any substances. Dennis Hopper was friendly and remembered when we'd first met when we were kids in Hollywood years ago. Had a long talk with Ed Begley Jr and Penny Marshall. She's supposedly set to direct *Bewitched* and I want to play Endora in it. I found it incredibly difficult to understand one word out of five Penny spoke, and couldn't figure out whether that was because of her accent or whether she was drunk or whether I was drunk. After half an hour I gathered that she wasn't interested in directing *Bewitched* in any case, and the usual story: 'The script's not ready'! Clint Eastwood sat in a corner looking terribly serious, as did Timothy Dalton. Shirley MacLaine came over and I asked her why she hadn't come to the Oscar *Vanity Fair* party. 'Oh, I forgot,' she said, not seeming too concerned about leaving Dominick without a dinner partner.

Talked to Anne and Arnie Kopelson and George Segal and Timothy Dalton. After two hours decided to hit another party, even though Dani kept insisting that Al (Pacino) was on his way. Didn't want to wait to find out, but bumped into Michael Douglas coming out of the lift and we hugged warmly, although we don't know each other that well.

Went to the Maple Drive restaurant for Elton John's Aids Benefit party. It was quite a happening, even though every hairdresser and decorator in Los Angeles had paid to get in. John Reid found us in the throng and took us into an inner sanctum to see Elton. He was wearing a new brown floppy hairpiece, quite fetching, and a lovely butterfly brooch *en tremblant*. His boyfriend David was there. Geoffrey Rush came in, the Oscar-winning star of the night, and we hugged too, although I'd only met him once before at the party after *Shine*. There was a lot of jostling and many people had too much to drink. After talking to Seal and Trudie Styler and lots of other people, we sat with Lulu and her husband. She was utterly sweet and complimentary to me. But I often find this quite embarrassing. She seemed to mean it sincerely, though. She looks great and we became a mutual admiration society. The photographer Firooz Zahedi came by, by which time I'd had enough to drink to ask him to photograph me because I thought he was a great photographer. Tottered out about one thirty. The diehard autograph hunters were there with their pens and bits of paper flapping in the wind, asking for my autograph, but holding on to Jeffrey with one arm and my bag with the other, plus my sanity after eight hours of drinking Scotch, I was unable to fulfil their desires. A couple of them actually booed me! 'I can't believe that,' I said to Jeffrey in the car, 'just because I wouldn't sign their autographs on scraps of paper.' 'It's a sign of the times,' he said.

Home at two. It's been a hard day's night – eight hours of schmoozing and boozing.

Wednesday, 26 March 1997

Called Aaron – yes, it's true! He's been having murders with Fox to see if we can change our air date because of Ellen coming out, but we can't. That's showbiz folks. Had another fitting with Nolan: do not like the black cocktail dress, neither does Judy. What are we going to do?

Dinner at Spago with Jeffrey and Judy. Spago has really gone off in terms of the clientele, although the food is still terrific. Not that I would know since I'm hardly eating anything, which is really a drag. I would love to get down to a hundred and twenty but it's like pulling teeth not to eat. The camera adds ten pounds always.

Thursday, 27 March 1997

Lunch at Le Dome given by Wendy Goldberg. Arrive promptly at twelve thirty; sister Jackie and Alana Stewart are already there. Wendy arrives twenty minutes late, clutching tiny Easter chocolate eggs which she distributes around the table. Irena Medavoy arrives, then we wait and we wait and we wait. Ann Jones shows up, then Bianca Jagger and then Barbara Thornhill. I have eaten half a cauliflower and cucumber as I'm permanently starving. Conversation is spirited, but not as spirited as it would be in London. Have to leave at two o'clock for a fitting at Nolan's. My stomach feels like I've swallowed six balloons. Judy tells me it's because of the cauliflower. Another fitting of the black dress; it's still not good.

On to the studio where *Pacific Palisades* shoots. It's next door to Van Nuys Airport – not good for the sound department. I visit my trailer, which is luxurious, and Monica, the hairdresser, is bustling around being bossy. Meet the producer, Peter, and the director, Chip. They couldn't be more charming, helpful and interested. What a difference to my first day on *Dynasty* when I felt cold antipathy from Forsythe and various others. Here they are welcoming me like I'm some sort of queen. I think people are quite impressed by the OBE. They don't seem to know what it means and they think it's like a knighthood – which it is!

On to the set where everybody looks to be about twelve years old and I meet a couple of the actresses. I notice the planes flying over during a take and think what fun this is going to be! Everybody has enormous enthusiasm for this show; I'm keeping my fingers crossed. Outside I meet Lucky Vanous, the hunk who's playing the Hunk. He is most famous for the commercial in which he plays the bare-shirted builder who drinks a can of Diet Coke watched by gobsmacked secretaries. Every time I mention this guy, girls drool. He's quite charming, good-looking and well-dressed. I comment on his suit and how good it looks. Try on the new wig, which is much lighter than my own hair and is, I think, different enough from Alexis to make it interesting.

When I get home, Nolan calls. 'What did you do to them on the set?' he asks. 'They all think you're great.' 'News travels fast,'

I say. 'What happened?' 'Oh, they all said you were lovely and gorgeous and charming,' he goes on, laughing, 'and Lucky went dashing into Eilish's wardrobe department to say excitedly that you liked his suit.'

Exhausted, I go to bed early, trying to lose a few pounds by eating only broccoli. I know Mummy used to say you've got to suffer to be beautiful but I'm permanently starving.

Saturday, 29 March 1997

Went with Jeffrey, Sacha and Erin to see Steven Berkoff's new play *Massage*. He said he'd like to work with me again – well, let's see if that comes off! It's is an avant-garde piece in which Steven's dressed as a woman, camps around the stage in mini-skirts and plenty of slap and is actually convincing and quite good. The play is mostly about masturbation, the language out-rageous, with detailed descriptions of the male organs – Steven takes delight in miming releasing them from their confines. We sample the new and supposedly hot restaurant Coco Pazzo, and then adjourn to the Sky Bar on the roof, which is filled with wannabees and have-nots. I'm greeted by a short gentleman who says, 'Hi, I'm Jackie Stallone's agent, we watched you on your court case. Jackie's going through the same thing right now and you gave her inspiration.'

I don't stay long. Young, so-called hip Hollywood is not my scene. Sacha says this isn't young, hip Hollywood. That doesn't really exist, except perhaps in private houses.

Easter Sunday, 30 March 1997

Jeffrey and I went to Jackie's for lunch and watched the part of the Oscar ceremony we hadn't been able to see because of the waiters getting in the way. Billy Crystal was unbelievably funny as the MC. Went to see Howard Stern's movie *Private Parts*, which I really liked as I'm a fan of his. Had early night preparing for tomorrow. I'm worried about this new wig; I hope it's going to be good.

Monday, 31 March 1997

Picked up by my driver, Linda, and driven forty-five minutes to the studios on Balboa Boulevard next to Van Nuys Airport, where we are shooting the first day of *Pacific Palisades*. As I'd expected, the studio is not soundproofed. It's a huge old warehouse that was a factory for making bombs during the last war – hope we won't be making one this time. The hairdresser brings the wig and to our horror and fury the stupid woman who made it has cut the whole top, crown and fringe so that the style is totally ruined and I look like a French poodle.

'I told her ten times *not* to cut it,' wails Monica. 'And I told her to keep the crown and top long.' This is really a blow since I wanted a different look: light brown hair with blonde streaks in it. Monica calls the wig maker, who is considered to be the best in this town, and patiently explains the problem to her, but the bitch hangs up! I throw a conniption fit which Monica, a fellow Gemini and Brit, understands, then we try on another wig and spray gold dust on it. But I *still* look like Alexis!

Finally at three o'clock I work with Kimberley Davies and Michelle. They are both in their mid-twenties, very cute, wearing short little frocks that look as though they cost seventeen dollars. As I am decked out in Nolan's black satin peignoir and velvet dressing gown, I am definitely over the top – however, I am playing her mom. Kimberley wears as much make-up as I do and coincidentally the same brand. I adore the director,

Chip Chalmers, and J.R. the lighting cameraman. He is the son of Richard Rawling, who was the great cinematographer on *Dynasty*.

I think the scenes go well and I'm quite pleased. Nolan comes over for a final fitting at seven o'clock with the dreaded black cocktail dress. I try it on but it still doesn't cut it. I'm too disheartened to tell Lucy the fitter to alter it again. Jeffrey agrees with me that it isn't flattering. After Nolan leaves, I show Jeffrey one of my dresses, a high-necked, sleeveless, long black dress, a combination of Valentino and Yves Saint Laurent. He agrees it is infinitely better and much more nineties. I do not want to look like Alexis in this show, which of course is rather difficult since we have the same face and voice and now the frigging wig.

I fall asleep at nine-thirty and wake at one thirty with this fearful ghastly Santa Ana wind rocking the whole building *again*. It's like being in *Wuthering Heights*.

Tuesday, 1 April 1997

Three months of this year have gone. I can't believe it. Linda drives me to a nightclub on La Cienega called The Gate, which used to be La Cage Aux Folles. Nolan arrives with 'the dress' but I've already told his assistant that I'm not going to wear it. He's quite upset and I'm upset too because I adore him, but it's more important that I look right in this part than hurting somebody's feelings.

I do a short scene with Lucky Vanous. He has a cheeky sense of humour and I think he will probably go far as he's studying acting like mad. Kimberley has done an excellent job of covering up her Australian accent to sound American. She looks very Barbie dollish, pretty figure and enormous lips (bigger than Ivana Trump's), rather small eyes and extremely bleached blonde hair.

Lance visits at lunchtime and tells me that she'd been around for quite a while and they have various mutual friends and he does not believe she's twenty-four as she has been on *Neighbours* for three years.

J.R. says that I look exactly the same as when I was on *Dynasty*, which is nice to hear. I call Aaron Spelling to thank him for the flowers he sent yesterday and he starts raving about the rushes and how great I look, blah, blah, blah. Here we go again. But we still don't know if this show is going to be picked up after six episodes, and even if it is picked up are they going to go with me? Jeffrey drops by the set after a meeting with ABC and says he feels sure that they will, but there's no such thing as a certainty in showbiz and horse-racing. The only certainty is that I have to keep my calorie consumption to under a thousand a day, and I'm eating aptly named rabbit food. However, it's paying off as I look slimmer.

Wednesday, 2 April 1997

Lead item in Army Archerd's column in *Daily Variety*, complete with colour picture. Jeffrey extremely excited. 'They never use colour,' he exults. Basic premise of article: Aaron Spelling's *Dynasty* darling Joan Collins is back, etc. etc. etc. Spelling is quoted as saying, 'We wanted someone to play a vixen and who's a better vixen – and she looks fantastic.' I am quoted as saying, 'The public will get flashes of my claws in the first episode but the character will have less of a hard edge.' I admitted it's great to be back in series TV. Well, it is. Still get that Norma Desmond feeling sometimes!

Judy and Max arrive from Vegas to stay in the apartment for a few days. It's really great to have them as she is more like a sister. I'm picked up at 4 p.m. by Linda, who is turning out to be a bit of a treasure. Work night location outside Laura's house in lovely downtown Encino. It's bitterly cold. Who says the California climate is great? I prefer Europe's weather. Every time I talk to somebody in London they tell me about the glorious spring they are having. I think the scene went well. Kimberley is quite a good little actress and seems to be improving. Our scenes have an edge.

I take the Bryers and Jeffrey to Eclipse, my favourite restaurant in LA, for a celebratory dinner.

Thursday, 3 April 1997

Janice French called to say that Russell Kagan and a business partner were in town and could I possibly fit them in for a quick meeting? Since it's still night shooting tonight, I agreed. Russ is a tough, hard, but charming go-getter. He has just put together the movie *Samson and Delilah* with Elizabeth Hurley giving us her Delilah, and various other biblical epics which are doing very well on cable. His idea is to take four or five of my books – *Prime Time*, *Love and Desire and Hate*, *Too Damn Famous* and perhaps my autobiographies – and to make movies or mini-series out of them. 'I know your potential in Europe is still huge,' said Russ. 'They don't realise that in Hollywood, because they never get to see the whole picture.' He asked me if *Prime Time* was unencumbered and I said yes, although I was slightly worried about Lance, to whom I gave a free option for two years, but he hasn't managed to get it off the ground. As fond of him as I am, nothing has come to fruition – and we have had endless discussions over the past two years.

A rich Greek's secretary called to try to set up a meeting. Betsy Bloomingdale had told me about him and said that if I ever had any money to invest, he was the man. Well, I do have the Random House money but I'm terrified of investors – been burnt too many times.

Went off to location at four. I must say they are treating me in rather a queenly manner. I'm the only one who has a large trailer with TV, kettle, make-up mirror, loo, shower and bed. Did an interview with *Access Hollywood*, a popular showbiz news programme. J.R. the DP came and checked the lighting, which is so sweet of him. 'Do I need a mohair blanket over the lens?' I joked. He smiled and said, 'Absolutely not.' This crew is so much nicer and friendlier in these first few days than the *Dynasty* crew were in the first year. There must have been some sort of block with everyone, and I think I know what the blocks were – Forsythe and Evans. Things weren't helped by the vicious rumours constantly perpetrated about me by, I think, Doug Cramer. I know it was good for their business but it wasn't good for my morale, constantly leaking lies to the media.

Rehearsed a confrontation scene with Kimberley outside the Malibu mansion. It was bitterly cold. All the rest of the cast were there, including Finola Hughes who has been working on daytime TV for the past three years. She is so sweet, a very good actress and ballerina. We made a forgettable film together called *Nutcracker* in 1982. Everyone watched as my double, dressed in identical white suit and wig, struggled with Kimberley's double and we fell into the pool, amidst much hilarity from the crew and my group of friends who were hanging out. We had a lorra lorra laughs. But talk about copying from *Dynasty*!

The crew, all huddled in anoraks and woolly hats, watched as Kimberley and I tentatively got into the water, which was heated to about a hundred and fifty degrees. It was actually quite pleasant, although my white skirt kept on floating up to reveal my pants. We drenched ourselves thoroughly then come up spluttering and splattering. I called her a bitch, which I hope they leave in. Unfortunately the writers had not given us any dialogue for this scene, so I threw in a few ad-libs. I wonder if this is what the producers think is going to rival Krystle and Alexis's fights. Got out of the pool to applause from crew and onlookers, then quickly changed. Linda, the new treasure, had bustled around getting beer, a bottle of Scotch, turkey burgers and sandwiches, which she'd laid out in my trailer. When we're on late locations the meal hours are ludicrous. Lunch is at four and dinner, if we're lucky, is at midnight or so. Finished the scene at one a.m.

Friday, 4 April 1997

Lunched at The Ivy with Steve Tellez, my new CAA agent. Well, he's not so new any more because he's been representing me for over two months. We discussed the ramifications of why the Spelling organisation have not signed me to more than three episodes, and why they are farting and fiddling about with my contract. I told him I wanted to continue in the series, and he agreed that I should, but said that they were not committing to me. I don't know why, but I realise it's probably to do with the fact that I make a lot more money than the other actors and also I am possibly not 'demographically viable'. Translation: 'too old'. That's my opinion. I think that network 'suits' are a cynical bunch of bastards – and that goes for all of them, charming as they are to one's face. I told Steve I really wanted to work on other projects and was hoping to play Endora in the movie version of *Bewitched*, for which, according to Justin, I am still a front runner. Hmm – they told me that about *One Hundred and One Dalmatians*, and Miss Close snagged that.

Lance joined us for coffee. He said he has the rights to the new Pamela Harriman biography, a tell-all tale of the world-famous courtesan and socialite. Another actress would play her in her twenties and thirties, and then I would take over up until her recent death at the Ritz Hotel swimming pool. What a cool way to die! Instead of just pitching this, Lance immediately started bringing up all my books – *Prime Time*, *Love and Desire and Hate* – and also pitched the 'Joan's World' project, which is this travel idea that Stella came up with. Seriously embarrassed as the table was suddenly covered in all my paperback books, I glared at Lance. Steve, the definitive smooth-talking, rather charming, businesslike Hollywood agent, was suitably attentive. I wonder how good CAA will be. After all, they do handle Aaron Spelling, from whom they make a minimum three million bucks a year, so I am but the tiniest cog in their wheel and it behoves them to make me dance to the tune of the Spelling organisation.

Bumped into Tamara Beckwith with a group of friends. She told me she is excited about Tara's wedding. Diahann Carroll and Jeffrey met for drinks in my apartment. She was looking extremely glamorous, and strangely enough we were wearing similar outfits: black tuxedo jackets, long skirts and diamonds. She is still limping from her two-year stint as Norma Desmond in *Sunset Boulevard* in Canada. That must really have been a terrible grind. She had to go up and down seven hundred steps each performance. Who says an actress's life is glamorous? We imbibed our latest favourite brew, orange Stoli, and then Nolan arrived and we shot off to L'Orangerie, which I consider to be the most sophisticated and glamorous restaurant in Los Angeles. It was Jeffrey's treat, so we had caviar with scrambled egg, absolutely delish, and I went off my diet for that course. It's a fight to the finish, keeping to 124 pounds. Had a wonderfully funny dinner. Nolan is so amusing and his stories about everybody from Joan Crawford to Carol Channing to Barbara Stanwyck should be made into a book.

Saturday, 5 April 1997

Conference call with Russell Kagan in New York and Janice French here. Russ says he's still hot to trot. One of the things I know about Hollywood and show business is that talk is very, very cheap and in plentiful supply.

Aaron Tonken called and said did Jeffrey and I want to meet him at Cartier as he wanted to buy me a present for introducing him to an actress whom he wanted to meet. I am not one to say no to a trip to Cartier, so off we trotted. We met in Cartier's boutique and I found a great pair of gold earrings, although at nine thousand dollars(!) they look somewhat like what one can buy at the costume jewellery counter at Saks.

Aaron is a bright young man who has made a niche for himself in America by putting celebrities together for parties for big companies, e.g. Cartier, and organising functions and charities, etc. He's just done Natalie Cole's big birthday party, and the 150th celebration of Cartier in New York, which he got Brooke Shields and Claudia Schiffer to attend. Quite a coup, that. We went and sat in a café on Brighton Way and he talked to me seriously about the fact that now was the time for me to try and make some money out of licensing myself and to be part owner. He sure is right there, and he said he is interested in helping me. While we were deep in conversation a woman who was dressed like a tourist came up and bent her head to look under my hat. I looked up and said, 'What can I do for you?' 'I just wanted to say hello,' she said, not giving a shit that she had interrupted a deep business discussion. 'Hello,' I said coolly and turned back to continue my conversation. 'I always knew you were hateful on TV,' she snarled. 'And you're obviously just like that in real life.' She stumbled off and I felt slightly shaken up. Aaron's eyes opened wide in surprise. 'Does that happen to you often?' he asked. 'Unfortunately, unless you interrupt anything you're doing and give them your full attention, there are some morons who think that because they see you on the box they own you,' I said. 'C'est la vie.'

Later, I dressed 'casual' as instructed and went to Candy and Aaron Spelling's house for dinner and a movie. Aaron said he had a cold. He gets more colds than any person I've ever met, but I think it's because he hardly ever eats and is extremely thin. Candy worries about him all the time. We sat in Aaron's study, which is completely lined with bookshelves containing leather-bound copies of all the scripts he's ever made, from *Mod Squad* to *The Love Boat*, *Charlie's Angels*, *Dynasty*, *Beverly Hills 90210* and *Melrose Place*. 'I gotta show you your rushes,' he said excitedly. 'They're just great and you look fantastic.' Nolan brought down the tape and I was pleased to see that I am not the only person who has difficulty with TV video equipment, as Candy couldn't work it and had to call the English butler to help her. 'He used to work for the Queen Mother,' boasted Candy. Aaron said, 'And he's quite a fan of yours!' Saw the night-time scene and the pool scene and thought they were OK, although I hate watching myself on rushes as I am super-hypercritical.

Dinner was sent in as they are having chef problems. Aaron read us a poem he'd written about Candy and her sixteen cooks. Their home is probably one of the biggest and most lavish in LA, but they are having to sue the builder for three million dollars because the roof is leaking and it's costing three quarters of a million dollars to get it fixed. Scaffolding encroaches around the front of the house, rather spoiling the view. During dinner we are informed that the last reel of *The Saint*, which we are supposed to see, has been left at Marvin Davis's house from last night. Aaron goes totally bananas. Minions are summoned right, left and centre to find the missing reel. Ah, the problems of the rich! The Spellings' screening room is about the size of the average Odeon, but much more comfortable. Cashmere rugs cover our knees as we watch the Val Kilmer starrer. I give it a four. The plots are so bizarre these days. I don't usually like Kilmer, but he's not bad in this.

Sunday, 6 April 1997

Went to see the Bette Midler film *That Old Feeling*. It hasn't had terrific reviews but the cinema was completely packed and we had to sit all the way down front and to the side, so Bette Midler looked extremely thin. I loved the film, as it's about an actress and there are some really witty and perceptive bits in it. I think most critics suck and they *hate* commercial films.

Monday, 7 April 1997

Worked at studio until five then rushed home to get totally tarted up for the press launch of *Pacific Palisades* at Eclipse. Wore new white St Laurent suit, quite simple, and went with Jeffrey. Masses of photographers outside. Was greeted with enormous affection by the CEO of Fox, David Hill, an Australian (natch), who seems jovial, avuncular and enthusiastic about the show. Peter Roth, he who originally turned me down then became my number one fan at Aaron's Christmas Eve party, was in high spirits. Did all the media press, *Entertainment Tonight*, *Access Hollywood*, E! Entertainment, Sky News, etc. etc. They all asked the same questions. 'Is this character like Alexis?' I fend them all off, humorously I hope, then Lucky and I get into a conversation. 'I hate all the media hype,' he says. Jeffrey told me that his agent, Joel Dean, said that Lucky wanted to know what my 'personal status was' because he would like to date me! I have a feeling he's a highly ambitious young man who has been married but the wife is no longer mentioned. However, he's jolly good fun and we posed for piccies with Kimberley and the rest of the cast. Then Peter Roth got onto the podium and made flowery speeches and introduced Aaron, who then introduced all the cast ending up with me. Lots of applause and more photogs – ah the glamour of Hollywood.

Joined Candy and Nolan at our table while Aaron was table-hopping excitedly. I sat next to Peter Roth, who was seriously over-enthusiastic about how fabulous the show is and how fabulous I am in it and sexy blah, blah, blah. I have learnt to take all of these things with a very huge tablespoonful of salt. If one believed all the good things then one would believe all the bad, and that would be fatal. George Christy, a columnist for the *Hollywood Reporter*, came over and plonked himself down at an empty seat at the table even though Jeffrey protested that Aaron was coming back.

George, who had called me two days ago to ask me to read and review a 500-page biography of Spencer Tracy and Katharine Hepburn, and was rather put out when I said I had a few things going on, ordered his food instantly, even though he wasn't invited. Talk about pushy. He did this at the *Larry Flynt* premiere too. After half an hour Jeffrey said that he needed to bring some people over to meet Peter Roth and me, who were sitting at the other end deeply engrossed in chat. George said crossly, 'Can't you see I'm still eating my dinner – can't it wait until I've finished?' 'No,' said Jeffrey, going pink in the face. With enormously bad grace Mr Christy finally got up and stalked off. Needless to say he did not mention the party in his column. Some gossip columnists and press are so much more difficult and demanding than any actor is. Aaron was extremely chuffed by the reaction to the show's potential.

Tuesday, 8 April 1997

We all worked hard all day. Had a complicated scene in which I am telling all the assembled young people about my life as the lady of the manor in Gloucestershire. I think it was quite funny. I certainly hope so. Eddie Sanderson on the set was desperate to get headshots of me and double shots with Lucky and me. Finally did the shots at eleven thirty. I wore the sleeveless black top and long Valentino skirt and Lucky wore a dark suit. I think the shots were OK even though we were both exhausted.

Wednesday, 9 April 1997

Christopher Biggins came to stay. Lunched with Gary Concoff, my lawyer, and Lance at Le Dome to discuss this idea for 'Joan's World', a half-hour travelogue in which I'll go around the world introducing everybody to the delights of the cuisine and the culture. *Lifestyles of the Rich and Famous* meets *Dynasty*. Gary and Lance looked like they'd had a bit of a row before I got there and Lance seemed sulky. Nikki Haskell was at the next table with Beverly Johnson. 'Hi gorgeous,' she gushed as she came over to the table. She calls everyone gorgeous – it doesn't matter if they look like a dog.

My new secretary, Christine, is a bit flaky. Other than the fact that she can't take messages properly, can't type and gets flustered at everything, she's quite nice. She has been spending the past two days trying to get my ticket to London sorted out, and my television to work. Both things seem to be too much for her. The trusty Linda seems to do things much faster and more efficiently, plus she's on the set all the time. After Gary left, Lance and I were joined by David Niven Jr, which was a giggle. Jeffrey came down and we grabbed some food. I'd told

Christine that Biggins was a big eater but even with the four of us at the grub only about 20 per cent was eaten. We then all went into the bedroom to recline and watch the first episode of *Pacific Palisades*, which had been heavily promo-ed on Fox's Channel Eleven. I was pleasantly surprised, as were Jeffrey, Robin and Biggins. It's really quite good and interesting, and some of the cast are excellent, particularly Finola Hughes and Kimberley Davies. Some are only OK and don't photograph well at all. As *USA Today* said in their review, '*Palisades* is pallid with too many gaunt and toothy actors in it. Let's wait and see if Joan Collins can add some spice.' Hah, rather difficult to add spice when Ellen DeGeneres is coming out of the closet in exactly the same time-slot. Anyway we'll see.

Thursday, 10 April 1997

Had a call from Jeffrey saying *Pacific Palisades* got a thirteen share in the overnight Nielsen ratings, which means it was watched by 8.9 million people. Not bad, considering it followed *Melrose Place*, which got a fourteen. I never understand these damn ratings, actually, but each point means millions. Plus they got the demographics, the magic 18–59 age group.

Biggins and I drove to Santa Monica to meet Miriam Margolyes at Shutters Hotel on the beach. It was a beautiful day, we had a simply hilarious lunch, then went walking along Venice Beach while Miriam kept on admonishing me to hide my diamond rings and bracelets as 'everybody gets mugged around here, darling'. The usual decrepit-looking beach-dwellers were strolling around enjoying the lovely weather, but there were a lot of the homeless too. Very sad.

Robin and I are just coasting now, and Biggins continually makes me laugh – he's such a tonic!

148

Friday, 11 April 1997

Fitting with Nolan in the morning and an interview with *Entertainment Tonight* at the same time. Supposed to meet Aaron Tonken for lunch at The Ivy but he doesn't show. Apparently his accountant has run off with three quarters of a million dollars. He's understandably pissed off. I know the feeling.

Drove to the beach to David Geffen's house. It's a beautiful house right on the beach in Malibu. Greyish stone and wood, very chic, laid-back and stylish. Geffen, who is a major mogul, greeted us and took us into the living room, where the new widow Sue Mengers was ensconced and wreathed in kaftan and marijuana fumes. I got a contact high from just being in the room. Ordering a Stoli orange vodka which came in a quart glass, got my own high. Alice Ferreira who was Tara and Sacha's nanny and now works for Geffen and is the Portuguese mafia in terms of housekeeping, gave me a big hug and said how much she wanted to go to Tara's wedding. Lovely conversation with her. Then Barry Diller arrived. Killer Diller, as he's known.

After dinner we went to Geffen's screening room where he ran Arnold Kopelson's new epic *Murder at Sixteen Hundred* starring Wesley Snipes and some truly boring girl. The film was so boring that I fell asleep, so remember nothing of it.

Sue was in very good form and when she mentioned Jean-Claude it was in the most normal kind of way.

Saturday, 12 April 1997

Caught the 11.40 America West to Las Vegas. Met by Max and Judy, all excited to see us. Can't wait to hit the tables, so we go to the new hotel casino complex called New York, New York. Robin and Biggins disappear and Judy and I hit the blackjack tables, where I get the most appalling cards and lose fast. Meet Jeffrey and go up to Hamilton's, which is George Hamilton's sophisticated cocktail bar on the first floor of New York, New York. It is dark, elegant and beautifully designed, a bit like George! It keeps all the noise of the casino out, yet one can go to the window and look down and see the bustling crowds playing their games. There's a piano which gives a distinctly thirties/forties feeling.

I have never in my entire life seen such a group of hideosities as there are wandering around in Las Vegas. The fattest people are the ones who wear the tightest shorts and the most lurid shirts. It is quite astonishing. It amazes me that people can walk around eating as though they're animals – stuff, stuff, stuffing their faces.

Play blackjack once more – my luck's appalling – then try the slots with Judy. I think slots are for cretins, but she seems to like it. I, of course, throw endless quarters in and get nothing.

Dash to the hot show in Vegas, *Jubilee*. We are escorted to the best table by a security guard, having almost got lost driving down the Strip. Downtown Las Vegas is a mixture of Leicester Square, Piccadilly and Times Square, with a lot less charm, and the street signs are unutterably confusing. It has changed totally since I first came here in the late fifties to see Sammy Davis Junior and Frank Sinatra at the Sands. It was a sleepy little desert town but unbelievably glamorous. In the great hotels everyone was gorgeous, chic and brilliantly dressed.

Jubilee has a cast of about a hundred and fifty performers, fifty of whom are bare-breasted showgirls. Every one of them is simply ravishing, with the world's most perfect bodies and beautiful faces. It's extraordinary that in a place where ugly people traipse around the casinos, the most beautiful people I've ever seen sparkle on stage.

I enjoyed the show, although it was far too long. The Bob Mackie costumes are fabulous, the girls wonderful, but the chorus boys are all far too camp, particularly a skinny Samson in the 'Samson and Delilah' sketch. Jeffrey went to see Engelbert Humperdinck. He tried hard to persuade us to go to Mr Humperdinck's opening night, but reason prevailed. Judy, Max and I go to Hamilton's bar again. George greets us, suave and perma-tanned as ever and smoking a big cigar. He is very much a cigar business mogul these days, importing his own and selling them very successfully. He is with his girlfriend Kimberly, a six-foot beauty. We have drinks with Sean Young and her husband. Sean and I discuss *Legends*, the theatre project that I've been involved with for two years. Then we go into the back of Hamilton's, which is called the Railway Car, a long thin room with a long thin table, which looks down onto the milling crowds. Have the most excellent claret – George really does know his wines – but it's almost midnight and we are utterly ravenous. The food which we had ordered earlier was practically inedible. We'd ordered caviar because George had suggested it, but all we got were two eye-bath-sized pots for eight of us! The steak was good but cold. Couldn't wait to get back to the tables.

George escorted Judy and me to a special cordoned-off room where he persuaded the management to take down the hundred-dollar minimum sign and make it a five-dollar minimum. It was fun to play, but my God, my luck is bad and I lost another couple of hundred dollars.

Sunday, 13 April 1997

I wake up to a huge blast of sun in my face from these tiny little windows. Luckily I've put on my eye-mask. Max makes pancakes, but I of course eat only fruit. I'm used to starving now but

I'm pleased with the result. Then we pack and drive into downtown Vegas. The boys want to gamble at Rio, the new casino hotel. Talk about garish. It's Carmen Miranda crossed with Margarita Pracatan in a Brazil gone mad. I can't face gambling for four hours, so suggest we go to the new fancy shopping mall. If there's one thing Judy and I really enjoy, it's a day of shopping. I find Katy a wonderful evening dress for Tara's wedding and several other good things, and Judy and I have a ball. Have a hysterical time on the plane back to LA. Meet David Niven and R for dinner at Hamburger Hamlet. We're all so tired we don't know what's hit us.

A young waitress whose hair is done up in nine million braids all over her head comes to take our order. I make the fatal mistake of complimenting her on her hair, which immediately means that she thinks I'm her best friend and starts saying to Biggins and Niven, 'Gee, I just love you guys, I just love you.' After the waitress takes their order she looks at me and says, 'And what would the little lady like?' Niven's eyebrows rose to the middle of his forehead as he sarcastically said, 'I think the little lady is having a turkey burger.' I must say I'm not keen on the overfamiliarity that passes for service in a lot of LA restaurants. But then, I'm just a dyed-in-the-wool conservative.

Monday, 14 April 1997

Work with a talented director called Jim Whitmore, son of that great old character actor James Whitmore. He is full of ideas, enthusiasm and zest, a big contrast to Les, the George Bush lookalike with about the same amount of personality. We shoot the airport scene, which is my final exit from the show. I'm impressed with Kimberley, she's getting better all the time. Get a message from Aaron, would I say something to her about her lip-liner as it's too much with those big lips of hers. I really don't think it's my business to do so, although she does have the biggest mouth.

Tuesday, 15 April 1997

I've given Linda, my driver, three tasks: one, get Tara's birth certificate from New York; two, get my address changed on my driver's licence; and three, organise getting me a new mobile telephone. I so admired the tiny little phone that George had in Vegas that I wanted one like it. She effortlessly manages all these things and I ask her if she would work for me, as Christine is totally hopeless and the office looks an even worse mess than before.

Work in outside-the-courtroom scenes with Kimberley. She and Lucky are practically the only ones I've worked with. It's unbearably hot and I'm wearing a black St Laurent suit with sweat pouring down my back. Finish in time to rush home, change and go with Biggins to meet Aaron and Candy Spelling and Nolan at Eclipse. Aaron is very excited about the show. He says it only dropped slightly after *Melrose Place* and he is just all around doggone thrilled. After ten minutes that famous movie star Mr Steven Seagal slopes over, says hello to me and everyone else, then plonks himself uninvited next to Aaron and proceeds to monopolise him for twenty minutes. He's pitching a project and Aaron, who is always charming to everyone, listens, smiling and nodding and looking interested. The rest of us cannot believe the effrontery of this asshole. After twenty minutes Seagal leaves and we get on with a fine dinner and plenty of caviar. Believe it or not, Mr Seagal returns towards the end of dinner to introduce his fat manager and says, 'We gotta make this deal.' He then says a fond farewell to Aaron and acknowledges neither me nor anyone else.

Biggins made a huge hit with the Spellings and I am pushing to get him a role in *Pacific Palisades*, perhaps as my butler.

Wednesday, 16 April 1997

A very hard day. Start off with my de rigueur twenty minutes in the gym on the walking machine in the morning. Joanna Poitier on one machine and Jeffrey on the other. Then give a *People* magazine interview to a young reporter who seemed nice. (Don't they always?) Go to the studio to shoot about nine scenes. God knows why they scheduled it like this but it's because they're trying to save money. They are making me do two scenes from episode six to shoot in episode five. This means they save half my salary. I think it's a shocking deal and I'm really furious but it's a 'personal favour' to Aaron. All my scenes are with daughter Laura, and I think they're quite good. She does have a bad habit, though, of taking the most unbelievably long amount of time to powder her nose and paint her lips on set. As one crew member laconically remarks, 'Shouldn't this kinda stuff be done in the make-up trailer?' Another replies, 'Well, we know who the pro is on this set.' Kimberley and I keep on dashing back to my trailer to watch the second episode of *Pacific Palisades*. Sadly, I have to cancel dinner with Billy Wilder and Audrey and Lenny Gershe at Le Dome. Work comes first.

We finish shooting at the unearthly hour of twelve fifteen. My nose looks like a potato, it's got so much 'flour' on it. I'm very tired. One of the production guys, Mr Silver, whom I've not met, comes oozing onto the set around eleven and tries to be charming. 'You know what I'm going to ask you, don't you?' he smarms oilily.

'Sure,' I say. 'You want us to take a forced call – but the crew are dead on their feet. They've been working unbelievably long hours, nineteen- and twenty-hour days. It's not fair to them.'

'You know, we're really in a bind.' Silver smiles thinly.

'You're in a bind because you're trying to get my scenes for an extra episode in,' I tell him. 'You're probably going to have to pay the crew more in overtime than what you would have had to pay me.'

He smiles sheepishly. 'Yes, I guess you're right,' he admits, 'but we really need a break. Would you take the forced call – just a couple of hours?'

'Let me think about it,' I say, and head back to the set.

When I tell Kimberley, she is in shock. 'I've got ten pages of dialogue and I have to shoot it tonight and it's already eleven,' she wails. 'I can't take a forced call.'

'Well, neither can I,' I say. 'But they always make you feel guilty.'

Some of the crew look worried so I ask the advice of George the wardrobe man. 'You shouldn't do it,' he tells me. 'You should not allow them to push you around.' He's absolutely right, of course.

'My union SAG says we must have a twelve-hour turnaround,' I tell Mr Silver. 'Sorry, pal. No-go. I'm not twenty-five any more and a girl needs her full twelve hours' break in between.'

I now become a heroine to the crew since that means they too can get a few hours' extra sleep. I don't know how these guys do it, particularly the camera crew, JR the operator, and the dolly grip, who are on set constantly.

Aaron called me Monday night to say that they would definitely know by Thursday morning whether the show was being picked up or not.

Thursday, 17 April 1997

Shoot interiors of Laura's house. First scene she and I are in peignoirs and Lucky comes in with just a towel around his waist. This is what we've all been waiting for, folks!

Lucky rehearses in a robe and when he finally strips off he has been pumping iron, I would think, for about six hours a day for the past thirty years – well, at least since he was six. He's also got a mahogany-coloured tan, darker than George H, which he admits to topping up. However, it's exceedingly effective when he comes in and says with tousled hair and a sexy grin to me: 'Coffee ready?' 'Sure,' I say, getting up to get his coffee. Laura looks utterly shocked and says: 'Mother, what's he doing here?' I look at her innocently, having handed the coffee to Lucky, and say, 'Darling, you never said I couldn't have a house guest.' Lucky and I then do a couple of ad-libs as he's sipping the coffee. 'Good?' I ask him. He looks at me with a suggestive expression. 'Great,' he says. 'Good,' I say. There's a certain chemistry there, which I hope will be captured on film.

After Lucky finishes, Kimberley and I shoot several more scenes. I'm so tired I don't know what I'm doing. I don't know how the crew can face it. The director, Les – aptly named, I might add, as he's not very good – does about ninety-four different set-ups for a scene that should only have four. What a relief when Jim Whitmore comes on but, poor guy, it's after midnight when it's his turn – the confrontation scene with Kimberley and me. We do our best, that's all we can do. Finish at 2.30 a.m. Insanity!

Friday, 18 April 1997

Another day of craziness, one meeting after another. Lunch with Sacha at Hamburger Hamlet. Sacha is a little gloomy because

Tony Newley is not too well, but I know he will be fine. At eleven o'clock Nolan calls. 'We've been picked up for thirteen episodes!'

Still don't know what thirteen episodes means in terms of my contract. I have finally signed it, but it does not specify that I'm going to be in every episode. I have a feeling I'm being used to get the ratings up and then possibly dumped. Well, nobody ever said television was a charitable institution. Jeffrey comes over at six with the schedule for New York, and how excited all the publicity people are at NBC. 'They'll do anything for you,' he said. 'If you have to come in at any time to do any promos or publicity, they'll send a company jet.' 'Hmm. Let's see when it comes time for the crunch,' I said. Then he showed me two pages in the *Star* tabloid, nice picture of me and one with Lucky, and one with Lucky and Kimberley. 'The witch is back' it was headed. How original. 'This is a barometer of public interest,' Jeffrey said, 'and you haven't even appeared on the screen yet.' There's so much optimism around that it's beginning to make me nervous.

Rush to the airport where I find I've put on these ridiculous hard shoes that are killing my feet. Phil, the charming British Airways representative, offers to go to Bally and buy me a pair of loafers – which he does, but they're so slippery on the soles that I almost fall down and break my neck. On the flight I find a new audio-video machine in the 747 'coffin' recliner.

'What is this for?' I asked the cabin steward or whatever the politically correct name is these days.

'Oh, it's to operate all your TV and movie channels, and you can also play bingo and send faxes,' he said proudly.

'I want to do neither of the latter,' I said, 'I just want to watch a film, but it doesn't seem to be working.'

'Ah, that's all taken care of,' he said. 'We have special technicians on board as this is the only 747 with these new machines.'

The young technician comes, fiddles around for fifteen minutes and announces ruefully that my equipment is not functioning. I'm quite cross as I like switching channels and that's one of the joys of travelling first class. Considering the bloody ticket costs over nine thousand dollars, you would imagine that this basic function would be working. However, I guess it's better than an engine being out of whack. They bring me a portable video and I watch *The Nutty Professor* and fall asleep.

Saturday, 19 April 1997

Arrive in London at three in the afternoon. Go home to see my beautiful new bathroom that the designer Geoffrey Plago has put in. I'm really thrilled with it.

Lazy day. Katy comes over at sixish and we do girls' things, trying on clothes for the different wedding ceremonies and the party the night before the wedding. She looks fabulous in the evening dress I bought her in Las Vegas. We watch the second episode of *Pacific Palisades* together. She thinks some of the actors are quite good, i.e. Lucky and Finola, but she doesn't like Kimberley, she thinks she looks like a Barbie doll.

Monday, 21 April 1997

London was freezing cold. Lunched at Daphne's with Stella and Sue St Johns. Food was good.

In the afternoon I had one of my least favourite discussions with PC and Gordon, my accountant, about where I am domiciled. It seems that the stupid, horrible tax people have decided to investigate me, even though they know that I've lived a lot of my adult life in America. I hate these grey-area situations.

Met Christopher Biggins at the Queen's Theatre. We saw

Marlene, starring Siân Phillips. Simply one of the best evenings I've had in the theatre since I can't remember when. She was staggering, terribly moving, and her emulation of Marlene in the last twenty minutes when she's dressed in the glistening Dietrich dress and white fur was almost creepy. Absolutely fantastic and I can't wait to see it again. Dined at The Ivy. So good to be back in civilisation. Saw various friends and had a lovely evening.

Tuesday, 22 April 1997

Met Katy and boyfriend Paul Robinson at Angel Bermans, the costumiers in Shaftesbury Avenue, where we tried on various Gatsby outfits for Alice Bamford's twenty-first birthday next Saturday. Katy looked adorable in a pink flapper outfit with a feather boa. Went to The Ivy again for lunch with the two of them; it's such a good restaurant, more like a club really. Paul had to leave to go back to work at Channel 5 so Katy and I had a girls' tête-à-tête, which was really nice. She likes this Paul, and he seems to like her, but she doesn't see enough of him.

Nolan called: 'Aaron asked me to tell you that you will definitely be in episode ten.' 'What?' I'm completely and utterly shocked, mortified and hurt. 'Episode ten? That means that they'll be doing seven, eight and nine – three episodes – without me.' 'That's right,' said Nolan. 'And Aaron put you into ten. The writers wanted to have you in eleven.' I thought it completely stupid and idiotic.

'Fox just seems to be using me,' I said, thinking of all those promos that I did and the back-breaking four days of publicity in New York. 'Using me to get ratings and then dropping me. The whole thing is insane. I think I'm being sabotaged in some way.'

Jeffrey told me, 'Everybody at Fox says it's madness and we will lose a lot of the publicity momentum.'

Sue St Johns came over for tea and I ranted and raved to her about the unutterable stupidity of the network. 'I think it's this Jonathan Levine who's got something against me,' I said. 'If, as everyone said, I'm good in the show, and I'm by far the biggest star, etc., how come they're going to write me out of three episodes? Even one quarter of a ratings point means something like half a million homes.' Neither of us could understand it and we drowned our sorrows in tea.

Thursday, 24 April 1997

Called Steve Tellez, my agent at CAA, whom Aaron insisted I go to, to say, 'Please tell Peter Roth that I have been totally available for work ever since I was signed in January. Whatever he says, even if you don't hear from him, please fax me one way or another.'

Bottom line: I do not hear from Steve Tellez. It's now Thursday and I'm quite pissed off. Spoke to Jeffrey yesterday, who faxed a full page of me in *TV Guide*, saying, 'Guess who's coming to dinner? *Pacific Palisades* new special guest star.' It is obvious they are trying out reactions to see how I pull for the ratings. Spoke to Charles Duggan, who said 70 per cent of America is not going to be interested in Ellen DeGeneres coming out of the closet, because most Americans are very middle-of-the-road moralistic. I don't believe him, but I hope he's right because I have never seen so much publicity about a forthcoming episode since JR was shot in *Dallas* in 1980.

On the good-news front, all is finally going well, I hope, with preparations for Tara and Michael's wedding.

Saturday, 26 April 1997

Drive down to Daylesford for the twenty-first birthday celebrations of Alice Bamford. Arrive at the house at four and have tea in the most beautiful of drawing rooms. Each room at Daylesford is more gorgeous than the last and Carole has done her usual exquisite job. I'm staying at the house, as are Robin, Ned Ryan and Biggins. My room is 'the Baron's bedroom' which is where Baron Heini von Thyssen lived when he owned Daylesford. Hugh comes in to tweak my coiffure, a fabulous bobbed wig which Linda, the treasure, found in LA. The *Private Lives* dress looks amazing and Hugh fixes feathers in my hair. Everyone troops down, the men look dashing in dinner jackets, hardly distinguishable from the waiters from the back. 'Hello, Joe, how nice to see you again,' says Ned jovially to an elderly man standing with his back to us. 'Oh, is that Joe Bamford, Alice's grandfather?' I ask Ned innocently as I'm greedily scooping up some caviar. Both young waiters holding the heavy trays of caviar and accoutrements start laughing silently and so hard I think they're going to burst. 'No,' says Ned patiently, 'that's Joe, their old butler.' This story made the rounds quickly. Another gaffe, for which I'm known.

Arrive in the tent at eight fifteen to find it only a quarter full. A band is playing jazz music as the theme is Gatsby. Carole and Alice look great in their beaded flapper frocks, Carole's albeit from Valentino and Alice's having cost three thousand pounds! We stand around endlessly, drinking and looking eagerly at the door for new arrivals. I start to worry about the bus that Katy and Paul are coming on from Victoria Station as by nine o'clock they still haven't arrived. Bit by bit people drift in. Patrick Donovan, Susan Sangster, Richard E. Grant and his wife Joan Washington, the Duke of Marlborough and his wife

Rosita, David and Serena Linley, the Fennells, Delevingnes, and hundreds of others.

It's boiling hot in the tent, and we are giggling at the young girls who have two-foot-long paper cigarette holders, which are getting into everybody's feathers. Katy and Paul finally arrive. It's taken them three hours on the bus but they both look adorable and she is in good spirits. Summoned into another huge tent for dinner at about ten. Carole has done her usual fantastic job of decorating. 'Who's the JC clone?' I ask, as a woman in black with jet-black bob and a lot of eye make-up comes rushing up to me. 'Darling, it's Louise!' she says. I prefer Mrs Fennell as her usual blonde.

I'm seated next to Theo Fennell and Richard E. Grant. Also at the table are Chubby Benson and Nick Mason, who I didn't recognise as he's put on so much weight, Lynne Pemberton, Patrick Donovan, Susan Sangster, and Michael Winner and his girlfriend Vanessa. The party is in full swing, but the music, when it starts, is so loud that one has to shriek at the top of one's voice. The food is excellent, the wine even more so. When the cabaret Kit and the Widow begins, Chubby and I scamper off to the loo as we don't think much of his rather crude and unfunny songs about Alice and the Bamford family. I'm dying to dance the Charleston but the disco is mostly modern and hard rock. Nevertheless, I twirl and shriek until three in the morning.

David Linley comes by the table to speak to Theo. He never, ever says hello to me unless I say it first. I stare up at him as he ignores me then finally say, 'Hello, David, how are you? Hello, I'm fine.' He looks startled. 'Somebody gave me one of your boxes from Dunhill, in New York,' I say, knowing that he's going to be interested in that. I'm right and he perks up and we chat for a second. Later Theo gets very drunk and insults Michael Winner, which isn't terribly difficult to do. Katy's a dancing dervish on the floor, indefatigable, Paul follows her everywhere and they seem very together. Long may it last. I can't believe that all of my children are happy in their relationships. Fingers firmly crossed at all times. Finally totter into the main house at 4 a.m., feeling much the worse for wear. All our voices are hoarse.

Sunday, 27 April 1997

Wake up to the most gorgeous English spring day one can possibly imagine. Stand on the baron's balcony and look out at this vista, so ravishing that one can only be glad, as they say, to be in England now that spring is here. Take a power walk around the huge property, which is kept immaculate. Biggins is sunbathing on the balcony and looking gloomily at the Sunday papers, which all forecast Mr Major's demise. We have a glass of champagne and try not to think about it. The bleary-eyed guests from last night arrive for pre-lunch drinks. There are about forty people, mostly adults. The young – Alice, her brothers and various others – having stayed up until eight or nine in the morning, don't show. Lunch is served at four round tables of ten. Sit with Biggins, Richard E. Grant, Chubby Benson and John Bowes-Lyon, and have hilarious lunch. Stand in a queue behind David Linley, who ignores me again, as does Serena. I'm not imagining it. John Bowes-Lyon, who is sitting next to me and is some distant cousin to David, totally agrees. 'My dear, he is a terrible snob,' says Bosie. 'He often doesn't speak to people and he's also a crashing bore.' That's for sure.

The lunch is loud and long and we finally get out of there into Steve's car at four-thirty. We give Bosie a lift back into London but we're all so exhausted we fall asleep in the car. Home at seven and it's back to packing those Vuittons yet again.

Monday, 28 April 1997

Wake up feeling that I can hardly talk. Throat is seized up from all the smoking and the shrieking. Steve drives me to airport and I buy all kinds of throat potions at Boots. Flight to New York uneventful except that I can't talk. It's extremely curious that when one whispers to people they whisper back. Jeffrey greets me in our two-bedroomed suite at the Plaza Athénée and comments on how exhausted I look (although thin, thankfully) and how my voice sounds a nightmare. I am so tired I don't know what's hit me. Call Evie Bricusse to tell her I can't possibly make the opening of *Jekyll and Hyde*, Leslie's musical, tonight as I'm ill. They're not too happy but I need the sleep.

Get into bed at seven and watch the tabloid talk shows, which are now heavily featuring Ellen DeGeneres and her new girlfriend, Anne Heche, the star of *Volcano*. The two women have both 'come out', are in love and photographed petting at a party at the White House in front of President Clinton. Not what I call good behaviour, but a great ratings spike. *Pacific Palisades* obviously won't have a prayer of beating their ratings, but Fox have brought me in to try to make some tiny dent. Spoke to Steve at CAA; he still hasn't heard officially when I start *Pacific Palisades*. I'm getting quite pissed off. I feel I'm being used for publicity reasons. Fox have taken a couple of ads in *TV Guide* with me in them and also the promos I made are on Channel 5, the Fox channel, constantly. I still find the whole thing weird. Try to call Aaron Spelling but he's recovering from eye surgery. He sure gets ill a lot.

Tuesday, 29 April 1997 – New York

Wake up feeling 100 per cent better. Jeffrey and I hit the gym, where two rude gentlemen are hogging the walking machines. Later we walk down Madison Avenue, which is looking fabulously spring-like. Go to NBC to tape the *Rosie O'Donnell Show*. In my dressing room Jeffrey is informed that the show is not going on today as planned but on the first of May, the day after my episode airs. Jeffrey goes ballistic. I don't blame him. The main reason I've schlepped all the way across the Atlantic is for this plug for *Pacific Palisades*. He goes into the corridor, voices are raised and the incompetent woman producer admits it's her fault. Rosie comes in. She is adorable, known as Queen of Nice on TV. When told the problem, she suggests that I come on at the end of today's show. She will change clothes, as will I, and she will say, 'Joan Collins is coming on tomorrow' and I will burst in to say, 'No no no, I want to come on today, Rosie, because *Pacific Palisades* airs today.' Have two six-minute segments on the show, which is good. When I ask Rosie if she remembers when we first met, at Swifty Lazar's Oscar party several years ago, she said, 'Yeah, I sure do, and when I was going in, everybody kept on shrieking, hey, it's Madonna and Kathy Bates!' Change, wait around, then do the tag for the show that will air on Wednesday afternoon. This rather cuts into my shopping time at Bloomingdale's, but I manage, with Ivy, the professional assistant at Bloomies, to do a bit of damage there. It is a most beautiful day in New York. Do telephone interviews with eight different journalists asking all the same questions, and they ALL want to know what I think about Ellen DeGeneres!

I don my bobbed Gatsby wig, new top from Bloomies and black suit. Blaine and Robert Trump pick me up and we go to a pre-opening of Le Cirque in the old Helmsley Palace building.

There we meet Aileen Mehle and her friends. The decor of this place is so hideous as to be almost comical. The original building, which was obviously listed as it was built at the beginning of the century, is classically rococo. There are beautiful eighteenth-century drawings on the wall panels, pillars and a heavily embossed ceiling. This has been covered by several plate-glass etched screens with what look like red and green footballs on them. The chairs are dark green and blue, also with balls on them – even the plates have this modern, ugly theme, no doubt to give the impression of the circus at Le Cirque. The food, to be blunt, is average, which also goes for the clientele.

Le Cirque was one of my favourite New York restaurants and I don't think this will be one of them. Nevertheless, dinner is great fun, though I have to send back my lamb as it's underdone to death. We all criticise everything like mad, then Sirio Maccione, the owner, comes up in his Versace brocade jacket and spills out his problems. He is being either blackmailed or picketed by PETA. This is a very out-there, pro-animal welfare group who are protesting against the use of white veal in restaurants. Since practically every restaurant in the world has veal on their menu, Sirio cannot understand why he has been chosen as the fall guy. We all sympathise. Aileen is vociferous in her condemnation of not only the animal rights activists but also Princess Diana and Ellen DeGeneres. When I ask her what she thinks about the latter coming out so publicly and flaunting her girlfriend, she says vehemently, 'It makes me sick.' When I ask her about Princess Diana she says: 'If she decides to come and live in New York, after a year with the novelty gone she'll be just another blonde divorcee.' Wow!

Wednesday, 30 April 1997

Unbelievably busy day. Leave hotel at eight-twenty to get to Fox in time for breakfast show. Halfway to the river I ask the driver, who barely speaks English, 'Where are we going?' He says he hasn't really been told by his dispatcher, but he thinks he's going to Fox. 'You *think?*' I say in my best Dame Edith Evans voice. After calling the Fox people (who seem to be somewhat incompetent) we find that the Fox studios are not at 80th and the river but at 25th Street and 7th! This necessitates a mad dash across town, the driver apologising profusely, Jeffrey yelling and me wishing I'd had more time to get ready. Arrive at Fox somewhat flustered and am whisked on to greet Tom Bergeron and Rita Rudner, who is co-hosting. When Tom goes off to do another spot, Rita suggests that when the camera finds us, she and I are locked in an embrace! We then break away guiltily, fixing our hair, looking embarrassed. This gets a huge guffaw from the studio audience and is another little dig at this Ellen and Anne thing. Airwaves are swamped with her. Ellen is on *Oprah* smooching with girlfriend Anne Heche, who looks to be a manipulating number to me.

I know we don't have much of a chance with *Pacific Palisades* tonight, even though I then go to another studio and do fourteen satellite interviews. Smiling charmingly and staring into a blank camera to an unidentified face. Totally exhausted but dash to La Goulue restaurant to meet Dennis Farina, Liz Smith's right-hand man. He is a sweet – as he puts it – 'forty-five-year-old queen', and we gossip madly about everyone from Judy Garland to – natch – Ellen DeGeneres. Have to spend the afternoon talking to Gary Concoff, my lawyer, as that creepy little Tom Chasin is planning now to sue me for, as he says in his letter, 'demanding the payment of my rightly earned commissions on *Pacific Palisades* to which I am legally, morally and properly entitled on all episodes. If not paid, I will pursue my legal remedies immediately.' All I need is another court case, but Gary rambles on and on. However, one must grin and bear it and although Tom Chasin wasn't very good, I don't think much of Steve Tellez and his CAA group either, since I have not heard from them and still don't know when I'm officially going back to *Pacific Palisades*. Loads of promotion for it of course on Channel 5, including the saucy promos I did, saying things like: 'If you think the women on *Melrose Place* are naughty, just wait till you get a look at us on *Pacific Palisades*.' How tacky. This all points towards the fact that I play a wicked, wicked lady.

Watch *Oprah* while I'm getting dressed for *Conan O'Brien*. She's interviewing Ellen, who's telling everybody about her coming out. Am bored to death of this subject and, from what I've heard, so is the rest of America. Tomorrow we'll know. Do the *Conan O'Brien Show* at NBC. He's a young, slightly manic, popular late-night talk show host who gabbles away so fast that one can hardly keep up with him. End the segment by doing the splits. Not dignified but, as Jeffrey says, 'It'll get those younger viewers.' Oh, these endless younger viewers the networks are all in search of. If they're anything like the younger people I see wandering around the streets sucking vacantly on cans of Coke and stuffing their faces with fast food, I don't think so much of them. Plus they seem to have the attention span of a flea.

Meet Evie and Dann Moss at Coco Pazzo with Jeffrey for dinner then Jeffrey and I dash to the hotel to watch *Pacific Palisades*. To say we are disappointed is putting it mildly. I think the show is terribly fragmented, badly edited and they have cut the party scene like an MTV video. The music is dreadful, absolutely dreadful, and I seem to have absolutely no edge what-soever. Am deeply disappointed. This ain't going to be no Alexis comeback, that's for sure. Never mind, I'll probably do a play in the West End. Much more fun.

Thursday, 1 May 1997

Hit the gym with Jeffrey then walk down Madison Avenue on this gorgeous New York day. Madison Avenue is now employ-ing special security guards paid for by the stores to keep away vagrants and muggers etc. I must say it's working, as the walk was a delight. Still got recognised, even in my headscarf disguise. Arrived at NBC to do the *Geraldo Rivera Show*. Everyone's talk-ing about the ratings sensation that *Ellen* had last night. She swept the floor all over America, getting a fifty – yes, a fifty share in San Francisco alone. *Pacific Palisades*, along with every other show, got slaughtered. So much for the endless publicity I'm doing. However, maybe it could have been worse had I not done it!? Geraldo is charming, one of the few interviewers who asks interesting questions, unlike Conan O'Brien, who rattles on and interrupts.

Dashed to 21 to meet Tom Dunne, Charlie Spicer and Steve to discuss the cover of *Second Act*. They liked my new epilogue and after much discussion, with me telling them I hated the cover as it was out of focus, we decided on a compromise.

I went on various errands around New York – Saks, Bendel's, Suarez. The pickings were slim. The weather was awful, pouring warm rain, and the Lincoln's air conditioner didn't work. So few mechanical things seem to work these days – there's too much technology, I'm convinced. After packing, went to the Plaza Athénée bar to meet old friend Adele Searll from South Africa. She pooh-poohed all the stories of unrest, muggings there, and said that I definitely should come in September when I have been invited to do a few more episodes of their top soap, *Egoli*. Then met Russ Kagan, who rattled on endlessly about ratings and how well his TNT series *David and Goliath* and *Jerusalem* had done. After about an hour he got to the point: he is interested in forming a company with me, with the help of Gary Concoff, to develop 'Too Damn Famous' for TV, and also some of my other books. I won't hang by the thumbs!

In a complete panic, as there's a thunderstorm, I finished packing and left to catch the plane in the pouring rain.

Talk to Nolan on my new mobile phone, which keeps breaking down. He hasn't heard that the cameraman on *Pacific Palisades* and all his crew, grips and electricians etc., plus Monica the hairdresser, have been fired. He knows nothing, except that I'm due back for Episode Ten.

'I still haven't heard officially from my agents,' I say. 'So, I'm just going to do what I have to do.'

Then Nolan tells me that Joel Wyner, who plays the plastic surgeon in *Pacific Palisades*, has been fired.

'Why?' I ask.

'Something to do with him having cut his hair in the middle of the episode. But,' says Nolan, 'they will be bringing in another actor in two episodes' time to play the same character.'

Television – a really caring community. Am so tired that I fall asleep in the Air France lounge and walk like a zombie when the flight is announced. The thunderstorm has stopped. Fall asleep immediately and sleep throughout take-off, flight and major turbulence. The plane is like something from the seventies. It compares most unfavourably with the streamlined modernity of British Airways.

Friday, 2 May 1997 – Paris

Ask for a toothbrush and toothpaste in the morning and the flight attendant informs me they don't have any on board. Charming. Have breath like a parrot's cage. Am even more unimpressed with Air France after the six first-class passengers are herded downstairs to mix with economy, standing stuffed together while we wait for the doors to open. Then, to add insult to injury, we are literally sardined into buses with a moronic driver who cares not that several of us have connections to make. It is boiling hot and the smell of humanity high. The driver takes sadistic pleasure in driving at sixty miles an hour along the tarmac, taking fast turns so that the people standing cannot keep their balance. No one meets me from Air France so I go into Luggage Claim. After waiting half an hour, I ask an Air France representative to help me. He shrugs indifferently and starts to walk away until I flash my Club 2000 Card and tell him my name. All is deference and charm as he summons two young Air France assistants, who unfortunately can do nothing about my luggage. Am desperately late for appointments with Tara and Stella, so finally I leave, giving instructions for my luggage to be sent to the Ritz.

Dash to Pigalle where, next to the old Moulin Rouge, I sit in a charming café and have a baguette and a cup of coffee and watch the tourists go by. Stella arrives and we go into the atelier of Dominique Sirop. He is a handsome young Frenchman who was Givenchy's second in command for eleven years, and before that an assistant to Yves St Laurent. Givenchy wanted him to be his successor, but that job went instead to the quirky, eccentric Alexander McQueen.

Then to Ritz to meet Tara, who is getting a little frazzled with all the wedding preparations. The invitations have finally gone out to the three events: the morning civil ceremony, the afternoon Jewish traditional synagogue ceremony under the 'chuppah', and the evening reception, grand party and dance at the Buddha Bar. Tara is full of excitement and plans as we go to the atelier of Jean Paul Gaultier, where I try on my evening dress for the party. Am not at all happy with it as it has a band across the bust which gives me a 1920s flat-chested flapper look. When I complain about this, I'm informed that that's what this band is supposed to do. 'Then we won't have the band,' I say. 'Make it like a proper bodice.' The young man, Steven, who is running the joint, is wearing a knee-length red and black kilt, thick woolly socks, big black bovver boots, a burgundy velvet waistcoat and matching jacket. He looks exceedingly hot and uncomfortable as it's about eighty-five degrees. Tara tries on the toile for her wedding dress, which I think is going to be fabulous, and also tries on her suit for the civil ceremony, which is a little funky, but that's what she likes.

Dinner that night at Le Doyen with Stella, Tara and Michael, and we talk of nothing but the wedding. Then to the Costes Hotel which is packed to the brim with trendy French intellectuals and nightlife habitués, all smoking and drinking and closely packed together. Meet Louis, who is in charge of the catering; he never stops sneezing. Try to speak to him above the incredible din, and manage to get through to organise my dinner the night before Tara's wedding. Hope it's going to be all right.

Saturday, 3 May 1997

Stella and I go down to the gym. Since she doesn't have any gym shoes and is barefoot and wearing a short T-shirt frock, this is somewhat hilarious. Then we go to Yves St Laurent on the

Left Bank where I proceed to do a lot of damage. Everything is really stylish and suits me and I decide I will get rid of lots of existing things in my wardrobe and give them to Stella or Katy or Victoria, my god-daughter, who like my things. We have a lovely civilised lunch again in the outside bar at the Ritz, then I take Air France to Nice, which is an infinitely better flight than New York to Paris.

Wednesday, 7 May 1997

Back in London, I get a letter from British Airways apologising for the lack of audio and video equipment last month and offering two round trips to Nice. Nice work. Lunched at Mimmo's with Stella and talked a lot about the wedding, and Katy joined us. Went to Joel and Son to buy some fabrics, then went to the opening of the new Escada boutique in Sloane Street with Stella and Didier. A complete nightmare, jam-packed with every face you've ever seen, plus three or four friendly photographers such as Richard Young. As Christina Estrada and Paula Tholstrup start rolling in, we rolled out.

Thursday, 8 May 1997

Lunched with Jonathan Lloyd at Harry's Bar. He's had somebody in his office go through 'Hell Hath No Fury' and they think it's salvageable, so that's good news, as I can't face writing another novel just yet. Spoke to my agent in LA, who said that *Pacific Palisades* now want me back for at least three or four episodes. Jeffrey called: the second episode aired last night and he said it was better and got much better ratings. Good.

Friday, 9 May 1997

Went to the gym at the Berkeley Hotel. It's very beautiful with a wonderful view of Hyde Park but the machinery is so high-tech I can't work it. Went to look at the swimming pool, which looked very nice, but I wasn't keen on the fact that everybody keeps staring at me or coming up and talking to me. I don't wish to get Princess Diana-ish, but it's nice to do one's exercise privately. Lunched with brother Bill at San Lorenzo. Business meetings all afternoon

Saturday, 10 May 1997

Lunched with Evie and Leslie Bricusse and Adam at Daphne's, where we saw several women our own age or younger who looked really elderly. Leslie complimented both Evie and me and said we never change – that is nice to know! Went for tea at the Delevingnes. My god-daughter Cara is so adorable, I'm quite mad about her. There were several other little girls there, all crazy for the Spice Girls. They put on the Spice Girls video and did Spice Girls dances. It's incredible how these five young girls know all the moves.

Prince Charles is all over the papers today being pawed and kissed by the real Spice Girls. He didn't look like he handled it very well, not up to his ex-wife's standard.

Monday, 12 May 1997

Went to see Katy's new bathroom in her flat, which looks very nice. Went to the Hill Samuel bank to recover an old safe deposit box of Ron Kass's [American businessman, former husband of JC from 1972 to 1983, and father of Katy]. Went into a private room and found the metal box totally stuffed with pictures of me, mostly from *The Stud* and *The Bitch*. There were also a lot of Katy and some of Ron, but none of his other children. It was very strange seeing these photographs, some of which had been taken out of my photograph albums from when I was a young girl, and some taken when I didn't know they were being taken.

Rushed to Philip Somerville to try on various hats for Tara's wedding. After ten minutes of trying on and making funny faces, Steve came in and said there was a paparazzo with a long lens taking photographs of me trying on the hats through the shop window. Charming. Somerville's assistant went out and asked the man what he was doing and he said: 'I just want to get some pictures of Joan trying on hats. I saw Princess Diana here last week and Madonna the week before, so I figured it was a good place to stake out.' They sent him packing and I took both hats as I couldn't decide. I'll try them in Paris. Dinner with Will and Sue Boyd at the Caprice.

Tuesday, 13 May 1997

Chili, a young cook, came over and we discussed the menu for Tara's shower on 12 June. Went to meet Peter Charlesworth and the director Patrick Garland and producer Paddy Wilson at the Park Sheraton Hotel. Discussed the ins and outs and ramifications of doing *Star Quality*, the Noël Coward play. It needs a lot of rewriting, but Patrick is willing to rewrite. Met Hannah Griffiths, a young reader who works with Jonathan Lloyd, who had read 'Hell Hath No Fury'. She liked it very much, but said it needed quite a bit of work. I asked her if it was salvageable and she said most definitely yes – and she'd thought this when she was reading it and didn't know that I had written it. Made a plan to work on it later in the year and then perhaps get it published successfully. That would be one in the eye for Random House.

Robin called and said that several friends of his had told him that I was looking tired and asked, was I 'doing too much'? I thought maybe I was, as I seem to be constantly thinking about the wedding, and whether or not this *Pacific Palisades* situation is going to resolve itself. In the past few days I've had endless telephone calls with agents, Jeffrey and various others about when I'm going to start. Of course, they are trying to make me do two episodes in one week. It's all a bit much and very unfair, particularly since I told them, when I originally signed, that I definitely had to be free for Tara's wedding in mid-June.

Dinner at The Canteen, which is owned by Michael Caine. Joined the Bricusses and the Caines for a jolly dinner. Michael was in good form – and why not? He's made five pictures in a year, so is understandably pleased with himself. Tried not to drink but it's difficult as dinners always seem to go on for at least three hours.

Wednesday, 14 May 1997

A lot happening today. Went to Tonya's gym and really worked out. Cathy Sloan and her builder went through my kitchen making decisions about what to do. I find it very confusing when somebody asks me what I want, since the kitchen is far from my domain of choice. However, battled on with the eighty million different suggestions that one can have for even the simplest thing like a hob or a microwave. Katy arrived for lunch and then brother Bill. Made them tuna-fish sandwiches which they both said were superb. I may not be much good at cooking, but I make good sandwiches and salads. Bill left, and Katy and I had a long talk. Then Fiona arrived to give me the works, manicure, pedicure, etc.

Went to meet Theo and Louise Fennell and Charles and Pandora Delevingne for a relaxing dinner at The Ivy. Theo and I are planning to sing at Tara's wedding, so we did a little bit of rehearsing at the table, much to the amusement of people nearby. From *The Cole Porter Songbook* we've chosen 'You're the Top' or . . . 'Anything Goes'. They don't write them like that any more, that's for sure.

Thursday, 15 May 1997

Left for Paris at the crack of dawn on BA. Thank God for them, they're so much better than Air France. Naturally the chauffeur wasn't there but he finally found us and raced to Dominique Sirop for another fitting of the mother of the bride's dress. It's very pretty, pale pink, and the hat that I got from Philip Somerville, also pink, looks very good with it. I think Dominique is a real comer in the fashion stakes and I tentatively ordered another dress. Met Tara at the Ritz for lunch on the terrace. It was a beautiful Parisian day and the Ritz is so unbelievably civilised. We went through our wedding list, shower list, list for the party the night before and then attempted to do *placements* for the wedding. This is going to be a complete nightmare, I can see, but at least I can place, in tables, the thirty or forty people I am involved with. It is very exciting. Went to a suite in the Ritz where Tara and Michael and I posed for photographs. They have done a deal for the pictures with an Italian press agency.

At Jean Paul Gaultier's again, I wasn't too happy with my dress, which looked distinctly matronly. However, they turned the sleeves inside out, which gave it a bit of oomph. Tara's dress was divine and she looked really pretty in it, although with a boned bodice I felt it should be more pulled in at the waist, but she said that she wouldn't be able to sing. Gianni, the Italian photographer, took copious pictures of this event. It's boiling hot in Paris and we're informed it's going to be ninety degrees the day of the wedding.

Took the nine o'clock Air France flight to Nice. The airport was completely jam-packed and luckily an Air France rep took me in a car to the plane, as I couldn't face another bus. The flight was uneventful until about half an hour out when lightning shook the whole plane and it was as though we were on a roller coaster. Immediately became best friends with the Englishman sitting to my right and chatted on gaily as I downed endless glasses of wine. It was really, really frightening but, as usual with incidents in planes, it didn't seem to go on for too long.

Tuesday, 20 May 1997

Joined Johnny Gold and Michael Brandon for an amusing lunch at the Belvedere, in which we all went down memory lane. I told Johnny that if he ever writes his book of reminiscences about his life as the owner and host of Dolly's and Tramp, it would be the most extraordinary look at the sixties, seventies, eighties and nineties. He laughed and said that he has to wait until most of the people are dead. He reminded me of when we were in Las Vegas in 1969 for Tony's opening and he was then dating Dory Previn, wife of André. He remembered when we were told that Sharon Tate had been murdered and he and I decided to come back from Vegas to go to the funeral. What a sad day that was.

I teased Michael about his experience with Heather Locklear on the *Dynasty* reunion. 'She went around telling everybody you tried to bang her,' I joked. He got slightly miffed. 'Hell, she was sitting on top of me with just a sheet between us, what was I expected to do? I'm only a guy, after all.'

Went to Harrods, head down, sunglasses on. 'Joan, Joan, Joan,' progressively louder, shrieked a voice. Reluctantly I turned to see Suzanna Leigh, star of sixties films and erstwhile friend. She said the usual platitudes, then said, 'I'm doing a book, I'm doing a book.' 'What kind of a book?' I asked. 'Oh, you know, you know, you know, a book.' I think she's not quite there and I remember Barry Langford telling me that she was having problems getting work. She's probably not even fifty yet. This business is so cruel to women. I remember when Suzanna was flavour of the month, dating everyone from Elvis Presley to George Best, and a very, very, pretty girl. Now she's just not. Didn't stop too long, as I had to order food for my birthday tea.

I hotfooted it to the Fennells' newly renovated house. It's very grand, very tasteful and three times as big as it was before. Hugged my god-child Coco, who is very tall for an eight-year-old. The evening was a birthday for Sarah Standing, and it was really good to see her and Johnny after months and months away. Adrian Gill and Nicola came, as did Simon Williams. I adore Simon, he is the consummate gentleman. Told him we'd been watching him in *Upstairs Downstairs* in the South of France and he groaned. 'Oh my God, that must be like you watching yourself in *I Believe in You* with Celia when you were eighteen!' 'But you were wonderful,' I said. He doesn't seem to think so. We made a plan to go and see Elspeth March on Sunday. A very jolly evening but we sat too long at table and didn't get up until twelve fifteen, by which time it was time to leave. Apparently they stayed up and did a singalong. Gave Theo *The Cole Porter Songbook* and told him to get the words to 'You're the Top' in his head as we're going to do them at Tara's wedding. He groaned too but I think he quite likes the idea.

Wednesday, 21 May 1997

Went to Escada with Sue St Johns. They have some really nice and very flattering clothes and I found the perfect powder-blue silk pants suit for Tara's civil ceremony in the morning. Went to the Caprice where Sue met Meryl and Shakira, and I met Una-Mary Parker, her daughter Baba and Katy. Una-Mary has taken to wearing a large chiffon headband around her head as I did several years ago. She is terribly sweet and nice and bought me a lovely present of a nineteenth-century silver bookmark. Went to Ivory in Bond Street with Katy to get various shoes for her wedding outfits. They're a bit overly solicitous in Ivory and a lot of staring goes on. One of the salesgirls went up to Katy and whispered in her ear, 'We've got somebody famous here today.' 'Yes, I know, she's my mother,' said Katy crossly. Went to the satellite interview place in Westminster and met Stella. Did forty-five minute satellite interview with very serious Argentinian interviewer asking me all kinds of deep analytical questions, which I tried to answer deeply and analytically.

Then as I was getting ready, the telephone rang. 'Joan,' said an angry voice, 'how come you haven't invited me to your wedding?'

'I'm not getting married,' I said.

'I know, I know,' he said even more crossly. 'But I should have been invited to your daughter's wedding.'

I started laughing. 'Nicky,' I said, 'you're joking, aren't you?'

'No, I'm not,' said the furious voice of Nicholas Haslam, interior designer to the rich and famous and chattering classes and somebody who I do not think I shall be trusting very much any more. 'I'm horrified that everybody has been asked and that you haven't asked me, one of your oldest friends. When I think of all the places that I've taken you, and you don't invite me to this wedding!'

I was completely dumbfounded. I tried to tell him in a kind way that if I invited all my friends there wouldn't be room for any of Tara's, but he was unrelenting.

'Am I to take it, then, that I am not receiving an invitation?'

'Yes, you're to take it as that,' I said firmly. 'You haven't been invited.'

'I saw Roger Moore last night and he asked me if I was going to Tara's wedding, it was very embarrassing,' said Nicky, obviously seething with rage.

'Well, Roger has known Tara since before she was born,' I said. 'He's a very close friend.'

Nicky went wittering on, and I have never been so shocked – at least not since Muck Flick cancelled my OBE party. What is coming over people in London? Are they all going socially bananas? 'I've got to go now, I'm going to the theatre,' I said firmly, and hung up.

Daphne Guinness and Robin arrived, and as we were in the car on the way to the theatre, I told them. Robin was not surprised. 'Don't get on his bad side,' he said. 'He's totally untrustworthy.'

Met Biggins at the King's Head pub in Islington and saw *Frankly Scarlett*, a weak spoof on the casting of Scarlett O'Hara in *Gone with the Wind*. Quite funny but much too long. Went backstage afterwards to see the cast, all of whom dressed in a dressing room the size of my bathroom. Since the female impersonator who plays Tallulah Bankhead, Bette Davis, Vivien Leigh and Katharine Hepburn changes about nineteen times, I can't think of anything more uncomfortable. On top of this they're paid the princely sum of a hundred pounds a week! That's showbiz, folks.

Thursday, 22 May 1997

Lunched at Harry's Bar. Sue St Johns took me as a birthday treat with Evie, very nice. Graham Payne, Noël Coward's boyfriend and keeper of the archives and executor, came for tea with Peter Charlesworth. We discussed doing *Star Quality*, but he said it was impossible to do it in 1998 as Noël Coward Productions were going to be put out, because the following year, 1999, would have been the Master's hundredth birthday. Talked about maybe doing it then.

Loads of calls between Nolan, Steve Tellez and Jeffrey about when I start *Pacific Palisades*. It has not been picked up for the Fall 1998 season but they are going to nurture it through the summer months.

Frankly, Scarlett, I don't think *Pacific Palisades* is going to hack it, not unless they make some of the situations and my character stronger. Called Diane Messina Stanley, one of the writers and show-runner producers. Having received the script, I tried to tell her a lot of the things that were wrong with my part – one of the main things being that I seem bland and too smiley and calm and let the girl, Kimberley, get away with all the strong assertive stuff.

'Oh, but that's the fun of it,' she cooed. 'You bring so much fun to that when we see that you are really being wicked and yet being so charming on the screen.'

'It's not coming across,' I said, having decided that I'm going to have to put my sling-backs firmly down in future.

Monica the hairdresser came over, she's visiting her mother from LA and she said the only way *Pacific Palisades* is going to be saved is if I bring some attitude to do it. She's right, so I guess I'm going to have to stop being Mrs Nice-guy on the set and do it the way I feel it should be done.

Friday, 23 May 1997

My birthday! Can't believe I've made it this long. It's all gone in a flash, quite terrifying really but one must not dwell on it. Spent the day answering the door to dozens of bouquets of flowers. So many people sent me flowers and faxes and cards. Carol and Anthony sent the most gorgeous Stephanopoulos orchids, completely beautiful and must have cost a fortune. Also Stella, Jonathan Lloyd, Harry and Cathy Sloan, Bill and Hazel, Rod and Maggie Tyler, Charles Spencer and David Wigg. Katy came over with some lovely lilies. Then Tara and Michael arrived on the Euro train from Paris, my brother Bill and then Pandora and little Cara. Had a lovely tea and opened presents. Telephone and front door going constantly.

Wonderful dinner party here. Some of my closest friends – the Bricusses, the Fennells, Biggins and Neil, Sue St Johns and Paul Raben – made the evening superb. Had ordered four hundred pounds' worth of caviar from Fred and we had it to start with in a baked potato. Chili the cook was very good. The Bricusses gave me an enormous Scrabble set with what looked like solid gold letters, and Biggins brought me a fabulous Aubusson cushion.

All in all, a wonderful birthday, saw all the people I love or talked to them or heard from them, with one notable exception.

24–25 May 1997

Beautiful spring day. Robin and I drove, with Steve, to Michael and Shakira Caine's in the country. Many friends already there: Dennis Selinger with dog (he is looking a little on the elderly side these days – Dennis, that is); Sue and Dick St Johns; Roger Moore and Kristina Tholstrup, his girlfriend. Kristina was in casual mode, which is unusual, as she is usually dressed up more than I am. She's better in casual mode. She is quite quiet and does not give a lot, but I think she is sweet. Emil Reilly, who is Shakira's oldest friend, half Indian and a bit of a soothsayer, told me that he had seen Katy and that he is trying to give her some pep talks about doing more; he's certainly right about that.

Sat between Michael and Roger at lunch. Michael gave his opinions on the current state of England, all of which are highly politically incorrect, but everybody seems to totally agree with them. Took a walk down to the river's edge, which was beautiful. Watched the boats go by. It's not exactly St Tropez but it has its own English charm, as does Michael's property. It must cost him a fortune for the upkeep. Lay lazily on chaises, gossiping with Emil. Michael is writing a book and doesn't care if he works or not, so he says. I don't believe him. Roger's off to do a film in South Africa and I said I might see him there in October. Kristina is devastated she can't give Roger his seventieth birthday in Paris as planned, but I told her why not give it a week or so later. Sounds logical. She thought that was a good idea.

Bank Holiday Monday, 26 May 1997

Another gorgeous day. Steve drove me to Denville Hall in Sussex. There I met Simon Williams and we went in to visit Elspeth March in the Old Actors' Home. Although it was a very nice environment and the staff seemed to take care of the elderly residents really well, it is still mind-shattering to think that any of us could end up there. Elspeth is now wheelchair-bound and can hardly see, but she is so wonderful and kind and reminds me of my mother. Went into the green room, where everybody was having a glass of wine. They were all, as the manager, Moira, put it: 'dressed to the nines to see you, dear'. Average age eighty-nine, youngest being about eighty-one, eldest ninety-eight. Some are pretty spry, like Olive Dodds, whom I remember from my Rank starlet days. She looked feisty and told me I looked great. Well, I felt like an adolescent next to everyone else. Then an old gentleman, properly dressed in a blue serge suit and tie and cane, shook my hand almost until it bled and told me that my father had been his agent and he remembered me when I was a little girl. Met a man called Patrick who also remembered me. 'We were at Maidstone Rep together years ago,' he said jovially. 'I'll never forget you because you were so pretty – still are of course,' he added hastily. We all laughed. I remember Maidstone well. I was a sixteen-year-old RADA student and Patrick, I think, was the character man. Everybody had beautiful manners, something you don't see much of today.

A local photographer came in to take snaps with Elspeth and Simon and me. Then we went into the dining room for lunch which was very much like school food. Never liked school food, which is probably why I was such a skinny kid, but there was plenty of wine, although mine tasted corked. The staff kept on shooting surreptitious snaps of me as I was lifting a forkful of cauliflower to my lips, but I did feel a great surge of affection for all these wonderful old thespians, particularly Elspeth. Took a little tour of Denville Hall and saw some of the elderly residents taking the sun in the walled-in patio, then visited Elspeth's room, which is about seven by ten but she loves it. There are no mementoes there except a couple of photos of her children Lindsay and Jamie Granger (she was married to Stewart Granger). In the main hallway as I was signing the guest book there were old photographs of Vivien Leigh, Noël Coward, Laurence Olivier and Richard Attenborough, who is the president of the home.

Simon is on the committee. He is such a charming, witty man and I do wish I saw more of him.

Came back to my flat which seemed unbelievably real and lived in with the hundreds of flowers and loads of photographs. I don't ever want to have to end up in Denville Hall, however well they treat you there.

On a youthful note, Katy came for tea. We sat on the balcony and looked out on Eaton Place, which looked quite deserted but charming in the hot afternoon sun. Off to Los Angeles tomorrow to get involved in the continuing saga of *Pacific Palisades*. Just read the new script and have to say that my dialogue is pretty dire. They can't seem to come up with any decent dialogue. Talk about trying to make a silk purse out of a sow's ear. Never mind, I'll just have to go into battle.

Wednesday, 28 May 1997

Trying to make a silk purse out of a sow's ear with this *Pacific Palisades* script is unbelievably frustrating. It's really crap. Certainly nowhere near *Dynasty* or even *Melrose Place*. A few people like Nolan (who has hurt his leg badly) and Jeffrey say the consensus is that the show ain't got 'it' at the moment. Added to this, Fox have removed it temporarily from the schedule, thanks to our totally appalling ratings against *Ellen*, and there is absolutely no publicity about it except for the occasional squib about me.

Exercised in the morning with Jeffrey and Joanna Poitier. Amazed how busy the gym is at six thirty! Went to Nolan's for fittings and they brought out some highly expensive Valentino and Givenchy outfits. The Valentino suit I chose for *Pacific Palisades* was a mere four thousand seven hundred dollars! I hope it keeps fine for them. Still trying to find out about episode eleven. The production company seem to think that I'm going to dash back from Tara's wedding for it. They also expect me to film my only two scenes in one day and only get paid for half my normal salary. It's quite disgusting. Steve Tellez, my agent, is getting really angry and says that he is only agreeing for me to do this to 'protect my relationship with Aaron Spelling'.

Judy and I watched the American Film Institute tribute to Martin Scorsese, which had a considerable lack of glamorous stars, with the exception of Sharon Stone, who seemed, as usual, terribly pleased with herself.

Thursday, 29 May 1997

Sped down the back steps to apartment 902 directly below me, into Joanna and Sidney Poitier's new apartment, which is in the throes of renovation. We went to the new Spago on Canon Drive which is where the old Bistro Garden used to be. It is a humongous place filled with Beverly Hills movers and shakers. Joined Barbara and Marvin Davis, who are unbelievably powerful in this town. Barbara is sweet and Marvin can be amusing. Different people came by the table to pay homage, including Sherry Lansing, Tony Thomopoulos and his TV presenter wife Cristina. Got into some interesting conversations with Sidney about life. He's one of the few people in this town who talks about something meaningful and deep. Spago food was absolutely delicious but the damn place was so noisy that one had to shriek. Owner Wolfgang Puck came over and we complimented him on the restaurant.

Everyone's worried about Sue Mengers, who has developed polyps on her throat and has to go into the hospital to have them removed. Called her and she said, 'Jean-Claude is waiting for me, he wants me to join him.' How macabre is that!

Friday, 30 May 1997

At 9 p.m. exhausted and having changed several times, I happened to see, by accident, a new schedule and 'day out of days'. To my horror I see that I am working on Friday when I had already planned on leaving at five forty-five for London. Spoke to Tim Silver, the production manager, who said, 'Oh, but we thought you could shoot all day on Friday and take the late plane.' Trying to read the different schedules by the light of a flickering torch was exceedingly frustrating and I was trembling with rage at, once again, being screwed up by these *Pacific Palisades* production assholes. Finished shooting at nine thirty. Judy made scrambled eggs, and we watched a good movie with John Malkovich and Andie MacDowell, who was excellent.

Saturday, 31 May 1997

Went shopping at Niemans with Judy. It is boiling, boiling hot. Went to the new Chasen's for a publicity lunch that Jeffrey organised for Aaron Tonken's charity for his children's theatre group. David Schwimmer, a hot young star of *Friends*, was hosting. Dozens of paparazzi outside Chasen's, which used to be the old Bistro Garden – it's all rather confusing with these changes of names of the restaurants. Inside, a lot of Z-list celebrities were quaffing some mediocre wines. Barry Krost, my sister's manager, and Mr and Mrs Al Grossman, whom Sacha is supposed to paint, were there too. They are very old, very rich and very ugly. He fancies himself as a wit and said to me, vis-à-vis my rather chic and simple straw Patricia Underwood hat, 'You look like you should be working in the paddy fields of China.' Ooh, ha-bloody-ha. I stared coldly at this ancient wreck, a huge grey curly wig perched on his decaying forehead, and said unwittily,

'And where did you get your tie?' Grabbed some cold salmon and salad and sat in the back room. 'I remember when Swifty Lazar used to host his Oscar parties here,' I told Judy. 'Those were the days.' We were joined by Suzanne Pleshette, Morgan Fairchild and Barry Krost.

Everyone started bemoaning that there are so few roles for women over forty. What else is new? Barry said that when the studio were looking for an actress to play opposite Robin Williams, aged fifty, they would not consider anyone over the age of thirty. 'It is extremely ageist out here,' Suzanne said. 'I'll never get into playing grandmother parts, I'd rather not work.' Hear hear, I'm not Joan Plowright yet. Suzanne then admitted that she was bringing out her line of couture clothes for pets on QVC. I guess she prefers that to acting.

Victoria, Judy's daughter, came over and I gave her a St Laurent jacket and dress, some clothes from Tara's wedding that she seemed thrilled with. I have now styled several of the guests. Went to new Spago again. Liked it better this time with Sacha and Jeffrey – sat on the terrace, were able to smoke and it was a gorgeous night. Don't think much of the service, it's terribly slow so we got through three bottles of red wine which left us all feeling no pain. Sacha was mortified that he had forgotten my birthday and said he would make it up to me – well, we'll see about that.

Sunday, 1 June 1997

People magazine shoot with photographer Neil. Monica, Judy, Jeffrey, Linda, Alicia and Sacha and Erin all in attendance. Wore several different casual outfits, which means that I probably can't wear them publicly. *People* magazine do not pay for anything, not even the hairdresser, so Jeffrey managed to get Fox Publicity to pay for Monica. She originally asked for seven hundred and fifty dollars just for the day! Hairdressing pays more than acting! Judy and Jeffrey were so appalled that they got her down to two fifty, which seems reasonable for three hours of relatively easy work.

Jeffrey and I went to an exhibition at Christie's of Hollywood memorabilia called *Classic Hollywood*. Most of this consisted of Claudette Colbert's old dresses and a lot of rather boring photographs of people like Milton Berle and his mother, Ingrid Bergman, Louise Brooks, etc. What was extraordinary was the fact that Christie's are auctioning such things as Claudette's Barbadian passport, her American Express cards and her Oscar, for which the estimate was $150,000–200,000! All sorts of intimate possessions of hers were on display and it was really quite sad.

Saw a movie called *Volcano*, which the critics trashed. I believe the critics don't know what the public wants. This was an exciting, well-made action thriller about a volcano that hits LA, with a good performance from Tommy Lee Jones and Anne Heche, who's the lover of Ellen DeGeneres. Don't seem to have heard too much about those two recently. Watched the Tony Awards on TV hosted by Rosie O'Donnell, who was the only person that the audience seemed to like. The applause for both Raquel Welch and Roseanne Barr when they came on was minimal, to say the least. I guess that Broadway doesn't like Hollywood.

Monday, 2 June 1997

Fitting with Nolan – I still seem to be losing weight which is gratifying. Lunched at Drai's Café with Joanna Poitier and Luisa Moore. Luisa seems completely obsessed by her ex, Roger, and his new lover, Kristina Tholstrup. She just can't stop talking about them, even though she keeps saying that he's out of her system and she doesn't care any more. It's perfectly obvious that not only has she been deeply hurt but she cares a lot. Joanna and I tried to be positive towards her and after forty-five minutes did our best to persuade her to change the subject, but she managed to get back to it. She said she was never going to give Roger a divorce, and that their kids had told her that if she did let him divorce her, they would never speak to her again. It all seems really ridiculous and sad. They've been apart three years. She should let him go.

At CAA, an impressive building in the heart of Beverly Hills, met with Steve Tellez and four other agents, average age twenty-eight (if that). All agents in Hollywood seem to look alike. They have bland, gung-ho faces and always seem terribly enthusiastic – to your face. But I'm sure that as soon as I left the building I was forgotten. Gary Concoff joined us and we tried to sort out these ghastly, never-ending problems with *Pacific Palisades* and the schedule. I am really fed up with the show now. They changed Friday's schedule so that I will be in a complete state about catching the five-forty flight. I must have time before the wedding (which they've known about since January). Also they are trying to persuade me to come back earlier than intended to shoot two scenes for just half my salary. I'm furious. I told Steve and Gary that I've seen the script, in which I have five scenes; I don't know how they are going to sort it. It's disgusting and I'm appalled that Aaron can allow them to stoop so low. I feel glad that I've not signed for more of this series as I'm not enjoying it.

Spent the afternoon going through my American galleys yet again for *Second Act* and finding endless mistakes. What kind of copy-editors must they have?

David Niven Jr picked me up and as we were leaving the building Marvin Davis came along in his stretch limo and said, 'Why don't you guys join me, Joanna Poitier and Frank Whatsisname for dinner at Mortons?' 'You mean Calcagnini?' I asked. 'Yeah, yeah,' he said. 'Well, my sister's away and I don't think she'd be too thrilled to see her fiancé and me at Morton's on a Monday night,' I laughed. But we went – Niven loves a free dinner. Had a very jolly dinner with the Davises and Niven, who is always charming and funny.

Wednesday, 4 June 1997

Lunched at the new Spago with Lance and Stephen Amezdroz. He is the Australian head of a company called Beyond who seem interested in putting up the money for 'Joan's World', a series in which I would travel all over the world revealing the delights of various exotic places. I think I would much prefer this to *Pacific Palisades*. I'm fed up with not knowing what I am doing and having no control and spouting awful dialogue. We still don't know whether the series is being picked up, we don't know when I will be wanted back. It's a mess. I'm going to be working solidly until I leave.

Packed, then went to Ray Katz's [Anthony Newley's manager] apartment for a cocktail party for Sacha, who had just painted Ray's portrait. Although he is eighty and looks pretty ancient, it was an excellent picture. Sacha had on display Gore Vidal's picture, mine, and several others. A very good turnout. Stefanie Powers, Connie Stevens, Michele Lee, Sandy Gallin, Suzy Pleshette and Lance, who'd brought along a few Australian producers. Two ancient crones who are mega mega rich and who Sacha is supposed to paint were there; Sacha said there wasn't enough money in the world for him to paint them!

Had a long chat with Michele Lee about how dysfunctional all the networks are these days. She was popular with them in the movie-of-the-week department, but now they've stopped returning her calls and she's been waiting over two and a half months to hear about a pick-up on a project. Absolutely typical. The networks are all totally screwed up. All they care about is appealing to the demographics: that 18–30 age group.

Thursday, 5 June 1997

Worked my ass off in *Pacific Palisades*, which quite frankly I think is becoming a large piece of dreck. I've never been so screwed around by a production company in my life. I find it highly upsetting. The director, however, Les Dalton, is a poppet. He confessed to me how dreadful the original scripts were, and how much work was needed to even make them palpable. Worked all day and into the night. As they had changed my call and had me working on the day I was supposed to be leaving for London, I had arranged with Tim Silver that I would do this. But what a long and exhausting day. Even twenty-four-year-old Kimberley looks drained.

Friday, 6 June 1997

After six hours' sleep got up at five to go to work. Les gave me a beautiful present of an old Greek coin and many of the crew came up and said how much this show needs me and please come back. Have seen the script for which they will only pay me half my salary for two scenes and it is actually five scenes – yes, five – scenes!! Talked to my agent and told him how unfair it was. Also talked to the line producer, Peter Dunne, and told him the same thing. He was totally appalled and said, 'How can they do this to someone of your calibre?' Quite. I'm disenchanted with all forms of television now, and quite frankly will not be at all sorry if *Pacific Palisades* doesn't get picked up. Judy and Max highly excited, and we all took the 5.40 flight for London.

Monday, 9 June 1997

Preparations for Tara's wedding are in high gear. Constant telephone calls to Tara in Paris and discussions of table *placements*, who's coming, who's not, etc. The layout in *Hello!* last week in which she, Michael and I were on the cover, was nice for her and she looked lovely. I looked ill at ease because, as Jeffrey said, 'You're trying not to upstage the bride.' Tara says that her wedding dress is utterly stunning. Well, that's good news. I'm not convinced that my Jean Paul Gaultier dress is going to be utterly stunning. To that end I whisked out the David Emanuel *point d'esprit* which he made for the aborted Muck Flick party.

Another kitchen designer came for another endless discussion of how to redesign my kitchen. Judy came over and was stunned at the price. Me too. In excess of fifty thousand pounds!!! I cannot believe how expensive things in London are, but this is the ball-park figure I've now been given by *three* different designers for a complete new kitchen and breakfast room plus appliances. Katy and I then spent an hour and a half going through her wedding clothes, tweaking and organising shoes, jewellery etc.

Tuesday, 10 June 1997

The sun is shining and Jeffrey, Judy, Max and Didier and I all trotted off to the Fine Arts Fair at Olympia. Full of the most beautiful things, nothing under about a million pounds. Saw three sideboards I'd like to buy but I don't happen to have that kind of spare cash on me.

Dashed with Judy and Jeffrey to Alex Harris, a jeweller in Old Bond Street who is going to lend me the most gorgeous amethyst and diamond necklace for the wedding, which is very kind of him. Then to Herbert Johnson, where I tried on dozens of hats for Ascot next week. All of this preparation is quite enervating. Telephone call from agent in LA. Bottom line is that he's spoken to Aaron Spelling who, much as 'he loves me' (ha ha ha!), will not pay me any more than an extra five thousand for the five scenes.

'Aaron said basically you can like it or lump it,' Steve said. '"If she won't do it for that then we will write her out of episode twelve or thirteen."' 'This means I will forfeit an entire episode's salary,' I said. Apparently they have no more money for anything and neither Fox nor Aaron will come up with the extra dosh. Steve purports to be as upset by this as I am, but as he is the packaging agent for *Pacific Palisades*, it's no skin off his nose, plus he's not even getting commission. Am deeply disgusted. What with the wedding and this new wrinkle in the *Pacific Palisades* situation, had to take another sleeping pill just to fall asleep. Keep thinking about how Aaron constantly said I 'made' *Dynasty*. What loyalty.

Wednesday, 11 June 1997

Talked to Peter Charlesworth. He too is utterly disgusted but thinks that I should take the five grand for episode eleven, then do twelve and thirteen, and then write a letter in which I say I must know in writing whether I am going to do the following episodes in blocks if the network picks up the show. I am fed up with being fucked about by these assholes.

Thursday, 12 June 1997

Day of Tara's shower. I wake up feeling terrible. Dr Northridge manages to fit me in. I ask him what's wrong, he says it's a viral upper or lower gobbledy gobbledy gobbledy gook. It's going around and it's caught on planes.

'Why do the three people I came with who were travelling Club and I was travelling First, not get it?' I asked. He had no answer to that. He said there was nothing one could do except the usual: aspirin, rest, etc., but that it was OK for me to go out.

Three o'clock and the shower starts. First arrivals are Tara and her mother-in-law Joslin, and Tara's best friend Lisa, closely followed by Judy and Stella. Tara is in good form. No trace of pre-bridal nerves. Then a ton of girls arrive, some of them my friends, most of them Tara's. Tara's grandmother Gracie arrives with Gina Fratini, Tony's girlfriend and live-in lover. Gracie, who is ninety-four, is in good shape – for ninety-four. However, she is not in as good shape as she was at ninety or eighty. There are not too many good things to be said about getting older. She is sweet and Tara is very solicitous. Then Erin arrives fresh from LA with the news that Sacha has been held up at Customs in London because of his portraits. This casts a bit of a pall but we continue. It was wonderful to see so many girls and women who really cared about Tara. We have a fine tea, catered by Chili, good sandwiches and scones and cream, of which I have a plethora, then tea then champagne.

After tea, Tara opens presents and everyone ooohs and aaahs about the various naughty bits, from Trashy Lingerie and Victoria's Secrets even. Then Tara has to leave to catch the Channel Tunnel to Paris, leaving us sitting around waiting for Sacha. Various telephone calls from various Customs officials saying Sacha is being held at Customs. Finally he arrives at seven o'clock having landed at twelve! Pretty shitty, I think. He's quite sanguine; I would have been going totally mad. Apparently he had gone through the 'nothing to declare' signs and he had two paintings that he had done, one of Kristina Tholstrup, Roger Moore's girlfriend, the other of Lily Mahtani. He says the Customs men were pretty slow, but he is being kind. They wanted to know why he hadn't declared them.

To cut a long story short, he had to wait to give them a thousand – yes, a thousand pounds, which is 17.5 per cent. I think the whole thing is disgraceful, outrageous, stupid beyond belief and I cannot believe that these Customs people haven't got anything better to do than to harass Sacha for five and a half hours about his own paintings when there are people coming in stuffed with drugs, gold, God knows what. We live in a world in which on every street corner, young perfectly able-bodied men sit rolling cigarettes, out of work. Yet they take my hard-working young son and interrogate and try to intimidate him, and then fine him a huge amount of money? But anyway, who said it was a perfect world?

We go to Egerton Terrace, Valentino's gorgeous house, to meet the group: the Bamfords and Alice, Robin and Valentino, Rosario the beautiful young princess of Bulgaria and Valentino's boyfriend Bruce. Valentino looks great and I am thrilled to see him. We haven't seen each other for over a year and we both keep saying how much we miss each other so why haven't we seen each other? Troll off to a society hostess's party at Claridge's for her daughter's birthday. It's supposed to be one of the major parties of the year. Everybody's dressed to the nines, diamond jewellery has come out in abundance. Walk into a heated sauna and see lots of friends: Jacqueline de Ribes, Nan Kempner, Lynn Wyatt, Doris Brynner, Charles and Pandora Delevingne. However, we find out that there are no *placements* at the party and everybody is in shock-horror, how can they do such a thing! Since I have hardly any voice left and the band is playing at full blast, it's hard for me to make a statement! Go into the furthest back room with Carole Bamford and Robin and Wendy and Ray Stark. A waitress comes up asking, 'Would ya like some stir-fries?' Carole and I look at each other in horror.

It is so jammed and so hot and all everybody can say is how dreadful it is that the hostess, who is trying to make a statement to her husband about how well she can function, is giving this totally naff party for people like Ned Ryan, Rupert Hambro, Princess Margaret, Raine Spencer, Serena and David Linley, Lord Bruce Dundas, Susan and Robert Sangster and their various children, and dozens of others. Everyone's complaining to each other in loud voices. The anti-class-warfare group would love this scene, I myself am thinking. Eventually Charles Delevingne oozes me over to where Pandora is sitting.

It is a bar rather than a proper place to have a party. Many people are saying they think this is the worst party they've ever been to. Chubby Benson sits with us. She is lots of fun. The food on offer is mostly lobster and fish and some sort of oriental stuff which I loathe. Good thing I stuffed myself with sandwiches and cake at Tara's shower.

All of a sudden a kerfuffle occurs. Rupert Loewenstein comes over bowing and scraping to bring Princess Margaret to our table. She is obviously bored stiff of whomever she's been with. A lot of gratuitous getting up and 'Hello, ma'am', 'How are you, ma'am?' I curtsy and she actually bestows upon me a thin grin. Ned Ryan, always in attendance, says, 'You know, Princess Margaret really likes you.' 'Bullshit,' I say succinctly. PM talks to Rupert Loewenstein, who's being extremely solicitous, and all of a sudden our table is the high spot. Nan Kempner comes over, oozes into a place, as does Lynn Wyatt, as does Wendy Stark, as does that ghastly Brett Sherwood. Princess Margaret looks regally around, cigarette in place, holding a large Scotch. She's basically saying to everybody, 'Come and worship at my shrine.' But it's 1997, folks, and nobody ain't worshipping at any old royal shrine. Granted we all get up and do a bit of a curtsy, but the bowing and scraping doesn't work any more – though I adore the Queen.

Anthony suddenly asks me to dance. 'Christ, I had to get away from that old bore,' he says as we twirl around the floor to some kind of seventies jazz band. People are cutting rugs, quite a few of them are young. Back at our table we're all having lots of fun. Even Princess Margaret, although many people profess not to like her, seems to be having fun and has attracted a whole heap of admirers. Valentino comes over. I must say he does look well and his boyfriend Bruce really looks great. Bruce and Princess Rosario are the best-looking couple there. My voice is in such bad shape that nobody can hear me. Rupert Hambro comes over for a dance and flirts as usual on the floor. Met Farah, the ex-Empress of Iran. She was very friendly. Very bejewelled. Sitting back and looking at the whole thing, it really is slightly déjà vu. Grown people all dressed up in their best, the women having spent thousands of pounds on their frocks – for what? For a party that isn't even a party. A dud really. Only because we got a good table together were we having fun.

Went home and practised my latest song for the wedding, 'Makin' Whoopee'. Trying to do it à la Marilyn, singing 'Happy Birthday to You' to President John Kennedy in 1962. The way I sound now, if I have any voice at all it will be a miracle. The world is very strange, as this party tonight has proved, but there will always be people who have money, there will always be people who will spend it in a way to have fun.

Friday, 13 June 1997

A typical Friday the thirteenth. Fiona came over for manicure, pedicure and the works, then Katy came over in a very bad mood. Judy arrived and we tried to dispense motherly advice to Katy. But one thing I've learned, you can never tell young girls anything about your own experiences since they simply take no notice.

Arrived at Harry's Bar with Carole for Judy and Al Taubman's lunch. Sat between Sally Khan and her very nice boyfriend, Maître Philippe. Also there, of course, Carole, Susan Sangster, Brett Sherwood and Signor Giotti, the ex-brother-in-law of Audrey Hepburn who seems to have had a coup de vieux. At the next table Valentino, Doris Brynner, Princess Rosario of Bulgaria and Va Va's boyfriend, Bruce, sat and critted our table. Halfway through a very nice lunch my voice started to go, and by the end of it I could barely squeak.

Came home, got into bed, called doctor – away, of course. Other doc suggested I go on steroids. Steroids? That seems a bit radical. However, I'm now down to zero talking practically. In a panic, I called Robin, who has gone to Paris. He didn't think steroids would be a good idea since they weren't prescribed by my doctor. The dressmaker came over for fittings and to help me pack. She went out to buy some old-fashioned Persian and Arabian remedies which consisted of sucking on the fermented hot seeds of a special kind of apple. Then eating some foul, gooey white substance that tasted like wet cotton wool. Did all of these things, plus the usual codeine, and took one antibiotic, although I'm not thrilled with the idea.

Fell asleep at nine thirty. Typical: telephone rang at ten fifteen and a nasal twang cheerily said, 'May I speak to Miss Collins please, Gary Concoff speaking.' 'I'm asleep and ill,' I screamed in a fury, adrenalin rushing. I was now wide awake, walking around the apartment, talking to myself. My voice seemed slightly on the mend, but my back was now out.

Does this always happen to the mother of the bride? Tomorrow's forecast: rain and thunderstorms. Great. Took half a pill and went back to sleep. Please God let the next two days go better than the last two.

Saturday, 14 June 1997

Arrive in Paris with Stella as scheduled and dash to the Ritz to meet Robin, Biggins and Neil, and Sue St Johns in the bar. It's overcast so we lunch there and have our usual shriek. Valentino is on the next table and I'm glad I'm looking reasonably together. Stella comes back from the Hotel Costes and informs me that instead of the long table for thirty-eight people they have been promising for the past four months, it has to be two tables of nineteen each. I'm quite annoyed about this as I've worked hard on the placement; however, we will work it out. Tara comes by. For someone who is being stalked by the paparazzi she is looking rather undone. No make-up, which is unusual for her, a rather unflattering hat and a dirty white raincoat. Valentino clocks the whole thing from his table and raises his eyebrows significantly. Tara and I go and fit the Gaultier dress in my suite with Sue St Johns – about eight people are there. Sue thinks the dress looks good, I am not convinced.

Try to rest, then meet Lynn Wyatt and the rest of our core group in the Ritz bar before we walk across the Place Vendôme to the Hotel Costes. Roger Moore and Kristina are already there, as are Judy, Max and the girls and various others. It is very hot but I am glad that it's not ninety degrees as the forecast threatened.

Katy and Paul arrive. She is wearing the purple dress she's been worried about, but it looks great. Everybody turns up looking wonderful and the placement is excellent even though it's a little crowded. The food is really good and the wine which Joslin and George Adam have contributed is excellent. I give Tara and Michael their wedding presents from me – a gold Cartier watch for her and a matching stainless steel one for him – which they seem delighted with.

Sunday, 15 June 1997

The day of Tara's wedding dawns! Start getting ready for the civil ceremony at nine. Creeping about the gloomy suite, I almost trip and think about what Jeffrey said about the Hotel Costes: 'I call it the Braille Suite.' I agree, it's much too dark. Wear blue silk Escada suit and pearls and go to Tara's room to see if she's ready. Panic and pandemonium reign. There are about eight people there, photographers' assistants, journalists, make-up artists, hairdressers, waiters. To top it all, when I ask how Michael is, she points to where he is sitting having his hair blow-dried at another dressing table. 'Don't you know it's terribly unlucky to see your bridegroom on the day of the wedding?' I ask, feeling somewhat old-fashioned. She shrugs and smokes a cigarette and I notice she's drinking champagne. She seems upset but I don't know whether she's nervous or not. 'He had to have his hair done,' she said. 'Where's your hat?' I ask. 'On the bed,' she replies. No more comment on that.

I collect Katy and Paul and Jeffrey and Stella, and we get in the car with black curtains at the window. In spite of Michael and Tara's precautions, the paparazzi are everywhere. We see none at the very nice Town Hall in Sceaux, which is the suburb where Michael and Tara will live. Tony and Grace and his son Christopher and our little family group all congregate. Michael is wearing a lime-green suit and quite a lot of make-up, but I guess this is for the benefit of the photographers. Tara's suit is very cute but the hat from Jean Paul Gaultier is a huge-brimmed affair made of clear amber beads and wire. It's very Gaultier but not quite suitable for the wedding. She was going to wear a straw hat with the black bow, very Chanel. We wait for Michael's brother, who arrives in a black pinstripe suit, several rings through his nose, ears and chin – yes, chin – and his black hair plaited into a pigtail that reaches to his bottom. He is about six foot four and quite an imposing figure, to say the least.

The civil ceremony is short and sweet, and then we are given a picnic lunch in a box and whisked off back in our cars. I talk to Tara's old nanny, who is seriously over-excited. Arrive at the Ritz with Jeffrey and Stella and go to meet the rest of the group in the bar. Katy and Paul take their picnics and go off to the park. We regale everyone with stories. 'Michael's brother looked like a deckchair,' announces Jeffrey solemnly. The sun is shining but it's not too hot and we're able to sit on the terrace, where I have the world's most delicious ham and cheese omelette and we are in mellow mood.

The synagogue where the religious ceremony will take place is full. Louise Fennell is looking fabulous in a huge hat. At six foot she can get away with it. The photographers, who I think are not terribly professional, take snaps of me fiddling about with Michael's tie and his mother fiddling with his hair. Jean Paul Gaultier has outfitted him in a white tie and shirt which doesn't fit. I can get half my hand between the collar and his neck. He is also wearing a rather curious arrangement that consists of black trousers with a matching overskirt and very long pointed silk shoes that turn up at the end. But as they say, they are artists and not your normal young-marrieds.

Michael walks down the aisle with his mother on his arm followed by me on the arm of George. I feel very emotional as we arrive under the chuppah where ninety-four-year-old Gracie is standing quiveringly and looking a bit frail. Then, to the evocative notes of *Lohengrin*'s 'Wedding March', we turn and I see my daughter coming down the aisle on the arm of Tony. This time I definitely start to tear up. Tara looks absolutely beautiful. The gown is seriously gorgeous and the masses of pale tulle that are caught up over her face and hanging down about ten feet and held by four adorable little bridesmaids look ravishing. She's carrying a beautiful bunch of orchids and has orchids in her hair and on her net gloves. It is a very stylish outfit. She is emotional too, her eyes filled with tears. Tony squeezes my arm and we gulp. Just think, thirty-three years ago *we* were doing this! He is looking well, although I know he's been having radiation for his health problem, which is sad. The ceremony is very nice, performed by a rabbi who received the OBE at the same time as me. He is quite a character, more like a television comedian than a rabbi, and he switches effortlessly from French to English and Yiddish. Then the couple exchange their vows and I hold Tara's bouquet and help her off with her veil while the ring is slipped on. Unfortunately, our backs are to the congregation so I can't see what is going on. I try to sneak glances, but I can only see Michael's family – and boy are there a lot of them! It seems that there are only about 20 per cent of our family and friends. Tony starts crying and I divide a Kleenex in half and give it to him, saving the other half for myself. Hope the waterproof mascara is working. Then Tara starts crying and so I donate to her the other half of my wrinkled Kleenex. She looks vulnerable and sensitive and sweet. I suppose this should be one of the biggest days of my life, and indeed it is, but everything has a surreal quality, especially when the rabbi announces that a collection is to take place. For what? I think it's unheard of to have a collection at a wedding and indeed many of the visitors have not come with money.

We follow Tara and Michael down the aisle. I am feeling proud and very matriarchal. We enter the private room, which is absolutely hideous. In spite of Jeffrey and Stella trying to organise things, the photographers do it their way, which means that in the picture we get the whole of the two families strung out in a long line. They put the babies and young children sitting down at the bottom and the old grans either side, but it's still too much since my half-sister Natasha is there too plus her husband and child, plus Hazel and Bill. The congregation streams into the street and there are massed paparazzi outside. Our cars are blocking the road and, as in the way of the French, everybody starts sounding their horns. I try to duck the photographers as per instructions but it isn't easy as I almost get knocked down in the process. Tara and Michael come out with the two huge bodyguards holding blackout curtains over them so they can't be photographed. Some of the paparazzi boo them. Charming.

Arrive back at the hotel and go gratefully into the Ritz bar, which has become our hangout. I think it went rather well, although I'm a little worried about the paparazzi shots since I know Tara's deal is for an exclusive and I hope it won't be blown by this.

Not much time to relax before I have to do a complete change of clothes. Put on Gaultier dress; it does not look good and I get lipstick all over it as it goes over my head, so have to switch to backup: I put on the black David Emanuel *point d'esprit* and then head down to the Ritz bar yet again for another fortifying drink before setting out for the party. At the Buddha Bar, all is mayhem and bedlam. The stairs are wooden and it is quite dangerous going up and down. There are about sixty people not in black tie who I have never seen before.

Roger Moore comes upstairs and we greet everybody. The music is loud and fun and people seem in a great mood. Tara is wearing a lovely beaded bolero and is in ebullient mood. Steve, who has come over from London to help out with the driving, drives Katy back to the hotel so she can change her dress because she says she can't dance in the long one. I sit between Biggins and Roger and opposite Theo, who is nervous about singing later. 'I told you I would let you off the hook,' I say, 'but you insisted.' 'I know, I know,' he laughs, 'but I want to do it.'

Suddenly I see zillions of people whipping out cameras. The bodyguards seem to have disappeared and half of the guests have Instamatics in their hands. It's not my problem – except it is, because I will have to stump up if Tara and Michael don't get the last third of their magazine deal. The food is excellent and finally Tony arrives with Gracie and Gina Fratini and sits at PC's table next to us. The dancing is great and Biggins and I do a wild dance which causes everybody to stop and do one of those things they do in 1940s musicals with Judy Garland and watch us! Tony tells me he's tired and can't stay up late. It must have been a very gruelling day for him and for Gracie too, who's looking peaky. I tell Tara that her father probably won't be able to stay and sing, and she says, 'Well, he must, that's the way it's been arranged.' I table-hop and have a great time giggling about everything. I see Katy dancing, she too seems to be having a great time.

Then Tara goes on the stage which has been erected in front of this huge thirty-foot-high Buddha. It is a wonderful room with plenty of atmosphere and everybody is in a great mood. She announces Regine, who gets up and gives us two of her better Edith Piaf-type songs. Tony has come by to say he cannot stay, which is really sad, and PC goes too, which slightly pisses me off as he is my agent and I wanted him to see me sing, but never mind. Tara sings and she has a truly sweet voice. I wish her career as a singer had taken off more. I am feeling no pain as she announces me so I got up on the stage in my black Emanuel *point d'esprit* dress, which looks much better than the Jean-Paul Gaultier, and gave them my rendition of 'Makin' Whoopee'. The background was the one I had rehearsed over the telephone with the pianist, and, immodestly I might say, it brought down the house. I introduced Theo, who did 'You're the Top' with me. Unfortunately, he didn't realise that you have to hold the hand-mike next to your mouth and he forgot his words a few times, but all in all it was great fun. Then the dancing started with a very good bongo, interspersed with fabulous disco music.

The cake arrived, a nine- or ten-foot edifice with sparklers sticking out of it, and much hilarity ensued as it came through. Tara and Michael were put into chairs held by several men and thrown up into the air seven or eight times, to the excited shrieks of the crowd. Everybody simply having a whale of a time. I was thrilled that everything went off so well and that the party seemed to be such a blast.

Monday, 16 June 1997

Robin and I went shopping on the Left Bank at St Laurent, then to the Ritz where we had lunch on the terrace. Robin proceeded then to tell me in detail a lot of facts about how I spoiled my children and how I don't dress well. All in all it was an unfortunate lunch. I thought it most unnecessary of Robin to tell me this and I was very depressed by it. I know he doesn't like social occasions, but Tara's wedding is something special.

Flew back to London very exhausted, and all I could do was

get into bed with a hot-water bottle at my back, which is killing me. A page of pictures appeared in the *Daily Mail* headed Mother of the Bride. The photographers had snapped some of the shots peeping out from the bushes. Tara was right about the paparazzi trying to get everywhere, although when I spoke to one of the staff at the party and told him of all the people taking pictures, he shrugged and said, 'What can I do?' Spoke to Tara, who sounded a little tense. Don't know why everybody sounds so tense, it's beginning to get to me.

Tuesday, 17 June 1997

I've had no word from my agent about when I will shoot my episodes. This is causing me great stress, not to mention my back is still horrible. Went to the doctor and he said my throat hadn't cleared up, and he wrote a letter to the *Pacific Palisades* people saying that I wasn't fit to travel. Called PC and told him to handle it, that I just couldn't face it, it was really getting me down. He agreed and said he'd never seen an artist treated so shabbily and that it wasn't too much to ask that, if the series was picked up, I should know if I was going to be in two or six episodes to be shot consecutively. I'd like to make some summer plans. Nevertheless, got myself together and went to Shakira and Michael's party at the Canteen for David Tang. Robin was in a foul mood, which he often gets into. He did a non-stop complaining monologue about how much he hated parties, hated people, hated going out, hated my family, couldn't stand this time of year in London, etc. He kept on saying this had nothing to do with me, it was just him blowing off steam. Fine, but it was draining.

There was no placement at the party but Conrad Black, the Canadian owner of the Telegraph Group, wanted to sit next to me, so I had Theo Fennell on the other side and Conrad's

beautiful wife, Barbara Amiel, on the other. Conrad was a fascinating, intellectual conversationalist and witty too. Robin, who
had said he wanted to leave early, was sitting at the other end of
the table next to Louise Fennell and Jan Gold [wife of Johnny
Gold, founder of Tramp nightclub]. I had ordered a taxi for
eleven fifteen and when I told him it was here, he said, 'You can't
leave a party so early.' 'I thought you wanted to leave,' I said. 'You
can't leave yet, nobody's left yet,' he said crossly. Went back and
schmoozed with Barry Humphries, Tessa Kennedy, Madeleine
Lloyd Webber and various others.

Princess Caroline of Monaco was with her new amour,
Prince Ernst of Hanover. Three people came up and patted her
on the back and said, 'Hello, Jan.' I gather they thought she
was Jan Gold, who is about fifteen years older than Princess
Caroline. Finally left and Barbara said how thrilled she was that
we came.

As soon as we got in the taxi, Robin snapped, 'You've got to
lighten up a bit, Joan.' I was so thrown by this statement that we
finished the trip in total silence. I don't know what's gotten into
him. He's becoming a pain.

Called Steve Tellez, my voice a disaster, and told him that I
was just not up to travelling. He said he would talk to Aaron. I
don't know what's going on. My life is in turmoil.

Wednesday, 18 June 1997

Woke up to a fax from Steve Tellez saying he's talked to Aaron,
who's very sympathetic towards my plight, wants me in the
show, has reworked the schedule and wants me to start work on
Monday. Rang Thomas Cook, trying to get a flight, either with
Sacha or with Judy.

Max, Didier, Stella, Erin and myself all got togged up and

went to Ascot. It wasn't a great day, quite blustery and all our hats were in danger of blowing off. Stella was wearing a very pretty lilac hat that matched her St Laurent suit, Erin was chic in a wide-brimmed black hat with a black skirt and beige jacket, I was in Escada pale yellow with a matching large yellow hat with cream ostrich feathers. Judy, however, had decided to wear a straw beach hat which I picked out for her a year ago to wear by the pool. Not quite the right look, but she seemed unaware. Visited with various friends: Carole Bamford, Minda Feliciano, Pandora and Charles Delevingne, the Fennells, the dreaded Nigel Dempster and the rather attractive Ross Benson, John and Melanie Randall and Ned Ryan, who looked three sheets to the wind and was with Sophie Rhys-Jones [now the Countess of Wessex].

Ascot doesn't hold a great deal of charm for me. Again they told me they'd lost my application to go into the Royal Enclosure, which Charles definitely sent in with his and Ned's. After lunch, during which everyone betted and I lost, they all tottered off in the rain to the paddocks, Royal Enclosures and other places, while I sat with Carole and chewed the fat.

Robin was in a bad mood again. Had a long, not very good talk with him on the phone. He said he was 'peopled out' – he never has liked this time of year in London. However, I do, so after Ascot I picked up Jeffrey and went to Conrad Black and Barbara Amiel's drinks party. Everybody was there, from Margaret Thatcher to Lord and Lady Dudley to Donatella Flick. Princess Michael of Kent was talking to Barbara Amiel. Barbara is a very beautiful and highly intelligent lady. Princess Michael was wearing an eclectic collection of garments, as was Vivien Duffield. Rocco Forte, Nicola Formby, Andrew Neil, Taki and many of the editors and writers from the Telegraph Group, which Conrad Black owns, were all having a ball. Conrad, however, was not there as he had been taken ill. Barbara Amiel joked that it was because he had so enjoyed being with me the previous night at dinner that he had come over all funny! Well, really.

Went to Mimmo's to meet Tony and Gina and Sacha and Erin. Tony was in great form. He looked 100 per cent better than he did at Tara's wedding, but now he wasn't having to schlepp around his ninety-four-year-old mother. I so hope these shots he's taking for cancer are working. We reminisced about the wedding, then he said he had to go downstairs as Gina was going to give him an injection. He apparently has to take quite a few of these. Jeffrey and I then left and went to L'Incontro to meet Blaine Trump. She was with a group consisting of Bea and Thierry van Zuylen, Bruce Dundas and his wife Ruth Kennedy. Aileen Mehle seems to go everywhere with Blaine. Blaine must like this as she's constantly in Suzy's column. Lots of faces from the party at L'Incontro. All in all, a rather jolly evening and as usual I burnt the candle at both ends.

Thursday, 19 June 1997

Yesterday PC sent a letter to Aaron Spelling saying that I insisted on knowing whether, if my scenes were picked up, they would be done in blocks or not. They're also nickel-and-diming me yet again about these five scenes in one episode that were supposed to be two scenes; I was told, 'Take it or leave it.' Well, I'm taking it, but I'm taking it with very bad grace, and the fact that they now say that they're not obligated to give me a return ticket from LA to London is galling and unfair. Have had several angry telephone calls with PC and the CAA agent and Gary, my lawyer, in the past few days, and it's all getting me down.

Had a depressing conversation with Robin. We're going through a bad patch. I guess all couples go through this and I know it's been exacerbated by the wedding and all of the attention taken away from him.

Friday, 20 June 1997

Katy is twenty-four today. She seems depressed about getting older. Well, join the club, darling! I pick up Jeffrey and we take the twelve fifteen to LA. I have that same old familiar sinking feeling as we drive through the grey overcast smoggy atmosphere to the apartment. Judy and Max are staying in with me. Got the call sheet for Monday. Yes, it definitely is five scenes, and I am totally appalled. Have been asking Steve Tellez for my contract, which finally arrives at eight thirty. What I see in it makes my blood run cold. Lou Patrick, the writer for Spelling Productions, has put down episode eleven, five scenes for $25,000, episode twelve same, episode thirteen same. Call Steve and started yelling at him but he's yelling back even more. I hold the phone away from my face so Judy and Max can hear his tirade. 'At least he's showing some emotion,' says Judy. Tellez is utterly furious that PC had the temerity to go over his head and send a letter to Aaron Spelling. He says in doing so PC intimated that he was incompetent. Well, somebody is and it's certainly not me. Eventually Tellez calms down and tells me that Aaron has agreed on $40,000 for the next two episodes. Getting money from this group is like getting blood from a stone.

I talk to Monica the hairdresser, who says the feeling is very bad on the show. The writing is truly dreadful and there is absolutely no publicity. Nolan says Aaron wondered why I came back on Friday instead of spending the weekend in London. 'Because Steve Tellez suggested I should,' I tell him through gritted teeth. God, the right hand doesn't know what the left hand is doing with this group. Nolan says that Aaron doesn't feel that Fox are going to pick up the series. Good. I am absolutely fed up with it. My scenes in episode 12 are so gormless I can hardly believe it. They have me saying things like, 'Oh Don, will you get me a cup of cool water, pumpkin?' I mean, really, are we back in the fifties? I'm hard pushed to say this stuff, and I even say it like it is sometimes, à la Victorian diva. For example, in the last show it was impossible to change this line: 'You wouldn't put your poor mother out into the street, would you?' so I delivered it in a cod, quasi-Victorian Grand Guignol way. I'm depressed. Hate *Pacific Palisades*, just want to be in Destino.

Saturday, 21 June 1997

Pottered about the apartment unpacking. Judy fixed some eggs, then Jeffrey, Judy and I meandered around Century City. I gazed at everyone and passionately wished I were anywhere but here. Went to see *Con-Air*, a movie with Nicolas Cage and John Malkovich. No wonder there's so much violence and anger in young people. This film is totally over the top in the pyrotechnics department, even landing a jumbo jet on the Vegas Strip! No mention made of the number of casualties this would have caused.

Wendy Stark and John Morrissey picked me up and we went to Irena and Mike Medavoy's house for a surprise party for Irena's best friend. There were a lot of forty-something women there. Trophy wives, supremely nipped, tucked and beautifully collagened, none of them looking older than twenty-nine. Some were pregnant, having their second family, since their kids are late teens and twenties. Michael and Pat York were there. 'I'm photographing lots of people in the nude,' she announced. 'Victor Drai has promised to do it.' I looked over at Victor, who has dyed his silver crew-cut blond; although his equipment is supposedly legendary in Hollywood, I don't really want to look at it. I think Michael is a bit pussy-whipped by Mrs York.

Also there was a woman whose facelift was so tight that I couldn't stop staring at her. She could be anything from forty to seventy. It didn't help that she was only four foot eleven. The music was very very loud and we stood around for a long time in the huge entrance hall, which was very draughty on a cool California night. Whoever said that the weather was great in California must have been mad. It's much more like Lena Horne sang: 'Hate California, it's cold and it's damp'.

In the dining room we found a crumpled brocade tablecloth on which five medium-sized plates were arranged. On two of the plates were small steak sandwiches – and by small I mean very small – a large salad of mussels and prawns – not for me, thank you – a huge thing of bread, a touch on the stale side, and some salad, most of which seemed to be mescaline and frisée, not my fave.

I sat in the den with Wendy and John, the noise of the rock music pervading the room. Michael Medavoy joined us, one of the major movers and shakers in Hollywood. His son, a minor mover and shaker, came in too. Everybody's got a deal, everybody's got a picture in the can, or working on projects. I took to the dance floor with John, who's a fabulous dancer, and we whirled away for forty-five minutes or so and were joined by Wendy. They wanted to go on to Richard Perry's for after-dinner drinks, but I folded up my tent. After all, it was nearly seven in the morning for me.

Monday, 23 June 1997

After a quiet Sunday, I arrive at the studios to find the feeling on set is still gloomy. This is the day that I do the five scenes for half my salary and I am not exactly being swift. I let the key members of the crew know what they are doing to me and everybody is shocked.

Finish at seven thirty and dash to meet Alan Nevins, Nolan, and Lorna Luft for the opening of *Master Class*. Faye Dunaway is good as Callas, even though her ass looks like it's been sliced off in a bacon-slicer. Everyone says Zoe Caldwell was better. I feel the play is repetitive – caught myself nodding off a couple of times. Allan Carr's there with Asa Maynor; the only other celebrities of note are Swoosie Kurtz and Steve Allen, and Mr Blackwell [Richard Blackwell, creator of the 'Ten Worst Dressed Women' list]. Not exactly an auspicious opening. 'Where are all Faye's friends?' I ask Alan Nevins.

Tuesday, 24 June 1997

I worked my ass off again in episode 11.

Wednesday, 25 June 1997

Lunched at Spago with Jolene Schlatter, Barbara Davis, Wendy Stark and Mary Hayley. At the next table were Candy Bergen and Carrie Fisher. Went to the Beverly Wilshire for an interview with Richard Barber for the *Telegraph*. I like Richard, but I really don't like giving interviews. In fact, the more I think about it, the more I'm beginning to dislike many aspects of my chosen career. Gary Concoff came for drinks to try and work out the deal with Lance Reynolds for 'Joan's World'. Gary always seems to put obstacles in the way of everything. Lance was exhausted – he'd just arrived from London and would be leaving for Australia tomorrow. We thrashed out 'Joan's World'. I told them I didn't think *Pacific Palisades* was long for this world. Met Sacha and

Erin at Hamburger Hamlet. Brought them *Hello!* magazine, which Lance had delivered to me. Fourteen pages and a cover on Tara and Michael's wedding. I must say the whole event looked spectacular and huge fun, as indeed it was.

Thursday, 26 June 1997

The day we were supposed to find out – and the axe dropped right on time. As I was going upstairs to the production office, George from wardrobe was coming down and he made a cutting motion across his throat. 'We're finished,' he mouthed. So it was true. ABC and Fox network had pulled the plug on *Pacific Palisades* even though only eight episodes had aired. It's really sad because the network never gave it a chance. It received very little publicity and had gone up against the *Ellen* episodes plus all kinds of basketball games.

Peter Dunne, the producer, made a rather cheerful announcement on the set and the crew looked glum. I immediately went and called my travel agent to make my booking back to London. Can't say I was particularly upset as the weather today was grey, overcast and chilly. Worked hard all day. The new lighting cameraman was quick but did not know how to light women and kept on telling me to 'keep my head up'. He shouldn't tell me to keep my head up, he should put some fill light in. Still, I guess now that we're cancelled, nobody gives a damn. Had another massage with Dr Shelley. Met David Niven for dinner and we went to Le Dome and had a giggle.

Friday, 27 June 1997

Worked all day from 5.30 until 10.30 at night, filming at the marina and various spots downtown. Did the tag of *Pacific*

Palisades in which my final line is 'I do love happy endings.' Ha Ha.

Saturday, 28 June 1997

Quite an interesting group at Carole Little's: Robert Altman, Ian La Frenais and his wife Doris, and various others. Saw the movie *Face Off*, with John Travolta and Nicolas Cage. How important stars like them can do such puerile shoot-'em-up *Boys' Own* stuff beats me. I guess it's the millions. Altman was so disgusted by the movie that he left and went into the other room to watch the fight with Mike Tyson. At the end we watched in horror as Mike Tyson bit off the other guy's ear! He has the eyes of a mad dog, it really is amazing. Sat next to Altman at dinner and we talked movies. He is seventy-something and a real old movie aficionado. He said he can't get a movie together unless he can attract the cast first, which is what he did with *The Player* and *Prêt-à-Porter*. I said I'd love to have been in *Prêt-à-Porter*. 'You should have pushed for it,' he said. 'Everyone else did.' 'I know, like Rupert Everett,' I said. 'Well, next time I do something, maybe we'll play,' he said benignly. 'That would be great,' I thought, knowing it will never happen.

Sunday, 29 June 1997

Went to Sacha's studio at the beach, which is really nice and very airy with plenty of space and great light. He's doing some good new paintings of landscapes and not concentrating just on portraits. Had lunch at their apartment, which overlooks the sea. It was a beautiful day. Walked along Main Street and bought some stuff at various boutiques. Picked up at five forty-five for one scene and was finished at nine. Went to Ray Stark's for a screening. David Geffen was there and he told me that Sue Mengers has got cancer. I'm completely shocked, as I thought she only had polyps on the throat. Val Kilmer came in. He's much more attractive and nicer in real life than I would have imagined as I've never taken to him on screen. Also Wendy and John, Ray and a girlfriend, and the super-agent who represents Faye Dunaway. He is obviously completely dotty about her. How wonderful to have an agent completely dotty about you. Had a very nice dinner then watched the worst film I've ever seen called *Austin Powers* with somebody called Mike Myers and the very pretty Elizabeth Hurley.

Tuesday, 1 July 1997

Although I am glad that the series has been cancelled, I still find myself incredibly depressed. In their usual fashion the *Pacific Palisades* people have managed to screw me up yet again. I worked Monday and now will not work again until next Monday, giving me a week to kill. At least the weather has turned nicer. Tottered about the apartment packing. Went to the Peninsula Hotel and did an interview for the biography programme they are doing on me on the Arts and Entertainment channel. They've already spoken to sister Jackie, Aaron Spelling, Robert Wagner, Sacha, Nolan Miller and David McCallum and a few other people.

Leonard Gershe picked me up and we went to Le Dome restaurant. Leonard was very impressed by the photographs in *Hello!* of the wedding; when Tara was three, she used to call him her boyfriend. I met Billy and Audrey Wilder there, and Sacha and Erin. Billy has aged a great deal – I suppose that's what happens when you're quite old – but he has flashes of the old humour. It's his hearing that seems to be most in need of a boost. But he certainly enjoys his food. A very sweet dinner with people that I'm very fond of.

Wardrobe called and said that if I wanted any of the clothes I wore in *Pacific Palisades*, I would have to pay 50 per cent of the cost! She sent me a list of various things, but I only want the two Valentino suits. I think Aaron should give them to me as a present since I've had to pay for half of my own LA to London ticket. David Wigg wrote in the *Daily Express*: 'Lesbian power puts the skids under Joan's soap.' I don't think this is a terribly nice thing to say. According to Jeffrey, Fox are trying to back-pedal radically; instead of saying 'we've been cancelled', they're saying that we 'haven't been picked up'. With five or six more episodes yet to air, they obviously don't want the viewers to get turned off.

Lance called from Australia where he was having talks with Beyond, the company who are hopefully going to finance 'Joan's World'. He seemed optimistic, but then he always docs. I adore Lance, but he's never been a strong closer. However I'm hoping that, with Stella prodding him, we will be able to achieve something.

Dined at Hamburger Hamlet with Alan Nevins. Gossiped about the book business and were gleeful that Michael Viner has been ousted from Dove Publications in a coup. Alan said the book market is completely flooded, that they are printing too many books and that HarperCollins just dropped thirty authors that they had given an advance to. It's all rather depressing. We then watched the last half of *Pacific Palisades*. Hot love scene with Lucky Vanous and Barbara Niven, who looked great. They've totally wasted her in this show. She is a good actress but most of the girls in our show are quite boring.

Thursday, 3 July 1997

Tried to call Aaron twice but he's either in meetings or screenings, or having eye surgery, or going to court – this according to Nolan. Nolan suggested I write to him and tell him that I'm having a problem with Tom Chasin, the agent suing me. Then Gary Concoff said I couldn't possibly put that into writing, so I wrote a semi thank you note to Aaron, who according to Nolan is allowing me to *keep* what wardrobe I like. Very kind, and this almost makes up for having only half a round-trip ticket. Had to buy another suitcase, so went to a cheapie shop on Santa Monica and got a large 'Made in Korea' for forty bucks.

Friday, 4 July 1997

The weather luckily is good for the great American holiday. Jeffrey and I hit the gym and thank God my back is now better. Charles Duggan arrived from Austin to spend the weekend; he is such a darling and we do have fun together. Sacha and Erin came for lunch, which was Nate 'n' Al's smoked salmon bagels and lox. Jeffrey came down for a drink while waiting for Diahann Carroll. She called at one fifteen to say she was going to be slightly late. Slightly late for Diahann is very late for anyone else. Diahann finally turned up at three! She presented me with a bottle of Cristal champagne saying, 'This is a present.' Then said, 'I think I'll have a glass.' I went upstairs to Jeffrey's apartment for cocktails and we were joined by Diahann. Went up to Allan Carr's for a July Fourth barbecue. Lots of mates there: David and Barbara Niven, Alana Stewart, Tina Sinatra, Jeanne Martin, Suzanne Pleshette, Jackie Bisset. A jolly time was had by all and we all drank quite a lot. Jeanne Martin grabbed me and told me about eight times how much she loved me, very sincerely. I remember how I caught her kissing my then boyfriend George Englund in a car several decades ago when she was married to Dean, but we were all young and frisky once. Then she told Niven endlessly how much she loved him. Maybe it's because it's July Fourth but there's a lot of love going around tonight.

Saturday, 5 July 1997

Met Niven and Barbara at Hamburger Hamlet with Charles, then met Alana Stewart at the Avco cinema in Westwood and we saw *My Best Friend's Wedding* starring Julia Roberts and Rupert Everett. Rupert has had incredibly good reviews for this. I can understand why. Rupert sends it up rotten and is a scream. I really like these feel-good films.

Went with Jeffrey and Charles to Carol Little's to see a screening of *Men in Black* with Tommy Lee Jones and Will Smith. It's taken eighty million dollars at the box office in two days and is the hit-hit-hit movie of the summer. I thought it was idiotic. Giant cockroaches who come and take over men on planet Earth. There is more shooting and squidging of cock-roaches, and all in all it was perfect for a nine-year-old boy's night out.

Sunday, 6 July 1997

Jeffrey picked me up at ten thirty and we went down to the 20th Century Fox vaults where they keep all the film from hundreds and thousands of old television movies and old movies. I narrated and hosted a one-hour documentary of movie song numbers that were cut from famous movies like *Down Argentina Way, Pin-Up Girl, I Wake Up Screaming*. They were all from Fox.

I ended with a clip of Robert Wagner and me taken from my first test for *Lord Vanity*. Even though I was only twenty, I was quite good. In fact I was actually better in this test than I am in *Pacific Palisades* some forty years later! Wagner was not so good and looked distinctly ill at ease in his eighteenth-century costume.

Did an interview for *In-Style* magazine. The journalist asked me a lot of questions about my apartment, then some incredibly intrusive questions about 'How much does a woman need to live on?' I said, 'This is a ridiculous question – who knows? Los Angeles is much cheaper than London, and London is much cheaper than Tokyo and every country is different and every woman's needs are different.'

Jeffrey's voice has completely packed up. It's this bug going around that's called the 'Los Angeles Lurgy'. No wonder. The air today is a soup of smog, exhaust and smoke from the forest fires. I'm not really happy living here, even though my apartment is lovely and I have good friends. I miss living near Katy and Tara, and all my friends in England.

Charles D and I zoomed to Spago. Outside, a couple of pho-tographers lurked. A strange woman with a lot of collagen in her face, black-dyed hair, black T-shirt with dreadful diamanté spangles on it, heckled me while I was being snapped. 'Hey, Joan Collins looks good – Hey Joan, you look good.' I thought she was a fan until, in the restaurant, she came over and said, 'Hey! It's Jackie. It's Sly's birthday today. He's fifty-one. Come and say hello, why don't you – he really likes yah.' It was Sylvester Stallone's mother Jackie! Stallone was with his entourage. Nolan met us and we had a most amusing dinner discussing Jackie and others. Watched Tony Curtis come in with his ten-foot girl-friend. Jaclyn Smith came by with her nerd of the year. She's such a beautiful and nice girl, why can't she get a decent guy? As we left, Mr Stallone came bounding over to greet me affectionately. I think he has great manners and he looked pretty good. I told him I'd read his article in *Parade* magazine today and he seemed quite pleased. I always find it good manners when actors go out of their way to greet fellow actors.

Monday, 7 July 1997

Up at the crack, exhausted but elated. It's packing-up day. It's over! Surveyed the sixteen assorted suitcases with dismay. But what can I do? A leopard can't change its spots. Arrived at the studio half an hour early after they informed me that they would be ready. I hate having to rush. Did a rather bad scene with Kimberley. Then I'm out of there. Fond farewells to George and Becky in wardrobe, Monica hair and Les the director. I don't feel at all sad or upset that I'm leaving *Pacific Palisades*. It was just a gig and not a very good gig at that. The fact that Aaron doesn't seem to care one way or another whether it's picked up, the fact that he hasn't called me back and just left messages with Nolan that 'he loves me' and the fact that, as Peter Dunn says, 'It's outrageous that you have only been given a one-way ticket from London to LA', has formed a pyramid of indifference in me. It's also reinforced my concrete certainty that I don't want to do another series in Hollywood. It's good that I did it because I got it out of my system, but I realise there will never be another *Dynasty*, and why should there? I'm going home to England and my family and that's all that matters.

Tuesday, 8 July 1997

Had a great flight on British Airways. Slept for seven and a half hours, thanks to copious draughts of wine and port. At home, pottered gently around looking gloomily at sixteen suitcases. Katy came to tea, obviously in very good spirits. She told me that Paul is moving into her apartment next weekend.

It absolutely poured, with torrential monsoon-like rain. Ned Ryan picked me up and we attempted to drive to a smart new place called the Putney Bridge restaurant. Although it had stopped raining, the streets were chock-a-block, so we left at eight thirty but didn't arrive until ten. Half of London's aristocratic and café society were gathered to celebrate David Metcalfe's seventieth birthday. Among them Mark Birley, Conrad Black, the Rothschilds, Ahmet Ertegun, Donatella Flick, Rocco and Aliai Forte, a slew of Guinnesses and Hambros, a slew of princesses of Hanover and Heskeths and Hindlops, Princess Firyal, the Weinbergs, the Wyatts and Uncle Tom Cobley and all. Sat at rather a fun table with Patrick Lichfield, Charles Spencer-Churchill, Cathy Ford and Jocelyn Stevens. The service was abominably slow and we didn't actually get our main course until about twenty past eleven, which caused a great deal of fury on the part of Charles SC, who never holds back, having just been vociferous in his condemnation of Prince Charles and Camilla Parker Bowles's affair. So many of the Englishmen there were terribly tall, so during drinks I said to Taki, 'I must talk to you, you know why?' 'Yes, because I'm the shortest man here,' he laughed. John Bowes-Lyon seemed half surprised to see me. I guess because, being one of Robin's closest friends, he wasn't aware I was coming and apparently Robin wasn't invited. Speeches were made, but it was impossible to hear anyone because the room was so long and narrow and everyone was sweating profusely. But all in all it was jolly good to be back in England again and see so many faces that I'm fond of.

Wednesday, 9 July 1997

Very civilised lunch at Harry's Bar with Sue St Johns and Doug Hayward. Princess Diana lunching in a corner, confiding closely with Prince Juan Carlos of Greece. Other familiar faces were scattered around. Biggins joined us for coffee and regaled us with jolly jokes. Then I dashed over to Katy's and we went shopping for a new armchair and potential storage for her apartment. It still astounds me how much more expensive things are in England than America. Don't understand why an armchair that's five hundred pounds here would be three hundred and fifty dollars in America. Still, I suppose that's the price you pay for being in a place you feel more at home in.

Thursday, 10 July 1997

Lunched with Stella and her young daughter Amy, and Katy, at San Lorenzo. It's still one of the prettiest restaurants in the world. The food is good even though the service is appalling, since most of the waiters seem to be relatives of the owner, Lorenzo, and have a habit of leaning across one diner to pass the spaghetti to another. The usual paps outside. Don't know why they bother to take pictures since they seldom appear. Checked in at British Midlands. British Airways cabin staff have gone on strike so the airport was heaving. So much for Mr Blair's New Labour reforms. There have also been major tax rises but everybody seems quite complacent about Mr Blair's agendas. Met Robin in the Midland lounge but didn't arrive at Destino until ten o'clock. Robin, tired and rather grumpy, put his elbow out lifting my six – yes, I'm now down to six – suitcases and nagged me for an hour about why I needed to have so many. I don't know why he doesn't make a recording of this moan, as we go through it several times a year.

Friday, 11 July 1997

Pottered, unpacked, repacked, drove to the airport and left for Paris on the six o'clock plane. The Ritz was, as usual, inviting. We had a delicious club sandwich and fell into an exhausted sleep.

Saturday, 12 July 1997

Dashed to Galeries Lafayette to buy twenty of the best hangers in the world, then dashed back and changed into major yellow fairy frocksuit and large Ascot-type hat, and dined at the Ritz bar where we saw various others who were also going to Natasha Fraser's wedding. Glen Birnbaum, Kenny J. Lane proudly showing off his new facelift, and Gil Shiva wearing a wonderful Caravani Italian suit. The wedding, held in a charming church near the rue de Grenelles, was filled with familiar faces. Sat beside George and Annabelle Weidenfeld and Tessa Kennedy. Nan Kempner and Ines de la Fressange were huddling, and Rupert Everett came bounding over. He's the new flavour of the month in America, thanks to his starring role in *My Best Friend's Wedding*. I told him he was great and he agreed! Natasha Fraser, the bride, had the most devastating décolletage on her Gilles Dufour Chanel white lace embroidered dress. The priest who conducted the Catholic service was somewhat camp, waving his arms around in the air and declaiming in an oratorial way. Annabelle Weidenfeld and I quite got the giggles. Outside I shook hands with Lord Longford, Natasha's grandfather, the old geezer who's always trying to get Myra Hindley out of prison.

He looked most ungroomed, having patches of white stubble on his cheeks, a shirt that was none too clean and did not meet around his scrawny neck, and rather badly uncombed hair. His wife, Lady Longford, seemed sweet. Antonia Fraser, Natasha's mother, was majestic if a touch on the plump side.

Arrived at a very nice open-air club off the Faubourg St Honoré for the reception. Beautiful Parisian day. Nan Kempner was wearing an Yves St Laurent jacket and above-the-knee skirt. Unfortunately, she has terribly skinny legs which are covered in sun blotches. This had led Valentino to say to her some years earlier, 'Nan darling, I love the animal-printed stockings.' 'These aren't my stockings,' she had said crossly, 'these are my legs.' *Hello!* magazine was at the reception, of course. Natasha told us she'd sold the wedding story for twenty-five thousand. Everybody's doing it these days, even Sylvester Stallone sold his story to *OK*. Robin not happy about being photographed, since he despises the press.

Considering it's a supposedly fashion-pack wedding, very few well-dressed women. Joan Juliet Buck, the editress of French *Vogue*, was beautifully dressed by Hermès and asked me where I got my outfit. I told her Escada and she seemed surprised. Escada are doing rather good things, I must admit.

Tessa Kennedy, who had her two grandchildren there, told us that the story of me not inviting Nicky Haslam to Tara's wedding had hit London with a vengeance, and asked was it true? I said, 'Yes, he doesn't even know her.' Ate a huge smoked salmon sandwich. Met Jimmy Douglas and Milton Seabra, who is a real old poppet and one of the richest men in Brazil. Jimmy gave his magazine, which contained references to Nan Kempner, to her. She perused it then said, rather surprised, 'Oh dear, it says I look like a skull on a stick.' Jimmy said he'd never been more embarrassed.

Sunday, 13 July 1997

Without a doubt I think the Ritz is the best hotel in the world. Drove to Wideville, Valentino's spectacular castle near Versailles. To say it is imposing is putting it mildly. It is a sixteenth-century castle set in exquisite grounds and even Carole Bamford said that it's extraordinary. Va Va greeted us in impeccably pressed pale blue jeans and matching shirt and T-shirt. He's put on a little weight but still looks iconic. We sat on the sunlit terrace where Giancarlo Giammetti, Tim Jefferies, Bruce and others were already gathered. Although it was drinks time, I seemed to be the only one who drank alcohol.

Valentino was pleased to see me and said, 'My dear, when I saw you at Sally Khan's I said, Joan is like my best and favourite girlfriend.' Very flattering to hear this, but I don't believe it. After a delicious lunch, he said, 'But my dear, you eat nothing!' 'That's why I've lost weight,' I told him. They were very complimentary about the fact that I had lost quite a bit of weight and Valentino said, 'Your skin is fabulous.' Nice to hear. It must be the new cream I'm using. After lunch, during which we gossiped and gossiped and gossiped, which Va Va and GG love, we were given a tour of the house, which is beyond beautiful. Robin thinks it's over-decorated but I love the print upon print and picture above picture. Valentino is of course unbelievably rich and has the best taste, and it all shows in his houses. He has five houses. Wideville, a villa outside Rome, a London house in Egerton Terrace, a house in Capri, a New York apartment and a magnificent boat. I believe Valentino is one of the very few people in the world who really knows how to live exquisitely.

Hated to leave but had to catch the plane. Real life descended at Orly Airport where the masses were leaving for the Quatorze Juillet. Arrived at Destino tired but happy to be home and watched two of the biographies that Kevin had given me. Audrey Hepburn's was particularly sad; I'm convinced that she probably got her cancer from the fact that she was so destroyed by the sad events of her life, i.e. divorces and miscarriages. Sophia Loren on the other hand, who had almost as bad a life as a child in wartime Italy, seems to be a great survivor. There's a lesson to be learned there somewhere.

Wednesday, 16 July 1997

Three days of relaxation then drove the nightmare route to Lynn Wyatt's. Changed in a dark downstairs bedroom which had neither loo rolls nor soap. The theme of Lynn's birthday this year is Afrique, so all my ethnic bracelets, ivory gee gaws and leopard-printed things were trundled out. An African band was playing tribal music so loudly that it was impossible to hear oneself talk. The terrace thronged with the usual suspects: Ricki and Sandra Di Portanova, Elton John and David Furnish, John Reid and Doctor James, Jerry Hall, rather magnificently pregnant and sporting her flowing golden locks, Joan Schnitzer and her husband, the ancient Irvin Levy, and Liza Minnelli. Liza has put on a lot of weight around the face, probably due to either drink or some kind of substance. She didn't appear to notice me as I was standing talking to Elton, and when she did she grabbed me and put me on her knee and hugged me, crooning, 'My baby, my baby, I've missed you.' Slightly embarrassed, as these overly excitable displays of emotion are rather cringe-making. Stood around for a very long time, then walked to dinner across the long wet grass of the lawn. I know this of old so wore not-new shoes. Sat next to Theo Fennell and somebody from *Women's Wear Daily*. Oscar Wyatt was at the other end of the table. He is rather a poppet and told me 'Honey, looking at you across that table you look thirty-five years old' in his thick Texas accent. 'I wish!' The conversation of the night was Versace's murder. Elton had been very upset about it as Gianni was his best friend.

Friday, 18 July 1997

Louise Fennell arrived to stay for a few days. The weather's not been too good but it's extremely relaxing.

Thursday, 24 July 1997 – London

Endless meetings in the London kitchen with Steve and Amanda, my interior decorator. I just hope the kitchen is going to look as good as they say, because it's costing an arm and a leg. Although my editor had some negative criticism on the book, on the whole I feel quite encouraged and think that I'm going to get it together by the end of September. If it's any good at all that will really be one in the eye for Random House, although I'm not pleased that I had to pay them 40 per cent of my American sales. Never mind.

Katy came over for tea. She seemed in good form. Paul was with her and PC and we went to see Jerry Lewis in *Damn Yankees*. Loved the musical and those songs that I knew word for word when I was a kid. Great star in the making called April Nixon who plays Lola, but Jerry Lewis steals the show. I just thought he was wonderful and incredibly funny, and what a pro. Went backstage afterwards to greet him. He came out in shorts and a black shirt, utterly dripping with sweat! For a man of seventy-one I thought that was pretty bold. We mwa-mwa'd and said how wonderful we thought each other. Paul, Katy, PC and I dined at The Ivy.

Saturday, 26 July 1997

Went to Adrian and Nicola's for dinner. He lives in the down-stairs flat and she has the upstairs. I think it's frightfully civilised. Adrian is divine and totally eccentric. On his mantelpiece he has the stuffed heads of about twenty monkeys. They look extra-ordinarily human and feel like billiard-balls. He has a huge portrait of Stalin over his bed and cushions of Mao Tse Tung. Richard E. Grant and Joan Washington also there, and as we were having cocktails a young man arrived whom I didn't recog-nise. I heard Robin say deferentially, 'Hello, sir, how are you?' and when he came in I realised it was Prince Andrew. He was with a very good-looking, terribly nice girl called Henriette Peace who, according to the tabloids, is his latest girlfriend. Great dinner, which Nicola cooked all by herself, and no staff so we could be really relaxed. Richard was being utterly outrageous asking Prince Andrew all kinds of really funny questions like 'Is it true that your father – er – sorry, the Duke of Edinburgh, bonked that hideous Anna Massey?' Andrew took it all with very good humour as he was being quite relentlessly teased by Richard, who was on a roll.

Andrew seems to have become a much cooler person since he and Sarah came to dinner with us seven years ago. We played a game called 'What have you never done?' and Andrew said he has never been to a supermarket and hasn't been on a bus since he was six. Richard then said, 'Have you and Henriette done it yet?' Andrew replied, 'It's a little difficult to give in to one's ardour when the paparazzi are on you all the time.' I understand, as it must be difficult for him.

Started dinner at nine fifteen and we left the table at two fifteen! It was one of the best dinner parties I've ever been to.

Monday, 28 July 1997 – Destino

Started working on 'Hell Hath No Fury' with Hannah's notes. I think it's pretty good, certainly as good as some of those so-called good novels I've been reading recently by Louise Bagshaw and Penny Vincenzi. Dinner with Stuart Grimshaw and Simon Sainsbury at their lovely house. Simon has developed Parkinson's, much worse than when we saw him a year ago. It's very sad.

Thursday, 31 July 1997

Donald Trump, that ungallant schmuck, has written something horrible about me in the *New York Post*. He said the story that he wanted to be one of Alexis's lovers in *Dynasty* is a lie. I know it's perfectly true because Gary Pudney told me. But Trump said, 'You know this isn't true, and you shouldn't write lies in order to get publicity. The last thing I would want to do in real life or television is to be your lover.' And I never said anything about it. What a gentleman! Sue and Will Boyd came for drinks and we sat on the terrace, watched the sun go down and the swallows swanning and Will, who is such a brilliant writer, gave me a lot of inside information about the publishing business.

Friday, 1 August 1997

Went to Voile Rouge beach to meet the Delevingnes for Cara's birthday. Where has the time gone? Poppy and Chloe, Ned Ryan and Mogens Tholstrup and his girlfriend Victoria Hervey all at the table. A hilarious lunch when Paul, the crazy owner, started bringing out the huge jeroboams of Dom Perignon and squirting the whole terrace with it. The fat prince at another table joined in with alacrity and the girls thought it was fantastic fun. I guess this is what everybody thinks St Tropez is like. Mad fashion shows, everybody getting drunk, incredibly loud disco music and people jumping and jiving and getting drenched with champagne. Well, it's true! Then they brought out the water hoses and it got so wild I had to leave.

Saturday, 2 August 1997

Lunch at Elton John's new mansion, the Pink Palace. High up in the hills above Nice, it is quite a marvellous spread, very modern. He's decorated it beautifully. We get the grand tour. Elton shows us his closets, which have about nine thousand Versace shirts, robes and scarves. He also has a wonderful collection of framed photographs by the world's great photographers. He shows me a book with photos from the fifties in the South of France and there is a wonderful picture of me, Mummy, Bill and Jackie that I have never seen.

Antonio d'Amico, Versace's boyfriend for the past twelve years, is at the lunch. He's very sad, understandably so, and has been having the most terrible nightmares – also understandable. Lynn is there, as well as an amazing selection of beautiful muscle-bound boys. Elton is adorable, as is his boyfriend, David Furnish, who's a real charmer! Elton's put on a pound or two, but it suits him, and he seems extremely happy. Paul O'Grady, also known as Lily Savage, and I have a bit of a shriek around the swimming pool. I do my lengths wearing a white towelling turban and everybody calls me Norma Desmond, but since I nearly drowned in a pool when I was four, I hate going under water.

Meet Kristina and Roger Moore at Tetou, the restaurant outside Antibes. It's great to see Roger, who is in very good form and getting ready to do a film in South Africa. He's also getting ready for his seventieth birthday, which he's not looking forward to. Well, who can blame him? He and Kiki are madly in love and I guess they will marry as soon as their divorces are final.

Tuesday, 5 August 1997

Dinner at John Reid's new house in St Tropez with John and Sarah Standing. Spoke to Stephanie Beacham, who is a house guest of theirs in London and having a most miserable experience being directed by Keith 'Blodwyn of the Valleys' Baxter in a Michael Codron play. 'I'm going completely mad,' said Stephanie. 'He calls me Celia all the time because that's the name of the character.' I told her perhaps the best thing to do would be to play the diva card. Stephanie laughed. She's a good sport and one of my mates from *Dynasty*.

Wednesday, 6 August 1997

Left at ten for the airport. Robin not complaining as much as usual about my suitcases – only five for this two-week trip. A prop plane to Sardinia then met by Tom, the Bamfords' major domo, and one small taxi. Naturally the bags would not fit in, so major drama. Robin furious, and we had to get another one. Waiting on board *The Virginian* were Carole and Anthony, plus her children Alice, George and Joe Bamford, and Christopher Biggins and partner Neil Sinclair, who works for British Airways. ... Had the most delicious tea. If food keeps up like this will rapidly become the size of a house. The boat is extraordinarily grand and my stateroom is wonderful, and there is plenty of room for my clothes.

7–8 August 1997

On the boat cruising around Sardinia. Absolutely divine and totally relaxing.

Friday, 8 August 1997

The Bamfords' staff went ahead to a local beach in Porto Cervo to set up loungers, tables, lilos, toys, etc. Everyone lay around chattering and sunbathing, then we walked along the beach. Lots of Italians there who unfortunately recognised me. Had delicious lunch and I tucked into a vast tuna-fish sandwich, having changed my bathing suit on the beach – rather cleverly, I thought. Halfway through lunch Anthony spots two paparazzi in the bushes with gigantic lenses trained on us. Joe and George went up to investigate and said yes indeed their lenses were on us. My heart sank; had they caught me changing my bathing suit? Had they caught me with tuna-fish hanging out of my mouth, or playing Scrabble with Biggins? Needless to say, it cast a slight pall over the picnic, so I beat it back to the boat. Went into Porto Cervo again to see the jeweller. I had been considering buying two pairs of earrings, my present to myself from *Pacific Palisades*. After what I went through, I deserve to spoil myself. Claudio, the jeweller, said that the paparazzi are all over the place and he actually called to find out what pictures they've got, suggesting that perhaps I could do a couple of posed shots in return for not having the hideous shots. No way, they said, the pictures have already gone off to Rome. Great.

I bought five sleazy Italian magazines. All of them feature celebrities changing into their bathing suits on the beach, looking hideous, showing their private parts inadvertently and even, as in the case of Valerie Campbell, Naomi's mother, sneaking shots of her in the bath. It's absolutely disgusting. 'It looks like a meat market,' said Anthony, and indeed the display of human bodies on the beach is most unfair. These celebrities are only trying to enjoy themselves but, indeed, it's not a pretty sight.

I'm slightly paranoid about the paparazzi. A ghastly sneaked picture of Robin and me appeared in the *Enquirer* last week, me in a bikini looking fat. But being on this boat is sybaritic luxury, the food is wonderful and the staff are great. Susan and Robert Sangster came onboard to stay for a few days.

So-called gala evening at the Hotel Cala di Volpe: I've never seen so many unattractive people, hideous outfits and ferocious facelifts in my life. The food was good but it's a fight to the finish to try not to eat too much. Then a dreadful Italian singer gave us a medley of his hits for about an hour; they all sounded exactly the same.

Tuesday, 12 August 1997

Beautiful day. Carole and I went to the beach where the usual set of loungers, lilos, deckchairs, tables, umbrellas and masses of towels had been set up. Was relaxing deliciously when another alert occurred. Alice spotted a pap trying to hide his camera behind a rolled-up towel. Shit, damn, hell. Joe solicitously arranged a deckchair behind me and I sat with my back to him in a big hat while the staff brought me tiny tomatoes and drinks. I'm reading the third ghastly novel I've read on this holiday. I cannot concentrate on the sheer boredom of most of them. Drinks onboard *The Virginian* at seven thirty. A new person has appeared, Prince Michael of Yugoslavia. Although he met Alice only once, he has managed to get himself invited. He's about thirty-eight and neither very good-looking nor very amusing. Judy and Alfred Taubman arrived with children, and

Massimo Gargia, an old Italian gossip-monger whom I've always thought is quite amusing but not to be taken seriously. We drank Bellinis for an hour and then our group went to a charming restaurant in Porto Rotondo called Gianna's. At the Hotel Cala di Volpe, I looked around at cruise ship Romeos and ageing Juliets with sun-dried skin and peroxide hair jumping around doing the macarena and John Travolta dances. Not a good scene.

Wednesday, 13 August 1997

Sadly leave *The Virginian*. It has been wonderful and I will miss everybody. Took Air Littoral to Nice – a prop plane, which I'm not keen on – and it got in terribly terribly late. Arrived in Nice with literally ten minutes to spare to catch the British Airways to London. Rushed around the airport like a blue-arsed fly, huffing and puffing as they took me through all the various red-tape things to make the plane. Having been harassed by paparazzi at the airport earlier, who wouldn't leave me alone, it was quite annoying to be informed by the uptight policeman at passport control that he wasn't going to let me through without my boarding card and that he had never heard of me. I find that being a celebrity definitely has its downside. People keep on taking your picture when you don't want them to and when you want them to recognise you, they choose to pretend they never heard of you. Arrived on the plane by the skin of my chinny-chin-chin.

London absolutely boiling in the middle of a heatwave. Flat seriously hot. *Pacific Palisades* is being trailered on Sky, using a lot of me. Dinner with Katy and Paul at Mimmo's. She looks wonderful and they seem very happy, having been living together now for five weeks! He does most of the cooking in the microwave and she does the washing-up. I hope this lasts.

Thursday, 14 August 1997

Dinner with the Bricusses at the Caprice. He filled me in on all the behind-the-scenes dramas on *Victor/Victoria* and the Raquel Welch debacle. Apparently Blake Edwards was completely vile to Raquel, saying: 'You can't act, you can't sing, you can't dance and you're no Julie Andrews.' The poor woman burst into tears and stalked off, as did Blake. Leslie was furious and told Blake, 'Since you cast her without telling anybody else, don't you think this is a little unfair?'

Friday, 15 August 1997

Took a very early flight to Nice, then the car met me and went to the Bricusses' house in St Paul de Vence for lunch with Gina Fratini and Tony. They were very relaxed and we had an entertaining lunch. It's nice to be friends with one's ex! Had to take two different grotty planes to Ibiza – one a prop – ugh! Arrived on the 'TM Blue One', and was met by an excited Valentino with his two adorable pugs Maggie and Molly, Giancarlo Giammetti, and a cute resident toy-boy, Sean, aged twenty-two. I was looking forward to a nice relaxing evening but no, it was off to Jacobo Etro's house up in the hills of Ibiza, where a jolly group was assembled. Jacobo owns Etro's in New York, which I really like. Rosalina and Todd – an ex-model and a bit of a hunk – a few assorted queens, and Lorenzo Quinn and his wife Giovanna. He's the son of Anthony and amused us all at dinner by saying, 'My father's made 360 films and so he's got about 360 kids!' It's true. The old actor is extremely virile and fecund; at eighty-two he's got a toddler and a newborn – and is being sued for divorce! Exchanged lots of bawdy jokes but I'm so tired cannot face the thought of a nightclub. Todd drives me home and at 2.30 a.m. the streets of Ibiza are crammed and jammed with singing kids on the make, pumping-iron studs, Essex girls looking for love, and dancing fools. We got stuck in a traffic jam, but I can see why Ibiza's such a tourist trap. It's a happening place for singles.

Saturday, 16 August 1997

Maria of Bulgaria has arrived to add to the houseboat party. They are minor royals, in their late twenties and rather sweet but shy. Sten, another stud-muffin, has joined us. I think he's for Giancarlo, who's fifty-nine. We sailed down the coast and snorkelled, dived, swam and lolled about. This boat life is too hedonistic and very addictive. Lorenzo and Giovanna took us all for dinner at a charming Andalusian place. Over paella, a lot more jokes and a lot more wine. What's happening in the real world, I wonder. The paps have focused on my presence and snapped Valentino and me tripping lightly along the quay. I almost fell off the gangplank – that would have given them a good exclusive. Princess Diana is all over the papers having a romance with Dodi al Fayed. He's sweet and quite quiet. I know him, as he stayed with Ron and me in the South Street basement several years ago. I chatted to him on the plane recently and he said he was going to London to find a new girlfriend! Well, he certainly did!

Sunday, 17 August 1997

Set sail earlier this morning to another gorgeous spot, and we all photographed each other like mad. Have been trying to do some work on book, but no time – too busy doing nothing. I love these floating gin-palaces.

Monday, 18 August 1997

Calm crossing. Woke at eleven forty-five surrounded by 'water water everywhere' and no land in sight. Thank God it's calm though. Hit Barcelona port at three. It looks ugly. Nothing but cranes and mouldering old ships and dockyards. Weather gloomy and hot as hell. Ate lunch inside the cabin then all eight of us crammed into a mini-bus to hit the high spots of Barcelona. I've always thought it was a deadly dull city, and in mid-August with 90 per cent of the shops closed, even more so. We were on a Valentino espadrille search, and ended up in some huge department store rather like the Beverly Center. Bought mags and British papers. VILE pic of me in *Eva 2000*, the scummiest rag in Italy. Back view changing bathing suit in Sardinia. So-o inelegant. They were very rude but since it's Italy, '*non me ne frega niente*'.

Tuesday, 19 August 1997

We set sail during the night for Costa Brava and when I opened porthole at nine thirty a magically beautiful rocky coast was visible. Back in a playground again, away from that ugly city. PC sent fax from *Daily Mail* of me on beach in Sardinia. Amazingly for the *Mail*, they were unbelievably complimentary, called me 'Belle of the Beach' and described me as having the 'figure of woman half her age'! Not bad. Must remember not to let pasta go to belly. Stopped in glorious cove called 'San Sebastián' so that the doggies could get to wee etc. They are adorable but quite spoiled. Giancarlo said there's a killer virus which has invaded the waters of St Tropez and Spain and they've closed many beaches – can't corroborate it though. Everyone on board very sweet and now we know each other we do a lot of teasing.

Valentino and Giancarlo often ask the most personal questions which, if I answer, I know will be discussed with others. Let's face it, we discuss Liz and Claudia and Linda and Sharon too. They love Sharon Stone who, Va Va tells me, took seventy-two pieces from a Beverly Hills Boutique saying, 'I must have them [free] for my forthcoming tour.' Well, I've got a forthcoming tour – but chance would be a fine thing! A discount is about the best I can hope for. Giancarlo, however, is somewhat disenchanted with 'Shazz', as Richard E. Grant calls her, so I think she might not get her freebies after all. Giancarlo has had gold injections from his Parisian doctor (quack); he suggests I get them for my nose to mouth-lines – which I didn't think I had!

Perfect day and perfect weather when we arrive in Cadaqués, a charming fishing village-cum-tourist spot. Built on a rocky coastline, all the houses are white and it's extremely picturesque. Not so the reality. Went ashore for a spot of sightseeing and the beach is stony and filthy and the river almost dried up and littered with plastic detritus. Ate in a charming fish restaurant but had steak. I'm OD-ing on fish. Very good review for *Second Act* in *Publishers Weekly*. Jeffrey says it's a rave. 'Sparkles with en-tertaining anecdotes' and 'You'll be glued to her barbed account of her battle with Random House.'

Wednesday, 20 August 1997

Another glorious day, so did much the same. Spirited discus-sion at dinner about Versace's death and the *circus* that was his funeral – over a hundred photographers in the church alone. Mama Mia! Nice piece in the *Express* about me in bikini. Set sail for France and the island of Porquerolles after dinner. Flat calm moonlit night across the Bay of León, which can be a choppy nightmare, 'tis said, but was unbelievably flat.

Thursday, 21 August 1997

Woke up to the sights and sounds of Porquerolles. These are the mountains that we can always see from Destino. Spent another sybaritic day going on the motorboat to the beach and photographing each other in every possible position. After lunch set sail for St Tropez. The harbour master was giving Luciano, our handsome captain, a hard time, so had to bugger around at the mouth of the port then come in to main harbour. It's strange seeing St Tropez through the eyes of someone arriving by boat. A crowd of about two hundred waited on the quay to watch us dock, snapping away with Instamatics. I must say the boat is an impressive sight – it's so huge that it has to totally turn around to fit into the big port. Our group descended and it was like a Hollywood premiere. Valentino wanted a shopping trip, so gawpers and paps followed us to Blanc Bleu, shooting snaps and standing around. So embarrassing.

I escaped with the sweet Belgian boy Sven and we went backstreet shopping. God, I love St Tropez. If you ignore the crowds, it is of such unbelievable beauty. Sven is in the rag trade, so likes schmutters. Bought great black leather jacket. Dined at La Table du Marché, not bad but too hot – then cruised around the village window-shopping. Valentino is very popular and kept stopping graciously to smile and be snapped.

Friday, 22 August 1997

Mad shopping all morning – then set sail again. Great excitement on board. Giancarlo spotted Princess Diana on the *Jonikal*, Mohammed Fayed's boat anchored outside the beaches of Pampelonne. He and Valentino grabbed massively strong binoculars and glimpsed her sunning with Dodi on the top deck. Then

Giancarlo jumped onto a water bike and zoomed off to their boat. Two men with machine guns greeted him, which didn't go down well with the fiery one. The boat was guarded by several menacing minders who pointed their Uzis at Giancarlo, who hastily left. He extended an invitation to cocktails on Valentino's boat to Diana and Dodi, which they declined. 'They want to be alone,' said the surly guard. What, in St Tropez in mid-August? Va Va is disappointed with Princess Diana. 'My dear, to abandon Buck House for the souks of Cairo – it's too much.' Went on Coco Plage and saw the nude beach, naked gays – not a pretty sight. Mostly between thirty and sixty, they revealed raddled bums and front bits in a sorry state. David Wigg and Matt were lunching there – dressed, luckily. Our boat was continually buzzed by noisy water motorbikes. Paps are around too, but they've got bigger fish to fry on the *Jonikal*. Dinner at the charming Vietnamese restaurant Kai Largo.

Saturday, 23 August 1997

The St Tropez market was jam-packed. Our last glorious day of boating. Marina Palma [socialite, and a good friend of Valentino] and her BF Mark came aboard. We all tried to swim off Coco Beach, but the water was too grotty. Went to Voile Rouge beach after lunch. They had just finished a champagne-throwing fest at the restaurant, and the place was a riotous mess and complete bedlam.

Sunday, 24 August 1997

Fond farewells to Valentino and all, then it was bye-bye boat and hello Destino. House looked spic and span.

Monday, 25 August 1997

Arrived in Copenhagen after lunch. Met by Peter Charlesworth and Raoul Meyer, Brigitte Nielsen's curly-headed husband, who whisked me through Customs fast. At the Hotel Angleterre twenty fans struggled to get photos and autographs. Among them was my biggest fan, Anders, whose T-shirt featured a dozen images of JC. Quite a melee. 'You're very popular in Denmark,' said Raoul. Stella was waiting in 'The Roger Moore Suite', a rather run-down arrangement with a makeshift air-conditioner and several photos of dear Rog on the walls.

Brigitte came for tea. Last saw her about eight years ago, when she was caught up in serious substance abuse. She now seems OK – glorious and unbelievably tall and very relaxed and amusing. Did the interview for *Gitta and Her Friends* in the hotel. It was desperately hot but her questions were quite clever and we talked for an hour. She must have a 44C bust and was clad in the shortest black Versace 'pinafore' dress, no stockings and black stilettos. An imposing sight. After, went for a relaxing dinner and chatted away. She said Stallone 'was trying to ruin my career at every turn'. They'd also been shivved by Viviane Ventura, who'd given her *two* dud cheques! 'I had them framed,' said Raoul proudly. Then we got on to the subject of her other four guests. 'Mia Farrow was delightful, as was John Cleese and Pavarotti too.'

'What about Catherine Deneuve?' I asked.

They exchanged significant glances, then Brigitte said, 'A total pain.'

'So stuck up and changing her mind every three seconds about everything,' said Peter. 'She wanted to eat, then she wanted to rest – then she wanted to sightsee – and we all had to jump.'

I thought this fascinating as Deneuve is always portrayed by the French press as an angel.

'She's a bitch,' said Gitta. 'But because she's such a bitch everyone's petrified of her, including the French press. So they'll never do her in – as they do with you and me,' she laughed.

A very good evening ending with us deciding to do a comedy together, which I shall attempt to write.

Tuesday, 26 August 1997

Peter said Raoul was calling Nordic Films today to see if they would be interested in my movie idea with Gitta, which I've called 'The Best of Enemies'.

Stella and I arrived at Destino. Weather muggy and overcast but fell asleep next to the pool anyway. Dined at John Reid's. He wanted to hear all the gossip from V's boat. He also wants to produce *Love Letters* with Roger and me. We'll see if that comes off.

Sunday, 31 August 1997

Was awoken at six thirty by a shattered Peter Charlesworth telling me that Princess Diana had been killed in a car crash. I believed I was dreaming so I said, 'I'm going back to sleep now.' Robin woke up and said, 'You're not dreaming.' We rushed upstairs, turned on the television and to our unmitigated horror found out that it was true. Woke Stella and sat glued to all the horrific events that had snuffed out the life of the most wonderful woman, whom I particularly adored, admired and defended constantly at dinner parties and to the press. She was misunderstood and maligned by much of the media and many people, but I believed she was a really fine person. Am as upset as I've ever been. Stella and I cried all day. It is too too shocking.

I had first met her at a charity ball for Barnardo's where we were both wearing Bruce Oldfield. Diana was exquisite in a silver lamé gown with big shoulder pads, and I wore white silk, also featuring big shoulders. We chatted briefly and the tabloids the following day screeched, 'Dynasty Di meets Alexis'.

The second time I met her was in Palm Beach at another charity benefit. She had been married to Prince Charles for two years, but it seemed that the honeymoon period was waning as they seldom looked at each other. When I was presented to her, she whispered, 'How do you stand it? How do you stand the attention of the press and paparazzi all the time?' I was some-what surprised but replied, 'Well, I guess you just have to try and ignore them as much as possible.'

'Not much chance of that,' she said, gesturing towards the many international photographers in the bleachers whose in-trusive lenses were trained on the princess. 'They follow me everywhere. It's as if I'm in a goldfish bowl. Do they do that to you?'

'Thankfully not that much,' I answered. 'But I agree it must be very difficult for you.'

'It's horrid,' she shrugged. 'But, I suppose it's part of the job.'

Our paths crossed several times over the years and she was always charming and seemed glad to see me, so it seemed im-possible that such a shining light was dead.

Watched television to see Prince Charles arrive in Paris to pick up Diana's coffin and bring it back home. It's the saddest thing I've ever seen. Television and the papers still full of Diana. Still feel unbelievably sad but am now feeling anger towards the paparazzi, who I've always thought were vultures.

Monday, 1 September 1997

Woke up feeling as though I had lost somebody very dear. Tried to work on my book, but who can work? London has apparently almost come to a halt, Katy was crying on the telephone, even Sacha, who was not a particular fan of Diana, called from LA and said he didn't believe how upset he was. Spoke to many friends who are bereft.

Tuesday, 2 September 1997

It was Charles Duggan's birthday last night so we tried to put on a happy face, even though the weather is echoing our mood – grey, dismal and raining. Lunched at 55. A young conjuror-magician called David Jarre – the son of Charlotte Rampling and Michel Jarre – came over and did some tricks as a surprise for Charles's birthday. He was very very good and we all tried to cheer up, but until the Saturday funeral is over I think that everybody's going to feel intense gloom until at least next year. And so they should. We've lost a most wonderful person who will never be replaced.

Dined at Le Mole, a lovely family restaurant. The owner came over and told us with a catch in her throat that Dodi and Diana had lunched there a month ago. She said they were alone except for Diana's two boys and were like any young family, very happy, laughing, no paparazzi around, and Diana was dancing outside with her boys to disco music. Can't help but feel close to tears again. But then I'm not alone, the whole world feels like this. I don't think they've realised what they've lost. Nostradamus said that the end of the world will come in the year 2000 after floods, famine, disaster, volcanoes, droughts and the death of the second messiah. The way that people are treating Diana in her death is as though she was the second coming of Jesus. I've lived through the deaths of King George VI, Winston Churchill, JFK, Elvis and Marilyn. I have not seen anything like this, and it's not even her funeral yet.

We gave a dinner for Charles. Stuart Grimshaw and Simon Sainsbury arrived with Sean Mathias, a very good young writer-director, and his friend Myer. Naturally all everyone can talk about is the dreadful events. Sean says that he has been completely deprived of television because Stuart doesn't have a set, so we dashed to the TV room to watch.

Wednesday, 3 September 1997

Everyone still feels a sense of unreality. Went to the Beaulieu Hotel for an interview for *Entertainment Tonight* in which they asked me many questions about Diana. Long interview, which I know they will cut to about thirty seconds – which indeed they did – then read Byron's 'She Walks in Beauty' for ITV. Byron died at thirty-six, the same age as Diana. Everybody feeling very gloomy. Every time I talk to Katy she is in tears.

Thursday, 4 September 1997

It was a very sunny, a beautiful day, but we were sad. Finally got into the car, drove to have dinner at the Bricusses'. Roger Moore and Kristina were there, as were John and Jan Gold and Errol and Ginette Brown. The talk was naturally of Princess Diana, although they didn't seem particularly upset. Everyone was talking about Elton John rewriting the lyrics of 'Candle in the Wind' to suit the princess. I thought it was a great idea, everybody else thought it was a terrible one. 'Marilyn Monroe is not really remembered by anyone under forty,' I said, 'and the lyrics were very apropos of Diana.' Stayed the night at the Bricusses' but had to have a large fill of television news before bed.

Friday, 5 September 1997

Got up early and went with Charles to a studio on the roof in Nice. A most gorgeous day and with Nice in the background I gave an interview for GMTV about Princess Diana. They said they were only going to give me six minutes, but I spoke for about ten. I felt quite impassioned and said things that I felt needed to be said. Returned to Destino in time for Patrick Donovan and Peter Charlesworth's arrival. Atmosphere at dinner was like a boys' locker room. Lots of dirty and bawdy jokes told, but at least it took our minds off what's going on.

Saturday, 6 September 1997

Spent practically the entire day in front of the television watching Diana's funeral. To say that we were all upset is putting it mildly. It was the most moving thing I've ever seen and a pall of gloom hung over us. To lighten the gloom we played poker later and a rowdy time was had by all.

Monday, 8 September 1997

Nigel Hawthorne and Trevor Bentham arrived and we of course did nothing but talk about the tragedy, then had dinner at Stuart and Simon Sainsbury's villa.

Wednesday, 10 September 1997

Patrick and I left for London. As soon as we arrived we went to Kensington Palace. I was astounded and astonished by the outpouring of quiet respect and love from the people. Flowers seemed to stretch for miles. I had brought some red roses and placed them to join the others. I read some of the messages, which were unbelievably touching. A couple of people recognised me and said gently that they were very glad that I was here. Met Katy and went to Mimmo's for dinner, felt extraordinarily tired.

Thursday, 11 September 1997

Drove with Peter C. to the airport via a circuitous back route and walked on to an American Airlines plane to do, of all things, a one-liner on *Coronation Street*! Worked with Vera Duckworth and Jack,* who were very sweet. They were filming a revival of the commercial that Leonard Rossiter and I did for Cinzano. Vera is dripping. I then arrive and say to her, 'Don't worry, darling, it washes off, I should know.' We finished at eleven thirty and I managed to get on the British Airways plane back to Nice.

Friday, 12 September 1997

Roger Moore and Kristina came for dinner in the afternoon, played rather an aborted game of tennis with Trevor and Nigel at Stuart's. We all feel sort of dried up and dull. Am trying to work on my new book but it's difficult.

---

* Played by Liz Dawn and Bill Tarmey.

Monday, 15 September 1997

These past days and indeed weeks since Princess Diana's death have passed in a sort of daze. It's now 15 September, over two weeks since she died, and we are all still grieving. I've never known such an outpouring of affection. Called Elton after the funeral and congratulated him on how wonderfully he performed 'Candle in the Wind'. He said it was terribly difficult and that he almost broke down a couple of times. Spoke to Valentino and Giancarlo Giammetti, who were at the funeral and said it was unbelievingly moving and that the young Prince William is exceptionally handsome. They always notice things like that. Drove into the Colombe d'Or with Paul, Adrian Gill and Nicola, who are staying here. Met Roger Moore and Kristina and had sensational hors d'oeuvres and the most magnificent truffle salad with *mâche*. Now that A.A. Gill is here we are all very conscious of what we eat! The Colombe d'Or is one of the most beautiful outdoor restaurants in the world. Drove back and Paul, Adrian and I sang the show tunes.

Sunday, 21 September 1997

The past few days have been more or less the same, eating, swimming, sunning, going out to restaurants and having lots of fun. Adrian and Nicola seem able to eat a huge amount yet remain thin, it's quite annoying really! But they're both great fun. Went to Tim and Virginia Hoare's and, after dinner, played a fierce game of poker with practically no-holds-barred odds. I was amazed to end up winning three hundred and fifty pounds. Our host, quite inebriated, lost over six hundred. Today we are packing up the house, as it is *pas de saison*. Really very sad. I have finished my new novel, which I'm now calling 'Three Women for Adam'. Jonathan Lloyd thinks it's a good title. I hope he's a good enough agent to be able to sell it. Not very happy about the fact that Macmillan put only six thousand paperback copies of *Second Act* on sale in England. I'm hoping that the tour of *Second Act* with St Martin's as the hardback publisher in the US will do a lot better. Not to be immodest, but it's a really good autobiography.

Gained six pounds, which is enough to make me want to slit my wrists, but I'm working on losing it. Brigitte Nielsen called to say that Mr Klit of Nordisk Films is very excited about the 'Best of Enemies' project and we are meeting on Wednesday.

Monday, 22 September 1997

My decorator called. 'Are you sitting down?' she said. 'Yes,' I said. 'Well . . .' she sounded embarrassed. 'They've delivered the kitchen but instead of it being in limed ash it's in dark oak.' I threw a complete fit. This bloody kitchen, I've been going on about it for months now and I've been staying away specially. They said my flat in Eaton Place looks like a pit. Absolute murders between Cathy Sloan and PC and Steven, who put the kitchen in. Steven insists I ordered oak, which of course is totally ridiculous as I was always going to have it the same as Cathy's. They have no written confirmation of any colour that I ordered the kitchen in. Everything else has been daily signed off on, so it is their fault, but they are trying to argue otherwise. But why would I want a dark oak kitchen?

Wednesday, 24 September 1997

Met Brigitte Nielsen, her husband Raoul and Jesper Klit at the Byblos. I have been writing the movie script madly and changed the title to 'Jealousy and Hate'. I must say I think it's quite funny. Had an excellent lunch in which we all seemed to bond and Mr Klit said he was very enthusiastic about me working more on the script. I suggested John Cleese might be involved too, and they thought that was a great idea and are going to call him.

Thursday, 25 September 1997

Left Destino in the most beautiful weather. Rushed around London doing various errands. Went to my flat. What a disaster! I simply cannot believe the rubble and the crap. I have no fax, no answering machine, no maid because Isabel is not only sick but has gone on holiday, no secretary, no kitchen, no fridge – it's a wonder I have a mind left. But I do have a beautiful daughter. Katy came to tea and looked great.

Friday, 26 September 1997

Drove to Kidlington private airport and boarded the Bamfords' incredibly chic and beautiful Falcon 900 JCB plane with Carole. Anthony was in a meeting. Flew in beautiful weather to Holland, where we were met by Teddy and Bea van Zuylen's chauffeur and driven to the Chateau De Haar. This is an amazing old castle built in the late eighteenth century by Teddy's ancestors. It belongs to the Dutch National Trust and the van Zuylens can use it for one month a year, which is when they have these grand weekends and house parties. Quite a good group there. Played several games of Scrabble with Tessa Kennedy, Lord Kenilworth, Duncan Maclaren and Maya Flick. Then had a very fine dinner indeed: the most wonderful Moroccan chicken. The chateau is unbelievably grand and quite intimidating, but I think it's rather overdone in terms of decor. After dinner, Issy van Randwyck entertained us. Sorry Biggins couldn't be with us because Neil was unwell.

Saturday, 27 September 1997

A most beautiful day. Went for a walk around the grounds with the Bamfords. All the other groups went off on bicycles, but I don't fancy my chances on one of those. Another wonderful lunch, twenty-eight people. Tomasz Starzewski arrived flushed with success from his fashion show. Then we took a car into Amsterdam and cruised the red-light district and saw a couple of transvestites who looked as though they were done up for *Dynasty*! Some teenage hookers were standing in the window in bikinis. I found that unutterably depressing as they looked so forlorn and vulnerable. Then we got stuck in a traffic jam in the porno street, which is also the drug addict street. I've never seen so many dreadful-looking characters in my life, stumbling around stoned and weird. All of them look as though they're from a Central Casting call for drug dealers – I expected Robert De Niro to appear any minute. There were even men sitting on the pavement mainlining crack. Carole and I became really upset and we hastily went to the flower market, which was more our cup of tea.

Issy sang again and Tess and I played some more Scrabble, then we started a game of poker with Teddy, Tessa, Robin, me and Michel David-Weill, an older gentleman who is seriously rich because he is the president of Lazard Frères, one of the great banks. Tessa lost heavily, I lost heavily and Michel kept getting unbelievable cards. I owed him $392, so wrote him a cheque made out to Michel David-Weill.

Gave my rendition of 'Making Whoopee' again tonight after

the poker. When Robin came back, he said that he had not been paid his winnings!

'Oh, it's only sixty-eight pounds,' said the millionaire David-Weill dismissively.

'That's not the point,' I said, 'a gambling debt is a gambling debt whether it's threepence or three thousand pounds.'

I was quite angry because Teddy, being the host and the poker banker, should have sorted it out, but he vaguely suggested I give Robin the sixty-eight quid. Since I've already given Michel David-Weill $392, this didn't seem quite on.

Sunday, 28 September 1997

Everybody trooped off to church. When Teddy came back I mentioned casually the fact that I had paid Michel my debt and Robin was owed £68. He said, 'Oh, Michel should have given it to him.' Since Michel had left, this was a little difficult. 'He's going to frame your cheque,' laughed Teddy.

Tuesday, 30 September 1997

Stella arrived and we took the British Airways flight to Warsaw. I've never been to Warsaw before and I don't think I ever want to go again. It was pouring with rain when we arrived and I felt like I was in Malaysia as the sky was that scary dark greenish-grey. Met by Anya, who runs the Elite Model Agency here (the backers for the charity I am doing). It took at least an hour to drive to the television studio, where I did an interview with a rather po-faced woman called Margaret. I had the usual plastic translator gismo in my ear, which makes trying to be natural rather difficult. It took another hour in the car on the way to the Marriott Hotel. Terrible traffic jams and such depressing buildings.

Stella and I kept giggling and said we would cut our wrists if we had to live here. Did more interviews and photograph sessions in the presidential suite, which is where Bill Clinton slept when he was here.

At the charity ball, I did a press conference in front of forty members of Poland's press. Everybody is still crazy about *Dynasty* here, as it's still relatively new. I made a speech saying how happy I was to be here for the children of Kwaczka, which is under water from the floods of two months ago. We then sat for two hours for a mind-bogglingly boring evening of speeches. Polish people don't have a huge sense of humour, but then I guess I wouldn't if I had to live here. Stella and I went to the bathroom and started giggling, and when we came out Anya and the bodyguard said, 'You were laughing!' 'Yes,' I said, 'we're English, we laugh.' Some guy came up and said, 'I've always wanted to ask you this question. What is the difference between Joan and Alexis?' I looked at him coolly. 'There is no difference,' I said. 'I am exactly the same person as Alexis.' He looked totally shocked. 'You are?' he said. 'Yes,' I said. 'Totally devious and impossible and bitchy, I'm not playing a part, I *am* her.' 'Oh, so it wasn't difficult to play it,' he said. 'No,' I said. He staggered off looking puzzled, but since that question is asked of me constantly I just felt I couldn't answer it any more. Had two Scotches to get through the evening. The auction was turgid, to say the least, and one of the models wore one of my *Dynasty* dresses. All of the models flitting around were between fourteen and eighteen and they have that look – Jodi Kidd, Kate Moss, long hair, no make-up, skinny bodies . . . And big thighs, I might add. Finally I escaped. Feel that I never want to set foot in Poland again.

Wednesday, 1 October 1997

London looked particularly glorious on 1 October.

Friday, 3 October 1997

Robin, Cathy Sloan and Daphne Guinness and I climbed into the car and drove to Greenwich to the most charming ramshackle house owned by Emily Patrick, the artist whose pictures we were interested in. Fell in love with one for Destino and another for Eaton Place, as did Daphne and Cathy.

Lunched at the Caprice with Biggins, Robin and Daphne. Biggins seemed excited about my script of 'Jealousy and Hate', which he likes very much as I want to cast him as my butler. PC is dealing with Jesper Klit and they want to do it as a television movie. I think it's more of a low-budget movie. Decided to rewrite script myself as I will be in Los Angeles after my tour, waiting for my London kitchen to be finished! Spoke to Sacha and asked if he would help me with the script and he was thrilled.

Tonya came over for my first workout in two months and said that I was not too bad. Played poker at Cathy's and had dinner in her divine kitchen, limed ash, which is what I was supposed to have! Understand that Steve, the kitchen organiser, has lost his job. I feel sorry about this but it was because of his total incompetence that I have been completely put out. I could sue, because they never had a sign-off as to what colour the kitchen was to be, but I've had too many court cases.

Saturday, 4 October 1997

Pack, pack, pack, pack ready for New York and LA. Do I ever stop? This flat is a nightmare. Lunched with Katy at San Lorenzo, so lovely, but it was terribly noisy there and there were so many faces from the sixties, all of whom seemed to have aged to the point that I hardly recognised them. Katy came back to the flat and looked at a few pictures of her father's that she would like to have in her flat as I'm having a major clear-out.

Sunday, 5 October 1997

Off to New York for the tour of my autobiography, *Second Act*. Hope it will do better than the hardback and paperback in England, which got very little support. Mind you, nothing's selling at all except Andrew Morton's disgraceful book on Princess Diana.

Arrived in New York: unbelievable weather, eighty-five degrees. Jeffrey was waiting at the hotel, so we caught up, then had an early night.

Monday, 6 October 1997

Up at the crack. Left at eight o'clock to do twelve satellite radio interviews. Did *Entertainment Tonight*, then met Carole, Susan Sangster and Jeffrey at Harry's Bar. Very buzzy. Fergie came in with David Tang and Lauren Hutton. She's over here to do Weight Watchers and, rumour has it, to take over the mantle of Princess Diana, although she denies this.

Dressed in my Badgley Mischka white suit, went to Mortimer's for the launch party for my book. Glenn Bernbaum, the owner, was hosting it, which was so sweet of him. St Martin's Press were all gathered excitedly, telling me that the book was selling very well. Oh please God, after those English publishers letting the paperback totally disappear. Very good turnout of press and friends. Arlene Dahl looking beautiful, Alecko Papamarkou, Taki, Nan Kempner, and Dominick Dunne, who says that his book about O.J. Simpson with Sacha's portrait of him on the cover is going to be all over bus-backs in LA. That is very exciting. Others there were Helen Gurley Brown and her husband and Mica and Ahmet Ertegun. All the New York papers are rumbling about how I am delightfully bitchy about besting Random House and there are lots of giggles about me referring to Joni Evans as 'raddled with orange paper skin'. Dann Moss, Tricia Guild and Richard Polo, Eddie Sanderson and many others also there, and various other New York luminaries including Carolina and Reinaldo Herrera. After the cocktail party, went into the back room where Blaine and Robert had a delightful dinner party for me for thirty people. Sat next to Robert, who was as usual delightful and making jokes about his brother wanting to be a TV star. Mick Jones of The Clash, Ann's rock star husband, sat on my left. He was very friendly.

Tuesday, 7 October 1997

Dashed to NBC for the *Today Show* where I was interviewed by Katie Couric, who wanted as many anecdotes as possible. Did *Bloomberg Report*, then dashed with Jeffrey and Jamie, the PR for St Martin's Press, to Donna Karan, where I bought a leather jacket. Then we did Saks Fifth Avenue, where I suddenly seemed to have become popular again as I am constantly asked for my autograph. It's amazing how when people see you on TV they are all over you like a rash. Did my book signing at Barnes and Noble, which seemed extremely successful, and Tom Dunne

of St Martin's Press was grinning away like a Cheshire cat –
good sign. When we left, two burly Irish-American policemen
escorted us down Fifth Avenue past the crowds, paparazzi and
fans trying to speak to me in the boiling hot sunshine. We finally
roosted in 21, where Evie Bricusse and Blaine Trump were already
waiting, later joined by Carole and Anthony and Alice. Only had
a short lunch, as had to then do several more TV shows. Hurried
back to hotel, changed clothes, dashed back to NBC and did the
Conan O'Brien Show. Told the Mickey Mouse story in which I
describe Mickey as having caught an expression 'that looks as
though a finger has been stuck up his rodent rectum'. Conan
thought that this was simply hilarious. It's a bit sophomoric,
this show, but I'm here to sell books not to make comments.
Changed again into long black lace trousers and off-the-shoulder
top and met the usual suspects in the hotel bar, then walked
across to Ivana Trump's apartment on Madison with Carole and
Anthony. I've rarely seen anything so badly decorated in faux
everything in my life. Velvet on the walls! And cornices painted
glittering gold!! Someone remarked 'There must be an empty
room in the Plaza because it looks like all the furniture from
that over-decorated hotel has been put here.' Zillions of people
in an overly hot room and far too many photographers and press
people. Ivana has a new boyfriend – a quite good-looking Italian who she whispered to me was wonderful in bed! Too much
information.

The Bamfords and I went to the elegant, beautifully decorated
Fifth Avenue apartment of Mr and Mrs Alfred Taubman. He
is the CEO of Sotheby's and she is a very glamorous lady who
lunches. The rest of the guests, however, were all pretty dreary.
Chatted to Gil Shiva and luckily sat at dinner between our host
Mr Taubman and Jamie Niven, David's younger brother – although he looks older. Was so exhausted could barely keep eyes

open. Managed to extricate myself at eleven thirty and tottered home to meet Jeffrey, who'd also had a dreary evening with Ivana and Nikki Haskell.

Wednesday, 8 October 1997

Filmed *Live with Regis and Kathie*. They are good sports and I did a good plug for the book. Then went to an interview with Charles Grodin. He used to be an actor but is no longer interested and has left off his toupee. Worked the *Joan Rivers Radio Show*. She's as frantic as ever and I don't think she'd read my book as she didn't know there was a story about her in it. Her boyfriend Orin Lehman tramped into the studio on his crutches while I was trying to tell an anecdote and Joan practically genuflected before him.

Jeffrey and I met Carole and Alice for drinks in the bar at the Plaza Athénée then dashed to Coco Pazzo, where the manager informed us that our dinner reservation was nine thirty and not eight thirty and therefore he had told our two guests Peter and Linda Bren to leave and come back in an hour. We were absolutely furious since everyone wanted an early night. So we sat at the bar drinking champagne and smoking with Hugo and Elliot Guinness, and Peter and Linda, who are friends from over thirty-five years. They are both great fun and I've lost touch with them over the past years as they moved to Paris. They don't seem to have lost their sense of excitement about life. They are leaving for Portofino tomorrow to check out a new boat and we vowed we would not lose touch again. Lots of compliments on how great we all looked. Blah-blah!

Thursday, 9 October 1997

Went to ABC to do *The View*, a new programme with Barbara Walters and Star Jones, who was at Blaine's the other night. Very feminist show with the de rigueur 22-year-old to balance the maturity of Barbara. Barbara furious backstage that I was telling the same anecdote about Prince Charles I've told on other shows and annoyed with the researchers that they had not put in the story about her and me. Went back to the hotel to organise my suitcases and Jeffrey's, as they'll be going to LA with Carole. This will be a big help. Worked the *Geraldo* show. He really is good, very interesting and interested, and the audience was fine. Left for Toronto on Canadian Airlines and arrived at a seriously dreary hotel. Had a ghastly salad in the room. Jeffrey and I were so tired we couldn't keep our eyes open.

Friday, 10 October 1997

Woke up at six and did six or seven TV shows plus a book signing, ending up with *The Dini Petty Show*. She is the Barbara Walters of Canada and wasn't too happy that I had to dash away to catch yet another plane. She was wearing black stockings with 'Bitch' written all over them in white, which she said she'd worn specially for me! Charming.

Left for Los Angeles, and I fell asleep while Jeffrey was totally engrossed in Kitty Kelley's new book, *The Royals*. He says it's absolutely riveting, although how much is true we don't know. Arrived in LA, which is suffering from serious wind again! Apartment looks good, even though all the plants have died. Went to the new Spago with Jeffrey and Carole. It's such a great restaurant but the only game in town since Drai's Café has closed already. That's Hollywood, folks.

Saturday, 11 October 1997

My typed script of 'Jealousy and Hate' arrived. It seems much better in print. Dinner party at Wendy Stark's. Nothing seems to have changed since I was last here. Jolene and George Schlatter, the Davises, the Poitiers, Mike Medavoy and his lovely wife Irena.

1998

Tuesday, 1 September 1998

After eight months of off-again on-again negotiations *The Clandestine Marriage* finally got a green light. I reported to Ealing Studios for hair and make-up tests where Nigel Hawthorne looked dazzling in a long, curly, ruby-red wig and more make-up than I wore in *Dynasty*. As Lord Ogleby he is superb casting. I saw him on stage three years ago, which is when I yearned to play Mrs Heidelberg. He and Trevor Bentham told me then that if the movie were made, I would get the part. Unbelievably for showbiz promises, this one actually came through, so I am playing Mrs H. in Trevor's wonderful, funny script.

The make-up lady applied a pale, powdered look on my face, but she had trouble with my tanned cleavage. The wig was fabulous, a towering edifice – high as a kite. Then crooked yellowish gnashers were applied over my teeth. No eye make-up and tiny painted lips finished the look. The corset was unbelievably uncomfortable, and I realised I needed to diet, but I finally looked extremely austere.

At four thirty, twenty actors and ten crew members sat around for a table reading. Then to our horror, producer Tim Buxton, head of Portman Entertainment, gave a short, embarrassed speech saying there'd been 'a tiny little hiccup' and the money that they were expecting had not 'hit the bank'. Since the country was on the verge of a stock-market crisis this was hardly surprising, but nevertheless a terrible shock.

On autopilot, I read through with the other actors, including Nigel, Timothy Spall, Tom Hollander and Natasha Little. Afterwards we were all invited into the Ealing bar for a drink on the company, where I asked Christopher Miles, the director, what was going on. He seemed sanguine and said he thought that it was just a clerical problem and by tomorrow all would be fine. Steve Clark-Hall, the Executive Producer, was not so sanguine and told me it was fifty-fifty that the movie would start at all. I downed a large vodka and felt seriously upset. I was really looking forward to this film.

Tuesday, 8 September 1998

Despite the dire warnings, everything progresses as scheduled – maybe things had been sorted? We went to our location and moved into our accommodation, a fifteenth-century monastery done up like a twentieth-century Idaho motel. I couldn't swing a cat in my room. Tried desperately to make it habitable but the lamps were about thirty watts, the TV was the size of a stamp, the bathroom was the size of a second-class stamp and all in all I was pretty unhappy with my digs. But I had dinner with the whole cast downstairs in the restaurant and Christopher Miles made jolly speeches, so that restored my spirits.

Thursday, 10 September 1998

The seventeenth-century house we were shooting in obviously hadn't been redecorated since then, but it had enormous character. After a pub lunch, amidst much jollity, I thought we would rehearse but we just walked around the house again. We met

Lord and Lady Needham, who owned this stately pile. They are very amusing. He looks like Terry Stamp and sounds a bit like him. He wore blue jeans and a ravelled pinstriped jacket, and the sleeves looked about to fall off.

Friday, 11 September 1998

Finally rehearsed my gazebo scene in the afternoon – a difficult scene with Tom Hollander and Timothy Spall. I run around the room angrily and finally slap a statue in the buttocks and then grasp its 'front bits'. Decided I cannot eat, as it's corset time tomorrow, so got into bed with a chocolate digestive biscuit and a glass of Scotch. Slept badly and had horrible dreams – no wonder, with that dinner.

Saturday, 12 September 1998

First day of shooting was a day of amazement. Hair, make-up and wardrobe were seriously over-stressed because they have ten principals to get ready for an outdoor scene and the forecast is rain. I was ready by ten thirty in the corset and the huge dress, which looked fabulous, but then I sat around until three thirty waiting for the weather to change. To say that the corset is uncomfortable is putting it mildly. I simply could not eat. No wonder everyone fainted all the time in the eighteenth century.

Monday, 14 September 1998

Ordered a tomato salad at the pub and with it came celery, rice, nut and raisin mush, cucumber, strawberry, pasta shells, pears in cream, lettuce, orange slices, raspberries, coleslaw and grapes! It was enough to feed a family for a week. No wonder Britain is following America in obesity. One of the cast members ordered the jumbo trout. Since he was only about four foot eleven, the trout was minimally shorter than him. The local publican, Deacon, gave an interview in the *Gloucestershire Echo* saying how impressed they were when I arrived. 'People say she is this super-bitch, but she actually *spoke* to people when she was in here!' he said. There's that bitch tag again.

I nicknamed the hotel Fawlty Towers as everything went wrong: they changed the postage-sized television set but the new one didn't get any channels. We could only play videos, but there were no videos to be had. The lamps were upgraded to 40 watts, but that was the highest they could go as otherwise the little flimsy petticoats they had as lampshades might catch fire. Ergo I could neither read nor watch TV.

Tuesday, 15 September 1998

We were going to shoot the scene in the orchard garden, but it rained buckets. The sun came out for a brief moment and then it rained again. It was a miracle that we got the scene at all. It was pretty hard being ambulatory in a mile-wide boned pannier dress, corset, huge wig with a huge, huge hat perched on top of the wig, particularly when the ground under foot was a soggy mess. The shoes that were specially made for me did not fit, so I had to wear my own boots.

Nigel looked so hysterical in his white make-up and rouged lips with tons of eye make-up and a ghastly red wig, I couldn't stop laughing, but he was simply wonderful. We shot a scene in which I'm supposed to be carrying a white poodle, but as I couldn't possibly cope with the skirt and the parasol and holding Nigel's arm all at the same time, we decided to let it walk alongside. As if to punish me, it decided to relieve itself in the grass and then rolled in it. To cries of dismay from the wardrobe department, the white poodle rushed up to me, brown all over, and brushed itself off over my mauve satin skirt.

Dined with Nigel and Trevor at a little inn in the nearby village. Our waiter was the campest thing since Kenneth Williams, and it was all we could do to stop giggling every time he came over to offer us some exotic delicacy. Trevor and Nigel gave me all the background action of the ins and outs of how this film got started and I'm amazed it ever did, but then I'm amazed that any film ever does. Nigel has had seven movies cancelled in seven months!

Tuesday, 22 September 1998

After a full day's work on Monday, during which the weather was superb (talk about luck), I received a call from my agent Peter Charlesworth to say that my pay cheque had bounced! Great. Went to London and spent the next day wondering what was going to happen. Apparently, Portman Entertainment had promised that Tim Buxton would arrange bridging finance until the money from the Rod Gunner Organisation (RGO) and Jonathan Staples, the main producers, came through at the end of September.

Portman had reportedly not met their obligations for some reason, so all the cheques have bounced. Spoke to Susan Boyd, whose husband Will is producing a film in November, and she said that they too have money problems and don't know if they're going to able to start. It seems as though it's dicing with death trying to get money for a film. Drove back down to the location on Wednesday and, even though nobody's been paid, spirits are high. A meeting was held in which the producers told everyone that somebody was going to South America to pick up the money, would come back via Madrid and that it would all be 'in place' by Friday. In spite of this spy-novel explanation, it's a measure of how professional the crew is and enjoying this film that they're all soldiering on without pay.

Wednesday, 23 September 1998

We had a problem with a black horse as one of the female extras went near him wearing perfume. This so excited the stallion that we were unable to shoot until he calmed down. 'He's really a big boy!' bragged the stallion's trainer proudly, as the crew tittered.

This corset is killing me and I can hardly eat anything but little bits, drinking about a dozen cups of coffee with tons of sugar for energy as my biggest scene is coming up.

Had a long meeting with the line producer in his production office to find out what's really going on. Basically, if the film does not get £800,000 by the end of today, which RGO had promised, shooting will stop. He showed me a pile of invoices and bills from people who rent out the caravans, the cameras, the costumes and feed the crew. It's a nightmare. Nigel said it's the worst situation he's ever been in. Me too!

Thursday, 24 September 1998

When we viewed an assemblage, forty-five minutes of cut stuff, it was wonderful – beautiful. The lighting, the costumes, the performances, the direction, were a joy. The producers were supposed to arrive with money to pay the crew by the end of the day but at four fifteen, while Tom Hollander and I were getting ready for our scene, the crew 'downed tools' and everybody went out to play football on the lawn. Tim Buxton arrived and gave a ghastly speech to the assembled throng, to the effect that there was no money to give them but that he hoped that they would all carry on working while he tried to get some more. Several of the crew were completely outraged. 'What am I supposed to do? I've got twenty-five pence in my pocket. How am I supposed to feed my wife and family?' yelled one. 'I'm very sorry,' said Tim, 'but I'm doing all I can.' Nobody has been paid for three weeks.

Saturday, 26 September 1998

The union rep gathered the crew in his office and told them that their salaries would be guaranteed and that they'd definitely get them. 'But when do we get them?' asked one grip. Then it started to rain, and I sent out for a case of wine so that everybody could drown his or her sorrows. I felt gutted. Tom Hollander's agent told him that he was under no obligation to work, and Hollander said he felt like quitting but I persuaded him not to. Then we all went inside for another meeting with the main producers, Rod Gunner (RGO) and Jonathan Staples, who had guaranteed eight million dollars for this film, which they had promised to deliver on 30 September. In the meantime, Portman Entertainment had guaranteed financing the movie, but we were told, in spite of the fact that they were advanced £200,000 by RGO, they apparently sank it into a Peter O'Toole film! Tim Buxton had left by this point, either to go to London to renew his efforts collecting funds, or simply to escape the wrath of the crew. I cannot believe it.

The crew were very sweet, saying they were doing their best, some even mortgaging their houses, but the bottom line was that the producers were supposed to come up with the money by the thirtieth and it is still only the twenty-sixth.

'So why did we start filming?' yelled one guy. There was an uncomfortable silence. The trouble is there were no leaders in this crisis. Christopher Miles was sweet, but he is not a strong ballsy guy, neither was Trevor, who was getting very upset. Earlier, when I went to talk to our production manager about the situation he literally cowered under his desk. They're wimps, except for Willy Wands, our first AD, who is also a producer. He spoke up, 'Look, I don't want to be here all night. Let's have a vote as to what we're going to do.'

So every department went into a corner and after two and a half hours everybody unanimously decided to stay with the picture, but only until Wednesday night. Unless the producers can come up with the money, we will fold up our tents on the evening of 30 September.

I decided to raise some money myself. I called half of my LA contacts and most of my London ones and spent two days on the phone constantly trying to save the film. One of the producers called and said the bank would be prepared to lend me half a million, but I would have to give my flat in London as collateral, which made my heart drop. 'I don't think that's a terribly good idea,' I said, and when I told my manager he was adamantly against it. Then he told me another story: allegedly RGO are not the knights in shining armour they're pretending to be. According to Portman Entertainment, RGO had not advanced any money. In fact, it was Portman themselves who paid the £250,000 to get the film this far and the story of a Peter O'Toole movie is a complete fabrication. Portman said that, because what they've seen up to now is so good, they want to take over the film. In the meantime, RGO and Jonathan Staples have disappeared off the face of the earth, the day before the promised money is due. To cap things off, a tabloid magazine ran the headline 'Joan's film collapses'. Probably word got out because of my fundraising efforts. Meanwhile the wonderful cast and crew carried on shooting as promised.

Monday, 28 September 1998

I decide to invest some money to save the film. I called Steve Clarke-Hall, who has taken over as producer from Tim Buxton, and told him that I might be willing to put up somewhere between two and four hundred thousand, and he was unutterably thrilled. He thinks that gesture would encourage Portman to finish the film. Of course, if they didn't they'd be sued for a million pounds by the producers' union, so why wouldn't they put in the million pounds and finish it? I figure my investment is safe. At least, that's my theory.

I had endless discussions about this. At a lunch meeting with my agent Peter, my bank manager and my lawyer, I tried to persuade them to let me access a certain amount from mortgaging my flat. We bandied this back and forth and they seem knocked out with the fact that I am willing to make this 'gesture', as they call it – some gesture! Peter still wants certain things, like me getting my money back before Portman, and that I get a producer's credit and a percentage of the film. Peter also agreed to put in a hundred thousand, as did Nigel, which is fantastic, so it was a good meeting. Then we watched fifty minutes of rough assemblage and were bowled over by it. The film looks like a thirty-million-dollar production. The acting and performances are great and the lighting and the look are exquisite. Some of my friends think I'm mad – so what? I believe in this film and I feel that it could be quite good for me making the transition from 'Bitch' to 'Old Bag'!

PC told me that he had to firmly put his foot down in his meeting with Portman that afternoon. He insisted that unless he and I got our money out first, before the bank, it was a no-go. They balked about this, but what else can they do? They have two options: either be sued for a million pounds or put in six hundred thousand and with our money make a go of it, so they can't really argue. PC called and said that the meeting ended at ten thirty in the evening and that it was really tough, but that we'd secured agreement on all points.

Wednesday, 30 September 1998

The day dawned and it was time for the announcement to the cast and crew, who had unanimously agreed to fold the film that evening if there was no money. Nigel and I stood in the grounds of the stately home, looking at their miserable faces. I told them there was a rescue package being organised by Nigel Hawthorne and me, but added, 'I hope you realise that my money is good, but I can't get it from the bank until tomorrow, so you will have to wait until then.' Then Nigel told them what a wonderful crew they were and then everybody applauded, which made me want to cry. The AD asked for a show of hands to see if the crew would wait until tomorrow and all hands went up, smiles all round – yes, they would wait until tomorrow. Lots of crew and cast came up and congratulated Nigel and me, hugs all around, quite emotional.

Had a quick bite in my dressing room with Christopher and Trevor, and tried to rehearse a scene with Emma Chambers, but she got slightly hysterical and rushed out almost on the verge of tears. That's all we need now – another emotional actress. Rushed back to London to meet bankers and sign papers. I am giving them this huge loan, which is costing me a fortune, but since I am supposed to get it all back first when the film is released, I feel more sanguine. It's still a gamble and I absolutely cannot afford to lose this money, so I pray the film sells enough tickets to pay me back.

Monday, 5 October 1998

Was awoken at five forty-five by a call from Tara saying she was in the hospital because her waters had broken! Called the AD to see if I was really needed at two-thirty in Gloucestershire. He said I could come in at three (gee, thanks!). Dashed to the hospital, where Tara was sitting up in bed smiling broadly and not having any labour pains at all. Drove to the country location to film the scene wearing my 'bald look', a short grey wig with curlers in the front which makes me look about as attractive as Olive Oyl's great-great-grandmother. Not that Mrs Heidelberg is supposed to be attractive, but this is truly grotesque. The scene went well, but I was becoming more and more tense because Tara, in spite of being induced at the hospital, was still not going into labour.

We did take after take after take, as the clock crawled around to 8 p.m. I made endless phone calls to the hospital to find out how Tara was doing, but they kept saying she's just fine. In the scene, the white poodle is supposed to go under the covers while I shriek, 'No licking!' but it's an untrained animal. Not like 'Verdel', the dog from *As Good as It Gets*, this one. He would not obey Christopher, who kept talking to the dog as though he was human. I finally lost my temper and blurted out, 'Why are you talking to the dog like he's an actor?' The lady who looks after the dog said, 'I'm not a trainer, I'm just a breeder, and I have no more influence on the dog than anyone.' Finally, I told the AD to give me a dog treat, which I placed between my knees so when Chris yelled 'action' and the breeder released the dog, it shot under the covers like a Scud missile. Finished the scene in one take! I dashed back to London to find new baby Miel wrapped in Tara's arms, both looking cute and fit. She was so teeny – you always forget how small they are. Tony and Gina were there, and it was happy families all round. Home for a four-hour nap, then drove back to Gloucestershire to shoot again.

Tuesday, 20 October 1998

At lunch with Nigel and Trevor we had a good old moan about everything, including Portman Entertainment, who took all the credit for saving the movie, never mentioning what Nigel and I did nor the fact that neither of us are getting paid. The producer makes no effort to return Peter Charlesworth's calls. We went to see an hour and a half of assemblage that looked good – touch wood. I'm not keen on myself, of course, but then again, I never am.

Wednesday, 21 October 1998

We shot the last scene of *Clandestine Marriage* this evening. It entailed the entire assemblage watching a play outdoors. In the script, a water tower built by my 'brother' Timothy Spall that runs various hydraulic innovations on the farm, is supposed to burst and drench the entire cast. The word came down the line that I'm not going to get drenched because the costume designer says the dress will be ruined, the hair designer says the wig will be ruined, and the make-up designer says the make-up will be ruined. That was fine with me! We watched the rehearsals, with the extras being completely drenched like a bizarre remake of *The Poseidon Adventure*. It was most impressive. Some other extras, ladies from Bath wearing their own eighteenth-century finery, were having conniption fits that they might be soaked, as they're sitting behind me, but the AD reassures one and all: 'It will just be like a fine Evian spray.' Finally, at 4.30 a.m. the 'fine Evian spray' comes down in a sort of chute and it's like having a bucket of water thrown all over me. Everyone was hopelessly drenched. The ladies from Bath were properly 'bathed' and in an absolute state, as all their vintage frocks were ruined. Everyone was screaming and yelling hysterically, and it was absolutely freezing.

One year later, after the film opened to tepid reviews and didn't do much business, I thought to myself, what a perfect metaphor that last scene was for my experience on *Clandestine Marriage*. For all the trouble I put myself through, all I got was soaked, literally and figuratively.

However, all's well that ends well as the Bard said – at least we made the movie, and I recovered my investment – phew! So, you still want to be in showbiz?

1999

Saturday, 23 January 1999

Wandering through the British Airways departure lounge, en route to LA, a man momentarily ceased his mindless prattle into his mobile phone to glance in my direction. In a voice loud enough to summon the cattle home from across the River Dee, he announced, 'Guess 'oo's just walked in?'

Instantly half the heads in the lounge popped up. I hastily slid behind a copy of the *Spectator*. 'Nah, I kid you not; and she don't look too bad neither. Wearin' a fur 'at, though,' he yelled.

Several people looked over towards me with a hint of disapproval. I mouthed the word 'fake' a couple of times and retreated to the furthest end of the lounge, muttering oaths.

30 January–6 February 1999

I've managed to escape the worst rigours of this exceptionally mild London winter with a brace of hedonistic trips; one to Mexico, the other to Egypt.

Before leaving for a trip down the Nile to celebrate Giancarlo G's big birthday, dire warnings were issued by various American friends. 'It's much too dangerous, you'll get shot,' warned one New Yorker.

'It's filthy – you'll get dengue fever, maybe even black tongue disease!'

'Don't eat anything except pasta and well-cooked meat – you'll be really ill if you eat vegetables or salad,' lectured another.

Bearing this well-meant advice in mind, and armed with every medication known to modern science, I arrived in Luxor with some trepidation.

The luxurious home for the week could best be described as a modern-day version of Cleopatra's barge – with a crew of almost fifty.

The Italian who had chartered this behemoth had none of the American phobias. They laughed when I talked of terrorists and feebly refused the delicious-looking salads, fish and vegetables.

I had stocked up on biscuits and dried fruit in Paris, just in case of attacks of acute hunger pangs while stumbling around some tomb or other. What an idiot!

The food was superb, not one of our shipmates contracted any deadly ailments, and within a couple of days it was back to the groaning buffet and to hell with the consequences.

Egypt is a total delight, as are the Egyptian people. Kind and dignified in their turbans and djellabas, there is an innate elegance in their bearing. It seems sad that more of them don't wear their traditional, stylish clothes, which all of us on the boat rapidly adopted as our own wear.

We shopped in the bazaars like mad, until I finally came down with caftan-fatigue syndrome.

It's quite incredible barging down the Nile: like being transported back to biblical times. Gazing at the banks of the river for mile after peaceful mile, you see no hideous modern infrastructure to bruise the eye; just mud-brick houses here and there, palm trees and a few shepherds tending their flocks.

Watching the little sailing boats gliding up and down the

river reminded me of a line of dialogue, fortunately cut, from a swords-and-sandals epic I worked on many moons ago, *Land of the Pharaohs*: 'Kiss me again, like you did on the felucca.'

Monday, 10 May 1999

Very glam party at glam Hotel Hempel for Valentino's sixty-seventh birthday.

Talked to Elizabeth Hurley, who has such a super sense of humour and is a great beauty. She just needs better films. The papers next day ran pics of the two of us with very flattering comparisons.

Chic party, although the Hempel is a strange ultra-modern hotel and the food was just little bite-sized dead bits on toast. Va Va's usual suspects were all there. My, he has a lot of hangers-on!

Sunday, 23 May 1999

My birthday and a nice surprise prezzie – I'm on the *Mail on Sunday*'s bestseller list! *My Friends' Secrets* is #4!

Gave a lovely party – good group – Diahann Carroll, Betsy B., Suzanne, Nolan, Alan, Niven Jr, Hugo Guinness, who follows wherever Robin goes, Alana and the Bryers. Michael Hollingsworth catered it very well.

Sunday, 6 June 1999

David Niven Jr invited me to a special dinner given by Liza Minnelli and Burt Reynolds at Chasen's on Beverly Boulevard. He picked me up, but when we arrived the place was covered in bunting, and it was obviously just a PR exercise to get celebs out to plug some product.

Liza, with her usual puppy-dog charm, hugged me hard and called me 'my baby'. Since I've known her since she was sixteen and I'm a decade older this seemed a bit odd, but she's adorable, which is more than I can say for the saturnine Mr Reynolds, who thinks he's hot stuff. I've always thought him overrated in the movie star department, and I gather he's not a very nice person.

The party was boring, so went to Anne and Arnold Kopelson's for a buffet. I love Arnold. He's so funny and he's made some of my favourite box-office hit films like *The Fugitive* and a dozen others. Jackie was there, and they love insulting each other brilliantly.

Monday, 28 June 1999

A party to celebrate thirty years of Tramp (at Tramp obviously). Went with Biggins and Theo and Louise and it really was a trip down memory lane. Great to see Jan and Johnny and so many friends. They played great eighties hits and I hit the dance floor like it was 1985!

Summer 1999

After being released from the constricting embrace of eighteenth-century-style corsets in *The Clandestine Marriage*, I found myself being squeezed into yet another set made of leather! At the irresistible request of Mr Steven Spielberg, flew to Hollywood to give my all as Fred Flintstone's prospective mother-in-law, Pearl Slaghoople – what a name! – in *The Flintstones in Viva Rock Vegas*. Elizabeth Taylor had played Pearl a few years previously in an earlier *Flintstones* incarnation with John Goodman. The costumes are the most outrageous and extravagant creations I've ever worn – which is quite an admission. Consisting mainly of beautifully cut leather, brilliantly coloured, they fit like a second skin – but only if the said corset is cinched into Scarlett O'Hara proportions and one eats like a sparrow. Hardly a gramme of fat was allowed to pass my lips. 'Thin is always in' within the Hollywood crowd.

Kristen Johnston is playing Wilma in white skin-tight leather mini-dresses, and she and I complain a lot about not being able to eat. Mark Addy from *The Full Monty* is playing Fred, and Stephen Baldwin, one of the notorious Baldwin brothers, is playing Barney Rubble. Stephen is like a 'will o' the wisp'. The ADs can never find him. He loves going off on a golf cart to explore the Universal lot.

At the end of shooting, I begged the costume designer to let me keep one of the totally iconic costumes – I wanted to auction it for my Shooting Star Children's Hospice charity – but they refused. They probably ended up being burned in a skip, like all of the fabulous costumes from 20th Century Fox and MGM which those studios in their wisdom destroyed.

Thursday, 30 September 1999

A very intellectual lunch at the *Spectator* offices.

Boris Johnson, the editor, has a deep, booming voice and looks like he brushes his hair with an eggbeater. Sitting next to him was Petronella Wyatt, who is rumoured to be his girlfriend, although he's married.

I sat next to A.A. Gill. How I love that man. He is so brilliant, and his articles and restaurant reviews are so right-on and funny. There were a lot of clever speeches by the likes of John Mortimer and Hugo Swire.

Tuesday, 26 October 1999

Andrew Lloyd Webber hosted a screening of *Joseph and the Amazing Technicolor Dreamcoat*. I thought I was good as Mrs Potiphar. My enthusiasm was slightly dampened by Mr Donny Osmond being quoted as saying, 'Joan Collins really loved running her hands up and down my body – she was really into it!'

Oh puh-leeze! In your dreams, Donny – it's called acting.

Thursday, 28 October 1999

Opening of *King Lear* at the Barbican, starring darling Nigel Hawthorne. I thought the production was ghastly. Huge rocks fell from the gantry during the big storm scene and missed hitting the actors by millimetres. I felt embarrassed for Nigel. It's the highlight of an older actor's career to play Lear, but this was such a miserable failure in direction and staging.

Dinner at the Barbican café with Nigel, Trevor, Robin and the Boyds. We all tried to be upbeat, but it was like a funeral. Nigel was extremely depressed.

Winter 1999

Just met President Clinton for the first time. As we waited for him in the Oval Office, an intern divulged, without a trace of irony, that 'the president uses the Oval Office mostly for business, but also for private matters'.

Suppressing a smile, I was suitably impressed when Clinton strolled in moments later, smiling affably and clutching a can of Diet Coke. The last American president of the twentieth century warmly greeted his guests, speaking to each of us as if we were the one and only people he'd been longing to see. This is an admirable quality, and a gift that precious few public figures possess.

My two partners in crime, Jeffrey and Robin, both sophisticated cynics, were greeted with great enthusiasm and were visibly entranced as Bill fixed them with his guileless blue eyes and chatted away.

He grasped my hands firmly; he has beautiful and expressive hands, by the way, and enormous feet. In his gentle Arkansas drawl, he asked all the appropriate questions. I must admit I was spellbound. The man has palpable sex appeal and is much taller and slimmer than I'd expected. He also has wonderful breath, but not from a surfeit of mints or mouthwash.

The White House photographer clicked away as the president pointed out a chunk of black rock that some astronaut or other had brought back from the moon. 'It's three and a half billion years old! Amazing, isn't it?'

I surprised myself by answering, 'Almost as old as me,' and he laughed.

After a further tour of the president's working offices we were next introduced to Buddy, the 'First dog'. He turned out to be a frisky character, who instantly developed an uncontrollable passion for my right leg. Maybe it's something in the water there, or perhaps he just likes high heels.

Washington was followed by a brief foray to New York, the most favoured destination for all gold-medallist shoppers like myself.

The high point was a dinner given by John Richardson, in what has to be one of the most stunning apartments in Manhattan.

Richardson is the author of the definitive multi-volume Picasso biography, and his long-awaited memoirs, suitably entitled, *The Sorcerer's Apprentice*, are due any day now in November. He is the grandmaster of raconteurs, full of humour and with a magical voice. His taste is as faultless as his manner and his walls are covered with personalised Picassos, and with Braques branded with affectionate dedications.

Nestling among all these is a ravishing jewel-like Lucian Freud of John, which somehow manages to convey the whole man on a tiny board hardly bigger than a postcard.

The Japanese have always been gadget-crazy, and at John's apartment I found myself face to face with one of their inventions: a washer-dryer loo. After dinner I entered this fearsome contraption, its various functions having been carefully explained to me. There were several buttons set into the side, with instructions in Japanese, accompanied by tiny, incomprehensible symbols.

After using it, I gingerly pressed the button which I thought was the 'hot-jet stream', only to receive a freezing fountain of water, which drenched me top to toe. Attempting to dry off, I pressed another button, and received what felt like 'Hurricane Floyd' up my thighs. I then pressed yet another and a scalding torrent shot out, causing me to leap into the air and yelp in pain.

Concerned voices called from the dining room, 'Are you all right in there?' Somehow, I doubt this eccentric contrivance will ever catch on in draughty old Blighty.

Monday, 8 November 1999

Roger Moore opened his new restaurant Hush in a dim, murky alley off Bond Street. Geoffrey Moore is running it. It's quite nice and spacious, but there are too many curving stairs.

Bumped into Victoria Beckham, aka Posh Spice. She was very

sweet, said I was her 'other mum'! She coerced me into giving an interview for her new Channel 4 documentary, and she was quite witty, but she has a rather strange new fringe!

Sunday, 28 November 1999

The Clandestine Marriage officially opened to the critics – ouch! But I got some quite good reviews.

Monday, 29 November 1999

Charity premiere at Odeon Haymarket. Wore a lilac Nolan suit. Nigel wore a beard and bright turquoise tie. He's still very upset by his horrible reviews for *Lear*. Tried to cheer him up by saying he should laugh all the way to the bank.

'My driver got paid more than I did,' he replied ruefully.

Very sad. He's such a great actor and a wonderful friend. He deserves better.

Tuesday, 7 December 1999

Elton's party.

Costumed, of course! So over the top, but divine. He wore an eighteenth-century white wig. I wore black velvet. It was a real festival of glamour and lots of fun, with many stars, a major turnout.

New Year's Eve 1999

It's the end of the century!

I can't get rid of the scary feeling that something awful is going to happen to the world. Either an economic collapse, a worldwide pandemic, like the film *Outbreak*, a civil war or total breakdown of social media.

Went to the bank to draw out some more cash. If something does happen, I think credit cards will become obsolete, so cash will be king.

Maybe I've seen too many disaster films, but I think it will happen one day.

Drove with the Fennells to the Lloyd Webbers' lavish mansion in Sydmonton to celebrate New Year's Eve. A fab evening. Madeleine had laid on a delicious dinner and we watched fireworks and drank Cristal.

Pandora and I went upstairs for a while to watch celebrations on TV from Australia.

Everyone seems optimistic and happy about the new decade.

2OOO

Tuesday, 4 January 2000

Dinner with Adrian Gill and 'The Blonde' (Nicola) and Dale Winton at The Ivy. Couldn't stop laughing all night. I adore Adrian. His wit is unsurpassable, and Dale has a biting, slightly camp delivery too.

A.A. and I reminisced about when John Reid wanted him to write 'Mrs Robinson' (*The Graduate*) for me, but I didn't want to be nude. Jerry Hall did a good job, though.

Friday, 14 January 2000

Flew to LA on Virgin – good flight.

Have a lot to do in the next few days, looping for *Flintstones* and screenings for *Clandestine Marriage*.

Tuesday, 18 January 2000

Fabulous dinner at Betsy's. She does give the most elegant and glamorous dinner parties in LA, or even NY for that matter.

Her Holmby Hills house is exquisitely designed and furnished, and she is indeed the perfect hostess in the old-fashioned way. I happen to love the superb crystal and china, the silver chargers beneath the Limoges plates and the marvellous flower arrangements.

The A-list dinner was in honour of Jim Billington, from the Library of Congress.

Nancy Reagan, Betsy's best friend, was as always resplendent in velvet and pearls. She sat next to Betsy but seemed quite hard of hearing. She spoke lovingly of 'Ronnie,' and everyone hung onto her every word. We all know he's suffering from dementia but don't discuss it.

I sat next to Leonard Goldberg (Aaron Spelling's business partner), who also has a hearing problem. He talked about several projects that he would like to put me in. Well, that ain't gonna happen! Just Hollywood talk. But it was a fab night.

Wednesday, 2 February 2000

Had been planning what to wear for tonight's Costume Designers Guild event for weeks, and the dress that Nolan made for me fits OK-ish, but it's not splendid and it's too tight.

Arrived at Beverly Wilshire to be greeted by lots of paps and fans cheering enthusiastically outside.

Inside, bumped into Sophia Loren (cool), Jane Seymour (friendly), and Harvey Keitel ('Joan who?')!

Presented the Distinguished Director award to Aaron, who was suitably grateful. But my God, he's so thin – too thin by half. Hope he's not sick.

Thursday, 24 February 2000

I agreed to be in a sitcom called *Will & Grace*, starring Debra Messing and Eric McCormack. I don't know who they are, but they're supposed to be 'hot'.

After months of negotiating, agreed to go on a mini tour of A. R. Gurney's *Love Letters* with George Hamilton. I love G. and we've known each other since the mid-fifties. He gave me a ride in his Rolls-Royce when he was only twenty, but even then mega-tanned and sophisticated. Charles D. will be producing and I'm excited to be back on stage.

Friday, 10 March 2000

Started rehearsing *Will & Grace*. At the table read ninety-four writers screamed with laughter after every line. It always happens. Bad sign.

Tuesday, 14 March 2000

Blocked. *Will & Grace* boring. I have a cute scene with a little dog to whom I keep feeding scraps. Then I get avocado goop pushed in my face, but it's funny and everyone laughed.

Wednesday, 15 March 2000

Shoot with audience from three till eleven. Exhausting. Lance and Judy watched, then we had a bite at BHH.

Tuesday, 4 April 2000

Arrived in NY late and meet Jeffrey at a ghastly hotel, the Phillips Club. Can't swing a cat in my room and no room service. Too late to go out for dinner and I have a ton of interviews and TV appearances to plug *My Friends' Secrets* and *Love Letters* tomorrow.

Wednesday, 5 April 2000

After the *Today* show, *Live with Regis and Kathie* and *Lifetime Live*, I prepared for a signing at 6 p.m. at the Rizzoli bookstore. Mirror in the bathroom is the size of a cigarette pack to do my hair and get glammed so it's tricky! Jeffrey said the producers won't change my hotel. Thanks, Charles. 'Diahann wouldn't stand for this,' Jeff teased me, as I was desperately trying to do my hair: I have no glam-squad.

Supposed to arrive at Rizzoli's before six, as I had asked Paul [Newman] and Joanne [Woodward] to meet for a quick hello. Traffic dire, so arrive at six fifteen to find a note from Paul: *We were on time, where were you?* Damn, really love them and they are very hard to get to socialise with as they hardly go out.

Signed for half hour, good turnout. Jeff said I should meet two guys from *Love Letters* who were waiting to meet me downstairs. Said hello to Max-something, who looked about fourteen, and Percy-something, who also looked young. 'You look very young,' I said to Max.

'I'm twenty-four,' he said.

'How about me?' asked the good-looking Percy.

'Oh, you'll do,' I quipped.

He asked me if I was happy about the NY hotel, and I gave him the full rundown.

'I was told you were happy here,' he said, seemingly puzzled, 'I'll see what I can do.'

Monday, 10 April 2000

Katy and I were met at San Francisco airport by Percy Gibson and Charles Duggan, the producer of *Love Letters*. He also produced my US tour of *Private Lives* and is a great friend.

We chatted happily in the car, and I gently admonished Charles about the fact that he wouldn't let me change my awful hotel in New York.

'That's not true,' said Percy. 'I called your press agent several times to see if you were happy there, and each time he said you were fine.' He looked quite concerned.

Charles piped up, 'I heard him telling that to Jeffrey on the phone.'

'Well, never mind.' I smiled at Percy, whose concern and sincerity were touching.

'We hope you'll like this one,' he smiled back beguilingly.

The hotel was fine; simple, spacious and close to the theatre. Contrary to some people's opinions, I don't go for the overdone and over-decorated deluxe suites and prefer more homey surroundings, especially since Katy was my companion on this tour.

So the two-bedroom suite, with a little kitchenette to make coffee and breakfast, was perfectly OK. The kitchen had been stocked with groceries, cookies and wine, and my favourite Casablanca lilies were on the table, as were the English newspapers, which Percy had found out I liked to read every morning.

'He is so considerate,' I remarked to Katy, as we unpacked.

'And cute too!' she giggled.

11–23 April 2000

In a misguided attempt to make everything 'friendlier' for the two-week stint with George Hamilton as my co-star, at the Marines Memorial Theatre in San Francisco, Charles suggested that George came to pick me up in the limo so we could both arrive at the theatre in time for the 'half' (thirty-five minutes before 'curtain up').

Percy and I were wary about this arrangement, but he had to

follow his producer's instructions to 'save money', and I didn't want to risk being considered 'difficult', so everyone agreed.

This worked for a few days, until George began arriving to pick me up later and later.

I started calling Percy, calmly at first: 'It's seven twenty' – the half was at seven twenty-five for an eight p.m. curtain – 'and he's still not here.'

'He'll be there, don't worry. He called and said he was in traffic,' Percy would calmly assure me.

The next night: 'Where the hell is he? It's seven thirty!' I yelled.

Again, the diplomacy, at which Percy excels, came to the fore: 'Don't worry, he's pulling up outside now.'

Jumping into the car, I berated George for his tardiness. 'You *can't* arrive this late. You've got to let me get to the theatre before the half: I have to prepare.'

But George didn't quite get it. 'Your hair and make-up are done: all you've got to do is change. Why do you need half an hour?' he said.

I stared at him bleakly, realising this could be a very long engagement. But I have to say George more than made up for this exasperating tardiness by being charming, witty, supportive and generous.

George is one of the funniest and most amusingly self-deprecating of actors. Backstage during intervals, Percy, Max, Katy and I would be in fits of laughter as George regaled us with his endless supply of anecdotes and jokes, and more seriously his exceptional knowledge of all things medical.

How he kept his tan during this cold April month I'll never know, but keep it he did.

Love Letters is a light two-hander in which the actors are seated next to each other reading their love letters from one another from the time they were teenagers until the death of my character, 'Melissa'.

There were some sweet laughs, but audiences usually went to the touring show just because they had been told that it's amusing and because many famous names had performed in it all over the US.

Charlton Heston and his wife Lydia, Robert Wagner and Jill St John, Larry Hagman and Linda Gray, Jessica Tandy and Hume Cronyn, and Uncle Tom Cobley and all, had played – often to packed houses. The actors liked it because they didn't have to learn lines and there were minimum rehearsals (only one day for us). It was an easy gig and a quick way to pick up a few bucks.

On our first matinee, George, Percy and I were sitting back-stage at the interval lamenting the lack of audience laughter.

'You know why they're not laughing,' I said, gloomily, 'because this play's not fucking funny!'

In San Francisco, George was dating the novelist Danielle Steel, so Katy, Max, Percy and I usually went out to dinner to-gether after the show. As often happens on theatrical tours, we all bonded together like family and exchanged many confidences.

Percy Michael Jorge Gibson was born in Lima, Peru, to a Peruvian father who was fifty-five at the time (and whose great-grandfather was Scottish; hence the surname) and a Scottish mother, forty-two-year-old Bridget Monahan, a schoolteacher.

Theirs was a tempestuous yet loving relationship, for Bridget was feisty and opinionated and Jorge was the typical South American macho man, the boss and the breadwinner with a temper and a touch of chauvinism thrown in.

In this respect he would not have been unlike my own father, a strict, hot-tempered, Jewish chauvinist born in 1902, just a few years before Jorge Gibson.

So Percy and I had much in common, for our fathers were of the same strict intransigent generation. There were more than thirty years between Percy and me, but that didn't matter one whit as the camaraderie between us flourished on tour.

Monday, 24 April 2000

George left the company and Stacy Keach joined us in San Diego to play the male lead.

As is common on tours, heavy press duty was required upon arrival at each town. Often, I had to rise at dawn to prepare for early-morning talk shows.

The first morning in San Diego, bleary-eyed and with badly applied make-up, I stumbled into the lobby to meet Stacy with the local press agent.

There, to my surprise and delight, sat Percy, with two containers of steaming Starbucks latte.

'It was too early for room service, so I got you a latte. I know you like it with four sugars.'

'You didn't have to do that,' I said. 'You don't have to be here.'

'I know, but I just want to make you happy,' he smiled.

I felt a great wave of warmth for this handsome young man, who was so completely dedicated to his job and to making his stars feel good; quite unlike many company managers I had known in the UK.

'He's the best company manager I've ever worked with,' said Stacy. 'Percy always goes above and beyond the call of duty, and that's rare in our business.'

Tuesday, 25 April 2000

I realised I'd run out of eyeliner.

'I'll get you some,' offered Percy.

When he returned, I opened the package to find a mascara wand.

'Isn't that it?' he asked, a bit confused.

'No,' I smiled. 'I wanted eyeliner. I guess you're not gay!'

'Afraid not,' he smiled back.

And that, as Claude Rains said to Humphrey Bogart in *Casablanca*, was the beginning of a beautiful friendship.

Thursday, 4 May 2000

The tour drags on. Katy had to leave, and Stacy's a bit of a home-body, so I've been spending a lot of time with Max and Percy, who I really like a lot.

Saw a matinee in Phoenix with P. and Max: *The Flintstones in Viva Rock Vegas*. Oh my God, there were only six people in the cinema. 'This is so embarrassing,' I said.

'Don't worry, you were wonderful,' Percy said. 'And don't forget it was #4 at the box office last week.' He is so sweet.

Saturday, 6 May 2000

Travelled to Austin, where for some reason I was given the keys to the city.

The preview of *Love Letters* at the Paramount Theater went very well, and Charles took George, Percy, Max and me to cele-brate at Gumbo's on the Lake.

Wednesday, 10 May 2000

A lovely day on Charles's boat on the river with Percy and Max. Just the four of us. A lot of laffs! I think we must all have the same blood group!

Thursday, 11 May 2000

Nightmare day. Had to do thirty-five 'blind' TV electronic satellite interviews for *Will & Grace*. Why I have to do these, I have no idea, but I think Alan slipped it into the contract. Anyway, I managed to plug *Love Letters* and Percy came with me. What would I do without him?

Saturday, 13 May 2000

Judy came to stay. So great to see her.

Dined at Four Seasons with Charles, Jude and P. Michael Caine stopped by to have a drink and tell some of his witty anecdotes.

I've known Michael since the sixties, when he was a suave man about town who'd just made *Alfie* and was catnip to women. He came to stay with me and Ron and our six kids in our Marbella house in the seventies. Michael had to sleep in the tiny maid's room, as we had so many children. As always, he was affable and fun.

P. and Michael hit it off and we all laughed hysterically for hours while the wine flowed.

Tuesday, 16 May 2000

Will & Grace aired and according to my agent it got great ratings 'cos of me. Oh, sure.

'NBC network loves you,' he crowed. 'They want to go forward with projects for you.'

'In your dreams,' I said, cynically. 'It's just Hollywood talk.'

'*The Flintstones* has grossed $28 million,' he said.

Sunday, 21 May 2000

Lynn Wyatt gave a great birthday party for me.

May 2000

Alan Nevins calls me from LA saying there's interest in me for a movie called *These Old Broads*. Probably the worst title I've ever heard, but he says that it's starring Debbie Reynolds and Shirley MacLaine, and that Elizabeth Taylor is playing the agent. It sounds very amusing.

Thursday, 1 June 2000

To NY for more publicity. Percy was there and he took me to see *Kiss Me Kate*. What a wonderful, marvellous romantic show. Absolutely loved it. P. is so adorable, he's a very special person.

19–22 June 2000

London is absolutely swinging. So many events, and Ascot starting soon.

Barbara Amiel and Conrad Black gave an elegant summer party, and Joan Rivers gave a cocktail party for Marylou Whitney.

Katy had a birthday and I went to the Serpentine Gallery party.

Thursday, 22 June 2000

Ladies' Day at Ascot. In a great box – Robert and Sue Sangster's. She looks gorgeous in couture. As usual, none of the nags I bet on came in at all, but everyone had such fun.

Saturday, 24 June 2000

Received the script of *These Old Broads*, which is not bad, I must admit. The part of Addie, which they supposedly are offering to me, is a sort of sexpot who has to 'bonk' her Mafioso lover to death. Better get in some practice!

June and July 2000

These Old Broads: the usual endless conversations backwards and forwards arguing about money, etc. Spoke to super-agent Toni Howard at Harry's Bar, who said that I should take this role, as every actress over fifty in Hollywood wants to do it, and although it is a television movie, it will probably be a theatrical feature in Europe and the rest of the world. Alan tells me they now want Anne Bancroft. Great actress, but she's not right for this role.

Tuesday, 25 July 2000

The London premiere of *Flintstones*. Even though I saw it in Phoenix, I took my three kids, who all dressed up to the nines.

Tara wore a short beaded dress in a pattern of the flag of St George and Union Jack. She looked amazing. She's working hard and her PR is calling her 'the original Tara', because of Palmer-Tomkinson.

Sacha is having some success with his paintings, and Katy seems happier now.

Late July 2000

Finally, definitely, *These Old Broads* has been green-lit and I am going to play the role. Hurrah! Love the role. They are going to rewrite it for me, being English. Quite a few squibs in the papers and every time I mention it to anybody they seem to get excited. I guess it's hit a nerve – we need some light entertainment now

Early August 2000

Nolan Miller comes to stay in the South of France and we spend many a happy hour going through magazines and discussing Addie's wardrobe for *These Old Broads*. Go shopping in St Tropez and find several over-the-top, cheesy outfits for her. I do not want to look like Alexis in the slightest. This woman is rich but supposedly has no taste and is trying still to be sexy. Well, I guess I can make an attempt.

Mid-August 2000

Director Mark Diamond and producer Ilene Berg call me. They have heard my worries about not being able to sing and dance well enough to keep up with Shirley and Debbie, and they assure me that they will give me lots and lots of rehearsals and that the choreography is not going to be Bob Fosse style. They sound very nice and are looking forward to meeting me. Spoke to Tom Korman to find out if it's true that Tony Curtis is going to play my Mafioso lover who comes out of jail for an 'assignation' with me and dies 'on the job'. He says Tony wants to do it, but they won't pay what he wants. It is quite a small part, but actors love to act. I mean Tony was a *massive* star. How the mighty have fallen.

Friday, 18 August 2000

A call from Nolan in LA, who is with Debbie Reynolds. I speak to Debbie, who assures me that she wants my dancing to look equal to her and Shirley's: 'We all gotta look good, dear, so it's important that we really work at it. But don't worry, we're not gonna let you down, dear.' She calls everyone dear, it's quite endearing – ouch!

Monday, 28 August 2000

Start rehearsals in Culver City with Peggy, our choreographer. There are three complicated song-and-dance routines; one is called 'What a Life', which we all try to learn while strutting around the piano. Then we try 'Boy Crazy' – or rather, we don't actually try and learn them, we try to 'get them down'. The other is the number that Debbie and I perform in a discotheque, the famous Judy Garland number 'Get Happy'. I'm terrified about the whole thing – to sing, to *dance*, with these two icons of musical comedy/movies is pretty awesome. We are working in a rehearsal room that has absolutely no air-conditioning. It's pushing ninety in LA so even I am sweating. Debbie insists on wearing her wig all day. Shirley and I just tie our hair back, and tell her to do the same, but she says, 'I only have three hairs left on my head, dear – I don't want anybody to see me like that.'

Monday, Labor Day, 4 September 2000

The week up to Labor Day started in a haze of rehearsals, rewrites, dance routines, falling down, minor arguments, discussions, fittings – I don't know whether I'm coming or going. I have a very nice driver called Dave who is saving my life as he's able to do lots of errands. Spent an afternoon with Nolan going through Addie's sixteen costume changes. I'm desperately losing weight – want to get to around 120 pounds; the camera puts on 10. The dances seem to be going well and I'm finally managing to get the steps in my head, which means that I wake up in the middle of the night with the strains of 'What a Life' going through my mind. Social life gone to pot. Spend Labor Day weekend with Judy and Max in Las Vegas.

Thursday, 7 September 2000

First table read. It reads well and quite a few laughs. More dance rehearsals in the afternoon. Debbie is still wearing a big wig despite it's only us in a closed set. It's over ninety degrees and she must be roasting. Shirley keeps telling her not to be so vain!

Friday, 8 September 2000

A gallery shoot on the Sony stage for Liz, Debbie, Shirl *et moi*. The assistant director arranges us in directors' chairs and introduces us to the assembled press. He stumbles on Elizabeth. 'Er, and this is Dame Taylor, er, Dame Elizabeth Taylor. No, er . . .

Ms. Taylor?' Finally, he capitulates and asks her what she wants to be called.

'*Daaaaaame* Elizabeth,' she replies in her unique nasal twang. 'I want eeeeverybody to call me *Daaaaaame* Elizabeth,' she trills gaily.

'Even on the call sheet?' asks the AD.

'And on my *chair*,' she beams back.

Shirley, Debbie and I giggle. Only Dame Liz can get away with this, but everyone loves her. She looks quite frail and can't walk very well. It's quite sad and she's also put the weight back on. When she was dating George Hamilton in the late eighties, he put her on a diet, encouraged her to get a deep tan, put her in Nolan Miller outfits and she looked utterly divine.

Tuesday, 12 September 2000

First day of shooting. We all have individual trailers in a car park on Wilshire Boulevard. Debbie and 'Dame Liz' haven't spoken for about thirty years, since Liz stole Eddie Fisher from Debbie. Debbie decides to bury the hatchet, so dashes across the car park to Liz's trailer – in her robe and wigless! A burst of flashbulbs ensues as the paparazzi who are camped around the car park record this historic moment. Three weeks on the closed set of rehearsals she has refused to take off her wig and this day she chooses *not* to wear it. The next day, the rags carry every cringe-making photo.

Wednesday, 13 September 2000

Worked from 7 a.m. to 11.30 p.m. with Debbie, shooting the 'Get Happy' number, working in a trendy disco. Huge fun and a huge number of gay fans, who are regulars at the club, show up to join in the dancing numbers with us. It's totally exhilarating and I think it looked really good.

Friday, 15 September 2000

We shoot the first number in the movie when we're all supposed to look young. Shirley turns to me as we're sitting in the back of a 1960s convertible. 'So tell me, what was my Warren really like?'

'Well, you should know – you're his sister!'

'C'mon,' she says, 'what was he like in – you know?'

'Overrated!' I said succinctly. End of conversation!

Wednesday, 20 September 2000

Dinner with Audrey and Billy Wilder at Morton's. He really is one of the most fascinating and brilliant people I know. He was complaining again that he can't get a project green-lit even though he's a multi-Oscar winning director. 'I'm over seventy,' he said with a twinkle in his eye. 'In Hollywood they don't want to even know you if you're that age.'

'Try being forty if you're an actress,' I said.

'Age is just a number,' said Audrey, raising an elegant eyebrow.

Friday, 22 September 2000

Shirley keeps following me around pushing an ice-cream cone into my face, which I say I don't want. 'Go on, have some – you're much too skinny,' she said. I wanted to say, '. . . and you're much too plump', but I held my tongue.

Sitting in my dressing room at lunchtime, trying to relax, Carrie Fisher storms in, lies down flat on the ground and wails,

'You've got to help me, Joan! I need some more good lines for Shirley!'

'Oh really? What about some good lines for me?' I asked.

She then closed her eyes and pretended to sleep. Carrie really is a little crazy.

The papers are making a lot of nasty snipes and innuendo about how Debbie and Shirley and I are at each other's throats.

'Not true,' Shirley tells them. 'We're playing three actresses who are bitching at each other all the time and maybe some members of the crew get the wrong idea.'

'We all love each other,' I chip in.

September–October

Mark Zunino comes into my dressing room looking worried. 'I was just watching rushes with Nolan, the director and producers and Shirley, she's not happy with your costumes.'

'Why? Aren't they in character?' I asked.

'Apparently you look too good, especially in the white jacket slung over your shoulders in the strapless top. She said she and Deb look drab.'

'That's ridiculous, Shirley is supposed to be this oh-so-serious actress, Deb is a Las Vegas hotel owner, I'm the Goldie Hawn-type floozie, we're all totally dressed in character.'

'I know,' he shrugged. 'I guess we gotta tone you down.'

Several days later I was told I couldn't wear the black lace 'Merry Widow' and would have to cover it up in a dress – completely outrageous! Maybe a touch of green eye here? Rather annoying, but Nolan and I had a good laugh about it.

Wednesday, 11 October 2000

These Old Broads finished shooting. I was sad to say goodbye to everybody, particularly Elizabeth, who I knew was very ill, and I wondered if I would ever see her again.

Friday, 29 December 2000

Took the 10.45 to Geneva, then Valentino's driver picked me up to drive to his gorgeous chalet, Gifferhorn, in Gstaad. Met by Giancarlo, handsome and debonair as ever, Marina Palma, Nati Abascal and the emperor himself, the fabulous Va Va.

Valentino Garavani.

The chalet is literally to die for, a feast for the eyes. It is so exquisitely decorated, every single inch suitable for a photo shoot in a digest, which, of course, all Va Va's houses have been in.

V is gracious, charming and anxious to hear all the gossip from London and LA.

GG teases me about the number of furs I've brought. I told him that Switzerland and Russia are the only places one can wear fur now without being slut-shamed or having red paint thrown all over you.

Lovely party given by Vivien Duffield and her boyfriend, Jocelyn Stevens. Taki there and we reminisced about our little romance in NY in the sixties.

Sunday, 31 December 2000

New Year's Eve. Valentino threw the most gorgeous, lavish black-tie party at the chalet. Divinely decorated, as were all the guests. Stayed up late, a great time.

2001

January 2001

Desperately trying to finish my fourth novel, *Star Quality*, but since I have not yet entered the twenty-first century in terms of computers (I can't even type), all my manuscripts are written in longhand, so need to be typed and printed.

The woman who usually did this for me in LA was not available, and I was frantically trying to find someone who could decipher my hieroglyphics, when Percy Gibson suggested that he could easily do it.

So he came to the apartment at ten o'clock and transferred everything to my computer.

Two weeks later, February 2001

I had appeared in an episode of *Will & Grace* and they wanted me to do another one, but they wouldn't send me the script, although the start date was imminent.

Eventually the script arrived the night before the first table read, and it was dire. I'd wanted to do it because it was a terrific show, and I'd enjoyed the last one, but to play a woman who insists on having an operation to get her shoulders extended by eight inches was frankly ludicrous.

'I can't do this,' I wailed to Alan Nevins. 'They want me to play a woman who gets a shoulder transplant, for God's sake. It's utterly ridiculous, but I want to do the show. Do you think they'll rewrite it?'

Next day Alan spent a morning of fevered talks with the *Will & Grace* producers, but they flatly refused. The gist of the conversations with Alan was 'Who does Joan Collins think she is? She's not doing *Dynasty* any more and we're a hit show. We're hot and she's not. Tell her we won't rewrite and she's gotta do it the way it is.'

When Alan told me on the phone, I became extremely upset, and broke down in tears. Mercifully, Percy was there with a tender shoulder to cry on.

Before we knew it, we were in each other's arms, and what we had both been thinking about for the past seven months finally happened.

It was the moment I always felt would occur one day and it was just wonderful.

Saturday, 10 February 2001

So now I was having a fully fledged passionate affair with Percy, who was quite honestly sweeping me off my feet. It was giddy, it was fantastic, it was all the romantic fairy tales that young girls dream about, but I was not a young girl. I was a woman in her sixties in love with a man in his thirties.

We tried to keep it a secret, but a few of my friends started to suspect, as we both had that heady glow that comes from being in love.

He was the best lover I had ever had, and I knew that the kind of passion we had for each other was terribly special; truly once in a lifetime.

Monday, 12 February 2001

Now Robin Hurlstone was eager to visit me in LA, but I kept putting him off. I had the perfect excuse of my looming deadline for my novel, *Star Quality*, so I told him I was writing morning, noon and night and that Percy was putting it all on the computer for me, which is true.

But Robin decided to come anyway. I was in a frightful bind. Should I tell him before he flew to LA? Should I wait until he arrived? Should I not tell him at all?

Robin solved it anyway. He and Charles Duggan flew out to LA to surprise me. They had only told me the day before that they were coming, so I was in a state of high anxiety.

Wednesday, 14 February 2001

Nolan Miller had a screening of an early print of *These Old Broads* for twenty of our friends at his LA apartment. Robin and Charles came, as did Percy.

It was an interesting evening, to say the least, particularly when the two first met and sized each other up. I sensed that male feeling of two stags at bay.

I was completely agitated as I tried to concentrate on the movie, sitting between Gore Vidal and George Schlatter. I thought the film was cute and entertaining, but I bet the critics hate it.

Saturday, 17 February 2001

Charles came to my apartment for drinks and I bustled about fixing them for him and Robin, being cheerful and chattering away.

I mentioned several times how well the book was going and how helpful and wonderful Percy had been, when suddenly Robin fixed me with a beady, accusing eye.

'This Percy fellow, you seem to talk about him a lot. Have you got a crush on him?'

'A crush? Don't be ridiculous,' I spluttered, but I literally felt my face flame. I don't think I had blushed since I was a teenager, but blush I did, and it was a hot crimson-faced one.

'My God, you're blushing! Look, Charles, she's blushing, it must be true, then.'

Charles, who had of course been with Percy and me all the time on tour, could not have been that surprised, as he had remarked on our friendship several times. 'She sure is,' he laughed. 'Maybe it's just the wine.'

Later that night, after Charles had left, I confessed everything to Robin. It was one of the most difficult things I have ever had to do. For someone who hates confrontation and hates even more hurting people close to me, it was intensely traumatic.

Sunday, 18 February 2001

Left for New York to do press for *These Old Broads*.

Robin stayed behind in Los Angeles, in my apartment.

Producer and sports promoter Jerry Perenchio had offered me a ride on his beautifully equipped private plane, which had been remodelled and decorated to seat just thirty passengers, in total luxury.

Although Jerry wasn't going to New York, there was a group of his American football associates on board. When I boarded, the flight attendant escorted me to a palatial stateroom, with a double bed and huge TV. 'Mr Perenchio wanted you to be comfortable,' she said, smiling.

I relaxed with a Bellini and rang Judy to tell her the events of the previous night. It had been extremely distressing to confront Robin with the news that I had become seriously involved with Percy, but I have always tried to be honest with people and tell the truth.

I could never do what a famous actor-friend of mine had done when he wanted to end his long-term relationship: he told his agent to tell her, 'It's over – give back my keys.'

Much as I loathed hurting people, it was clear to me that the Hurlstone relationship had been frozen in a not very mutually rewarding rut for several years, and that Percy and I had fallen madly in love. I didn't know what the future held, but I felt so strongly about him that nothing else mattered.

As the plane took off, and I saw the shoreline of Santa Monica far below us, I noticed a stream of yellow fluid coming out of the plane's fuselage.

'The plane looks like it's sprung a leak,' I joked to Judy.

Then there was a knock on the cabin door and an agitated attendant stammered, 'We're sorry, Miss Collins, but we've developed engine problems and we have to dump fuel over the ocean and go back to base.'

I was horrified and, coupled with my emotional state of mind, I burst into terrified tears.

Back at the terminal we were told that the plane couldn't function, and we were to be put on a smaller plane. The crew told us that Mr Perenchio was 'very upset and doesn't want to ruin your trip'.

I called Jerry, who was absolutely mortified. 'We've never had any problems with this plane in the ten years I've owned it. I guess I'll just have to buy another one,' he joked.

And even though I was upset, he made me laugh. I've always loved how the truly rich live, especially when they appreciate it.

Jerry's stand-by plane to New York was quite small, and as I sat between his football friends I couldn't stop crying; I had hated hurting Robin and I felt I was being unfair to Percy with my vacillating and refusing to commit. The football pals asked me if I was OK, and, drying my eyes with my second box of Kleenex, I assured them it was just a bad case of hay fever.

February–March 2001

Met with Robin again, in my London flat, to reiterate that I wanted to end our relationship. He did not take it well, becoming upset and insulting about Percy and calling me ghastly. I reiterated how upset I'd been when he had refused to accompany me to Buckingham Palace when the Queen would give me my OBE in 1998.

'You said "I'm not going to bother for a silly OBE. I'd go if they would give you a damehood,"' I reminded him.

Not a happy evening.

Decided to go to Forest Mere, a health farm, and retreat for the weekend to make the final decision about what to do.

After three days of staring zombie-like at the ceiling, thinking back over my years with Robin and what kind of future I had with a man who not only couldn't stand most of my friends, my family and my children, but who also made me feel insecure, I made my decision.

Robin Hurlstone packed his toothbrush (which is all he ever kept at my flat), and shortly afterwards Percy Gibson and I left to begin our new life in New York City.

And when people said to me 'What about the age difference?' I blithely replied, 'Well, if he dies, he dies!'

Sunday, 25 March 2001

LA Oscar night: 73rd Academy Awards. Watching on TV at home.

The annual Oscar Frocky-Horror show was a pleasant surprise this year. The lollipop ladies, with their enormous heads and social X-ray bodies, stayed at home, and the coast was clear for a dazzling array of old-time Hollywood glamour.

Led by Julia Roberts and Catherine Zeta Jones, the majority of the actresses were as elegantly dressed and coiffed as yesteryear's movie queens, Grace Kelly and Ava Gardner.

Most of them seemed actually to have washed their hair, eschewing the straggly, greasy, rats'-tail look so beloved by Hollywood 'stylists'. Many of these latter-day self-titled ambassadors of fashion wouldn't know style if it were served alongside their decaf cappuccino.

There were, however, a couple of ghastly exceptions. The singer Bjork was persuaded to dress as a dying swan, complete with lolling head and beak, in a creation that wouldn't have looked out of place perched on a Skegness landlady's spare loo roll, while Juliette Binoche was being strangled by a surfeit of faux-pearl necklaces, cascading down her chest to her thighs, and hideous Toulouse-Lautrec laced-up boots.

But the full horror was the silicone-lipped/-breasted Pamela Anderson. Revealing all the taste and refinement of a hooker on holiday, she chose to buck the system in denim hot pants and teeny-weeny white shirt, which struggled bravely to contain her pneumatically false assets.

Accompanied on one side by her camp, pink-shirted 'stylist', and on the other by our own dear Elizabeth Hurley, she brought trailer-trash fashion right into the twenty-first century.

At the end of the evening, she and Liz announced that they

were about to take a jacuzzi together. The mind boggles. Oh, Liz, you really need Hugh to get you back on track. Who will be your big date next year – Mickey Mouse?

I was delighted that Russell Crowe won Best Actor for *Gladiator* and Benicio Del Toro Best Supporting Actor for *Traffic*. They are about the only actors in movies today who have the macho he-man appeal of a Clark Gable or Spencer Tracy, and I bet they're not 'in touch' with their feminine side.

Monday, 16 April 2001

Well, P & I are finally 'coming out' properly. Connie and Randy Jones threw a fabulous cocktail party for us at their stunning Park Avenue apartment. Amazing balloons on ceiling and a spectacular guest list: Ivana T, Kitty Hart, C. Z. Guest, Phyllis George, Bianca Jagger, Carolyne Roehm, Marylou Whitney and George Hamilton. Percy loved it and I love him! So did all the ladies!

The news slipped out that I'm going to do *Moon Over Buffalo* in London.

April 2001

Tara was mugged last month. Not at midnight in a dark, nefarious alley or near a run-down council slum; she was mugged in broad daylight, waiting, with her baby in a pushchair, at a bus stop in Maida Vale.

Tara was one of the lucky ones. The mugger didn't bash her about and break a few bones, as so often happens in these cases. He just viciously ripped the gold watch off her wrist, causing shock, pain and bruising, but fortunately no lasting physical damage.

I was in New Zealand, working on a movie, when she rang.

When I told members of the crew what had occurred, they expressed amazement that not only does such an incident happen in one of the most supposedly civilised countries in the world, but it is considered a quite common event. There is little crime in New Zealand, and the denizens of Auckland can go safely about their daily life without the gnawing anxiety that thousands of innocent Britons who have been attacked and mugged are forced to live with.

London is now the crime capital of the developed world, and no one is doing a damned thing to stop it. Since Labour took office four years ago, street crime has soared and is expected to rise even further.

If New York can solve its street-crime problem, as Mayor Giuliani did several years ago, by adding 28,000 cops to the 12,000 in Manhattan, why can't Ken Livingstone do the same for London?

I live in SW1, an area of London that several years ago was considered so crime-free that the powers that be decided to close the Gerald Road police station, the only one in our vicinity. Since then, there have been dozens of muggings in my neighbourhood, including a particularly brutal attack on John Aspinall and his wife, as well as on the *Spectator*'s exceedingly fit columnist Taki.

At a charity event at the Savoy recently I asked Ken Livingstone what he was going to do to clean up London's streets. He gleefully informed me, 'I'm determined to get all private cars off London roads.'

'So how would I have travelled to this event?' I enquired, dressed as I was in full evening drag.

'You'd take the bus or Tube,' he gloated, 'or go by bike.'

Thanks, Red Ken, and how on earth am I supposed to pedal a bike in Jimmy Choo stilettos and white chiffon?

Thursday, 12 April 2001

Took the one thirty BA flight to New York and was delighted by our new digs at the Flatotel on West 52nd Street. Even though it's a hotel, it has a cosy 'at home' feeling, so this is Percy's and my first home together!

After my sojourn at Forest Mere, to try and put my life in order, I'm so delighted and happy that I chose to be with Percy. And I'm not listening to the horrid gossips who say it will never last.

Monday, 16 April 2001

Our first public appearance together, at the GLAAD awards. We took my friend Jack Rich of Tommy Hilfiger with us for support. He said it was the right thing to do, as we had to make our relationship public eventually.

Masses of press and photos and the usual stupid questions about the age difference.

I wore a black chiffon Nolan blouse and pants, and P. in black tie looked majorly handsome.

An amazing astrology forecast in this month's *Vogue* for Gemini: 'Time to settle down, and become a contented Cinderella, complete with Prince Charming, castles and solid values like commitment and patience.' Wow! Hope it's true.

Just realised I've been a working actress for fifty years. Is this something of a record?

Tuesday, 17 April 2001

Premiere of *Moulin Rouge* at Paris Cinema, West 58th Street, given by *Vogue*. Quite a gala evening and I loved the movie:

Nicole Kidman, so gorgeous, and Baz Luhrmann made it a feast for the eyes and ears. Ewan McGregor was excellent too.

When we arrived at our aisle seats they were occupied by a very large man and his date. Even though P. showed him our tickets he refused to move. He sat hunched over in his seat, staring blankly at the blank screen, totally ignoring the pleas of the usher to move, 'because you're in the wrong seat'. What a putz. Eventually the usher had to show us to another pair of seats.

I was surprised that the very large man was Donald Trump, who I've known since he and Ivana gave me a fabulous launch party at Trump Tower for my perfume Spectacular in the mid-eighties. Well, I was very popular then, not so much now, but nevertheless to pretend he didn't know me was rude.

The party after *Moulin* was quite good, even though we were seated at Harvey Weinstein's table and didn't know most of the people. Seeing Harvey eat was not a pretty sight, he literally slobbers!

Friday, 27 April 2001

Kenny Lane gave a lunch for Princess Michael of Kent at his small apartment on Park Avenue.

Very chic guests including Princess Ariana von Hohenlohe and her sleek man-about-town husband Dixon Boardman, and the legendary Mrs (Brooke) Astor, who at the age of ninety-something took a shine to P. and flirted outrageously with him. I thought she was adorable, funny and so chic.

I like Princess Michael, even though she talks a lot; maybe that's why the press call her 'Princess Pushy'. She is a lot nicer than they like to make out.

Saw *Rocky Horror Show* at the theatre with P., Jack and his boyfriend. Such a scream.

Friday, 4 May 2001

Flew to Cincinnati at the invitation of Marylou Whitney and her much younger husband, John. Older woman, younger man; seems quite in vogue these days!

P. working, so went with Nolan. Stayed at Brown's Hotel in Louisville. I love Nolan, he's a fund of fascinating anecdotes about actresses from Joan Crawford to Barbara Stanwyck to Lana Turner. Told him he should write a book.

The Black-Tie Charity Celebrity Ball was packed with celebs from Kid Rock to Bo Derek, Roseanne Barr – her usual loud and vulgar self – Crystal Gayle and, to top it off, Miss Pamela Anderson, a vision in hooker-chic. As usual it was fairly dull; all celebs were on best behaviour.

Saturday, 5 May 2001

Kentucky Derby Day. Very exciting, even though I'm not a pony lover. Marylou gave a lovely lunch, also attended by Helen Gurley Brown and others. I lost on the gee-gees, as usual.

May 2001

Robin has taken to encouraging our mutual friends not to see me any more. It seems to have worked with John Richardson and Hugo Guinness and the Bamfords. It's sad, after twelve years, that he is so spiteful. He also refers to me as 'That ghastly woman'. Charming!

First there was 'road rage', then 'air rage', and now I've witnessed a new phenomenon close up: 'shopping rage'.

My friend Jack Rich, who like me majored summa cum laude

in shopping, accompanied me for a day of NY boutique brows-
ing, which we liken to fishing trips.

We spent twenty minutes with a salesperson in a Fifth Avenue
store, carefully selecting various items, then followed him to an
empty till, where he began totting up our catch.

'Hey, man! What the hell are y'doing?' yelled an angry voice,
from the back of the queue, behind the other till.

The salesperson muttered that he'd been helping us and started
to ring up my purchases with my card.

'Hey! Hey! Hey! You must be star-struck, man. We was here
first. Let Alexis get in line behind us.'

I turned to see a very big and very angry young man, with a
chip on his shoulder the size of Texas, oozing fury. My glance
seemed to enrage him even more, as he continued to berate the
hapless salesperson.

'Get me the manager! You ring that store manager, right now,
d'you hear?'

The five poor wretches in front of him hung their heads in
embarrassment, trying to pretend they weren't there, while my
salesperson continued totting up.

'You're a star-f***er, that's what you are. A f***ing star-f***er.'

The guy was rabid by now. If he'd been a dog, he'd have been
foaming at the mouth.

I didn't need to hear any more venom. Any second I expected
a .45 to be pulled and I could see the headlines: 'Actress Dead in
Shopping Shoot-Out'.

I grabbed Jack's arm and my plastic from the salesperson, and
we left the building.

Not cowardice, believe me. I simply wouldn't have been caught
dead at The Gap.

Friday, 18 May 2001

Sardi's for dinner with Percy and Jack.

The Manhattan theatrical restaurant, owned by Vincent Sardi, is renowned for its walls crammed with hundreds of framed caricatures of 'above the title' thespians, from the early twentieth century to the present day.

Depending on their box office grosses, the Great White Way's most popular current stars will have their cartoons, now brilliantly executed by Richard Baratz, displayed prominently in either the foyer or at eye-level in the ground-floor dining room.

Dominating the entrance are Susan Stroman, choreographer of the absolutely fabulous mega-hit *The Producers*, and Reba McEntire, the eponymous heroine of *Annie Get Your Gun*.

Reba is a joy in her show, and when we had dinner together last week I was astonished to learn that she had never acted on stage before this January, even though she's been one of the most popular female Country & Western singers in the States for years.

After dinner, Percy and I went on a quest for my own drawing, done while I was on Broadway in *Private Lives* in 1992. Not surprisingly, I found myself upstairs, relegated to a frozen Siberian tundra, populated by long-forgotten theatrical names, of whom the only one I recognised was John Barrymore, directly to my left.

Friday, 25 May 2001

Attended a screening of *Pearl Harbor*, dined again at Sardi's.

Just as coffee was being served, a fat orange cockroach, who had taken up quarters under the urn, skittered across the pristine white tablecloth, bold as brass.

I emitted a girlish scream and Percy gallantly swiped the horrid little arthropod on to the floor, where it sought refuge under a neighbouring table.

The bug-eyed occupants of the next table had clocked the entire action, and the women went into Victorian 'Damsel-in-Distress' mode, daintily lifting their skirts, and their legs, out of the way.

The maître d' rushed to our table to assure us there would be no bill, and that this was a most uncommon occurrence.

'I suppose they usually stay in the kitchen,' I remarked.

A few nights later we called Sardi's to book 'a cockroach-free table for six, please' – which was greeted with a distinctly humourless attitude.

But, lo and behold, as soon as we entered the foyer, there was my caricature, in pride of place, sandwiched between Reba and Susan Stroman.

I've since decided to hire the cockroach as my agent.

Monday, 28 May 2001

Memorial Day dawned fair and fine, and Percy, Jack and I gladly accepted the invitation of Admiral Don Hayes to visit the aircraft carrier *John F. Kennedy*, docked at Pier 36 on the West Side of Manhattan.

The fleet had been in town for several days and the streets thronged with young sailors of different nationalities savouring the Big Apple's traditional 'Fleet Week'.

The ship was certainly a memorable sight, twenty-three storeys high, with four acres of flight deck and a crew of 5,200 able-bodied men and women.

On the dock, little stalls sold JFK baseball caps and T-shirts in anticipation of the throngs who would tour 'Big

John', as it is affectionately known in navy circles, that afternoon.

We were fortunate to be offered a private tour, during the time that crew family members were invited on board. It was, to say the least, impressive and quite exciting, culminating in lunch with the admiral, in the officers' mahogany-panelled private dining room, surrounded by paintings depicting eighteenth-century naval scenes.

I commented on how extremely well decorated the room was, to which the admiral proudly responded, 'It's all due to Mrs Kennedy. When this ship was finished, the First Lady came on board, and didn't like the dining room, with its austere white metal bulkheads, one bit. "This doesn't do justice to the president's memory," she told the captain. "I'd prefer the walls to be panelled in mahogany." "I'm sorry, ma'am," said the captain. "No American warships are allowed to have wood in them. It's flammable." "What would it take for this dining room to be decorated in mahogany?" she asked. "An Act of Congress, ma'am," the captain replied.'

The admiral sipped his iced tea and continued. 'So guess what?' he grinned. 'Two days later a bill was passed in Congress stating that only ships that are christened *John F. Kennedy* were allowed to have their dining rooms panelled in wood.'

That Jackie sure had the power and she sure knew how to use it.

Incidentally, the US Navy is the only 'dry' navy in the world. We were told the crew is allowed two beers on board, but only after they've been at sea for more than forty-five days.

After seeing the sheer magnitude of firepower on board, I can appreciate that you wouldn't want any drunk drivers at the helm.

As the admiral escorted us off the ship, the queue of people waiting on the dock for their tour was almost a mile long. 'How much do you charge for the tour?' I asked, brazenly capitalistic.

'Ma'am, the American taxpayer paid for this ship. The least we can do to give back something, is to let people visit for free.'

'And, just out of interest, what are the operational costs per year?' I enquired, thinking of the seventy planes, gallons of petrol, and twenty thousand meals consumed daily on board.

'One hundred million dollars, ma'am,' said the admiral, smiling proudly.

Hefty tab, I thought, especially since I found out it takes them three weeks to sail to the Mediterranean. Surely any war would be over by then?

2002

January 2002

I always knew that the popular press fudged the truth, but my recent engagement revealed to me just how they fib with fantastic fanfare, and how frenetically fanciful they can be.

The truth seems not to enter into their concoctions. The *Evening Standard* printed, on its front page, that while lunching at an Italian restaurant on New Year's Eve, I announced that I had been married to Percy that morning.

According to other patrons (whose names are conveniently withheld) the happy couple (that's us) 'flashed their wedding rings' (which didn't exist), 'quaffed champagne' (which I abhor), 'ate lobster' (which I'm deathly allergic to) in a '£600 meal' (which is ludicrous for a lunch).

Although my PR, Stella Wilson, called to deny this claptrap, several red-tops ran the story the following day, quoting those impeccable sources – two bus-boys and the restaurant owner, who garnered a ton of publicity for his spaghetti joint, which we had patronised only because the greasy spoon across the street was jam-packed.

Then the 'Showbiz Editor' of the *Daily Mail*, Alison Boshoff, printed the same story, plus various other fabrications the following day, refusing to reveal her 'impeccable sources'.

These turned out to be a *New York Post* mention, based on a series of fake email messages, purporting to be sent by a 'close family friend' but in fact sent by a person (or persons) unknown, who faked email addresses for people in our family who don't even know how to work a computer.

Talk about the bad fairies not being invited to the christening. Venomous and spite-filled as these emails were, it didn't prevent the newspapers from printing them without checking the source.

As a matter of fact, far from checking these apocryphal tales, they were embellished and reused by, among others, the *New York Post* columnist Neil Travis and Cindy Adams.

Monday, 11 February 2002

Full page, yet again, in the *Evening Standard*, written by Harriet Arkell revealing that we would be spending our honeymoon in a £92-a-night quaint bed-and-breakfast on the outskirts of Auckland. This, too, was immediately repeated as fact by the many sheep masquerading as reporters in the press.

Then, out of the rotting woodwork crawled Glenys Roberts, sixty-five, a hackette for the *Daily Mail*, who had a certain cachet with a group of my friends some thirty-five years ago when she was married to the popular Mayfair tailor Doug Hayward.

This woman had done a couple of hatchet jobs on me and people close to me before, so I was no longer on speaking terms with her, but she had the unmitigated gall to call herself 'one of my closest friends'. Having intrusively doorstepped some of Percy's and my relations and friends, she wrote two pages of tripe about what a mistake my marriage to Percy would be and how my friends were horrified, then sauntered into P's mother's care home to interview her, pretending she was a close friend of ours!

Because I've been an actress since I was sixteen, most of these jibes affect me like the proverbial water off the fowl's back, and since Percy has broad shoulders we countered by sticking two metaphorical fingers in the air and sent legal letters denying their allegations and lies. Once, we even got a retraction – in small print – on the back page.

But it certainly did affect other people in our lives. Just because I've married Percy, why should his relatives be placed in such an untenable position?

People talk about freedom of the press with regard to celebrities and the duty to put them under the magnifying glass, but what about the freedom of those who are related to or are friends of celebrities? Why should they be exposed to the glare of the spotlight?

Early February 2002

The run-up to the nuptials and I'm super-excited. Several F-list celebrities whinged to the media about not making the cut.

One person, who would go to the opening of a root canal, has protested that as he is yet another of my closest (or was it closet?) friends, he therefore deserved to be on the guest list. I found the whole thing amusingly bitchy, yet rather pathetic. Get a life, dear.

Nolan, Rene, Mark, Kenny J. Lane, Lynn Wyatt and Linda and Peter Bren flew in for the wedding. Nolan bringing my gorgeous pale lavender dress.

Late February 2002

After our wonderful wedding came the honeymoon, and Malaysian Airlines, which boasts flight attendants as glamorous as any fifties film star, and airline cuisine that is hard to top, flew us not to a B&B in New Zealand (who'd ever believe that?) but to Kuala Lumpur in twelve hours, without turbulence but with lots of caviar.

We were then transferred to Pangkor Laut resort, an idyllic island, where we now languish hedonistically on the most gorgeous private beach in the middle of the Indian Ocean, complete with golden sand, emerald sea, our own pool and all mod cons. It's heaven, and I'm relishing every lazy second.

* * *

Monday, 9 December 2002

Bumped into Mr Trump again, coming out of the Minskoff Theatre, after the opening of *Dance of the Vampires*, starring Michael Crawford. Mr T. had obviously heard that we are house-hunting in NY. He patted P. on the shoulder and boomed, 'You gotta come and see my new apartments opposite the UN buildings, they're great.' He also congratulated us on our marriage and was extremely friendly – unlike last time we met.

One week later

Went to see Donald Trump's apartment. The huge building is unbelievably windy because it's opposite the UN building. The apartment was small, badly designed and altogether nothing special, but over-priced as usual.

'Mr Trump will give you a special price,' confided the realtor.

There was no closet space to speak of, which is no good for me with my amount of clothes and masses of cases. It's really just a pied-à-terre for UN ambassadors. 'Mr Trump would really *love* for you to live here' trilled the realtor. 'Do you watch his show?' 'No,' we said, and scurried off. Who *does* he think he is?

December 2002

There are many things I love about New York, but one of the most attractive is the enthusiasm and joie de vivre possessed by many of the population, from the cheery Korean deli on Lexington to the sleek sophisticated vendeuses at the Fifth Avenue boutiques, New Yorkers seem to be bursting with unbridled optimism in spite of 9/11.

I'm thrilled with our new apartment on 57th Street, but cab drivers on the whole are sullen, surly and often verge on the abusive. In New York, Mayor Bloomberg has attempted to ease congestion by creating 'through streets' (or 'thru streets' as the quaint efficiency of American English requires) every six or so blocks.

On these 'thru' streets, drivers are not allowed to turn left or right until they reach a considerable distance from where they first turned, the aim being to give drivers who want to go across town a thoroughfare. Similarly, the main avenues are closed off to right or left turns into these streets in order to ease the flow of traffic.

This has *massively* increased congestion in NY, and horns honk ferociously all day long, but at least Bloomberg admits that it's an experiment and if it doesn't work by the New Year it will be a relatively simple job of removing some misspelled signs.

I have been roundly criticised by some of the press for 'deserting' to the United States recently. The more boring truth of the matter (and therefore less saleable for the press) is that I have always been fortunate enough to keep a place in the US, and I had merely exchanged the dubious smoggy delights of LA for the razzle-dazzle of Manhattan, where I've spent the past three months slaving away on a daily soap opera called *Guiding Light*. To say it was hard work is like saying Jihad is a bit of a bore.

Acting in a daytime serial in which fifty-five minutes or more of taped film must be shot daily is the showbusiness equivalent of boot camp. I haven't worked so hard, or felt so pressured, since I was raising my three children all by myself.

I had thought that a prime-time serial like *Dynasty* was reasonably tough, since we had to get fifty minutes of film in the can in six days, but that was a sun-kissed holiday on the Riviera compared to 'daytime'.

To commit to memory anything from fifteen to forty-five pages of dialogue *every day* you need the mind-bending concentration of Uri Geller and the stamina of an SAS operative.

There is no proper rehearsal time, which as any actor knows is essential. When the time comes for blocking camera moves the mayhem from the lighting crew and technicians manning the cameras makes concentrating on not getting clocked by the boom mic an imperative, never mind the lines.

We then 'dress rehearse' three or four or five scenes, which take place on the same set, and immediately shoot these scenes one after another without a break.

This is like performing half of the first act of a play without rehearsals, and it is admirable that the wonderful actors with whom I worked do it so seemingly effortlessly. I consider it a great accomplishment personally that I was able to keep up from day one.

'You get used to it after a while,' grinned Ron Raines, who has been in *Guiding Light* for nine years. 'You train your short-term memory to learn all this stuff real fast and then by the next day you've forgotten it, but even after nine years it's still pretty tough.'

2003

Sunday 27 July 2003

Sad to hear about the death of Bob Hope, although hitting 100 is a fabulous record: almost like batting 1000.

I worked with Bob several times on his television variety shows and in a movie, *Road to Hong Kong*, with Bing Crosby. In the four previous 'Road' films, Dorothy Lamour had played the female lead but in *Hong Kong* she was deemed by the Hollywood hierarchy to be too old at forty-seven, so I was cast to play Bing's love interest at almost forty years his junior. Bing was taciturn and grumpy through most of the movie, in stark contrast to Bob, who was a bundle of laughs all shooting-day long.

Reportedly one of the last jokes he made two weeks before he died was on his birthday: when asked, 'How does it feel to be a hundred?' he quipped, 'Up until noon I don't feel a thing, then it's time for my nap.'

What a trouper – he'll be missed.

Early August 2003

The sizzling temperatures of the past week are breaking all known records, so I've spent most of my time in my pool and the oasis of air-conditioning in my bedroom.

I live high in the hills a few miles from St Tropez and we've had several bad scares.

Last week, the forest fires came within a mile of the villa, so the local *pompier* decided, through some marvel of French logic, to ensure our safety by putting a large lock on the barrier of the access road from my house to the main road, thereby effectively annulling our escape route had the fire caught in the forest surrounding us.

The Mistral winds were tearing along at 80 miles an hour, and coupled with the 100-degree heat and the smell and sight of smoke, I was, well, scared.

Saturday, 16 August 2003

Blair is pulling a Mugabe and rigging the referendum on the Euro. His plans to allow 700,000 non-citizens living in the UK to vote on whether or not we must have this pesky little currency are cynical, to say the least. Since the French adopted the Euro, the cost of running my house in the South of France has risen by almost 30 per cent.

Everything has gone up so dramatically that one can only summon a Gallic shrug and mutter 'C'est la vie'. The bill for two cafés au lait at Sénéquier comes to €10, when it used to be a couple of pounds not long ago. Groceries are much more expensive than in England. I was charged €8 (roughly £6) for six lemons at the St Tropez market, and this in a country where lemons are local produce.

This currency looks and feels like stage money, and I find it impossible to differentiate between a €1 coin and a £1 coin. I've joined a committee that demands a fair referendum, in the hopes that the voice of Britain will be heard. Let us pray.

Tuesday, 19 August 2003

One fallacy about St Tropez is that it's constantly jumping with celebrities, though indeed one or two can occasionally be spotted: Liam Neeson and Natasha Richardson venturing down from their house in the hills for a dip in the unpolluted sea, Rod Stewart plus leggy blonde Penny jumping off a boat and clowning around for the paparazzi before sitting at the wooden tables at Club 55.

'Auntie Joan!' he yells, bright orange shirt flapping in the breeze.

'Uncle Rod!' I respond from under my floppy hat that keeps the sun's deadly rays off my face. 'Why don't you wear orange?'

'Why don't you wear a big hat?' he grinned. I've known Rod from the seventies when we'd play charades at Jackie's.

Friday, 24 October 2003

Today was the last flight of Concorde. I was thrilled to be going on this historic trip, but gutted that this fantastic plane will now be mothballed forever. It meant so much to so many business people, who could leave London early morning, arrive in New York for lunches and meetings and take the magic flight back to London in time for dinner.

P. and I arrived at JFK as instructed at 6 a.m. It was dark and empty. 'Are we the first?' I enquired of the charming special services representative.

'No, you're the last,' was the reply. 'The party's been going on for hours.'

We checked in without luggage, which in itself is a personally historic event. I managed to pocket a couple of Concorde luggage tags, which I understand are now selling on eBay for £17, along with various other mementoes from the iconic aircraft, including memorabilia catalogues, safety cards and a bathroom sign. God only knows how they took that off.

Going through security I bleeped – too much bling – and was then subjected to a rather undignified and barefoot body search, which would have been normal except for the mass of New York press that awaited us. Fortunately, they gallantly declined to photograph the humiliating experience.

In the departure lounge there was a party atmosphere. Luminaries and celebrities quaffed champagne and gave interviews to the eager American and British press.

I said how tragic it was that this magnificent piece of cutting-edge technology was going to be phased out and I hoped that another company, perhaps Virgin Atlantic, could keep it going, as had been reported.

Just before embarking, I popped into the loo, and while combing my hair, was asked by a nervous BA press officer if I would do her a big favour. 'But of course,' I replied graciously. 'Do you have a pen?'

'Oh, I don't want your autograph,' she said, 'but would you mind not mentioning Richard Branson?'

When the flight was called, the entire New York British Airways staff lined up to say their goodbyes to everyone, most of them with a tear in their eye. It seemed as though the entire airport ground staff had stopped what they were doing and stood on the tarmac to wave and cheer.

On board, champagne was passed around lavishly as we privileged few buckled up and prepared for the last ride.

I clutched my husband's hand as the brakes were released and the power of a sudden 250-mile-per-hour acceleration lurched us against the back of our seats, as if we were in some insanely powerful hot-rod competition, and then the plane majestically soared into the air like a beautiful and graceful prehistoric bird.

The passengers were an eclectic group. One couple had paid £40,000 for the privilege; there were several businessmen who had crossed the Atlantic at least twice a week for God knows how many years; there were also a few prize-winners.

Back in steerage (although all seats are considered equal) sat some distinguished members of the press, along with a sprinkling of ageist hacks.

The dancer Darcey Bussell helped start the autograph-collecting frenzy, and the staff did a game job manoeuvring trolleys and trays down the tiny aisle while battling TV cameras and photographers.

Suddenly Jeremy Clarkson, in a snit, threw a glass of water all over *Mirror* editor Piers Morgan, and there was so much hilarity that Piers implored us to come back and join the fun.

We attempted to get back, but there was such a crush of people that it was impossible. Then, as we approached Heathrow, the announcement brought a sense of solemnity to the cabin. Everyone fixed their gaze intently out of the windows as London passed underneath. Cars stopped on the M4, and people waved at us from the fields. The flight attendants walked down the aisle, bidding 'God speed' to the regular faces they had become so accustomed to seeing once or twice a week on that NY-LON run, thanking them for the memories shared.

Everyone felt slightly choked up when we landed on that runway, seeing those thousands of people who had turned out to say 'Goodbye' to their favourite, never-to-be-replaced aeroplane. A memorable experience.

2004

Sunday, 22 February 2004

Pickings are extremely thin on the ground for this year's Oscars. I don't particularly like any of the nominated films, and the few I thought had merit did not get a look-in.

However, there is one stand-out performance in an excellent movie. Charlize Theron as the eponymous Monster gives simply the best performance I've seen since De Niro in *Raging Bull*. Shorn of her make-up and eyebrows, wearing false ugly teeth, a mottled complexion and stringy hair, and having gained thirty pounds, this ravishing beauty is nothing less than astonishing, in not only her physical but her character transformation as well. This performance goes far beyond last year's prosthetic nose. If the Academy Award voters don't give Charlize the gong for Best Actress next week, then there ain't no justice.

Speaking of performances, the great musical comedy star Ethel Merman had a London musical written about her entitled *Call Me Merman*, which I heard thrilled audiences and which I'm sorry I missed. Merman was not only a great belting performer, but also a witty lady, as evinced by this exchange between herself and her then husband, whom she loathed, Ernest Borgnine.

Upon returning home after an audition with a producer, Borgnine asked Merman, 'So, what did he say about your fifty-year-old face?'

'He thought I looked just fine,' replied Merman.

'And what did he say about your fifty-year-old tits?' he asked again.

'He said they looked fine, thank you,' she again replied.

'And what did he say about your fifty-year-old ass?' he insisted.

'He didn't mention you!' came the reply.

Funny she was, but even she was trumped by the outrageously camp Tallulah Bankhead. After Merman enthralled Ms Bankhead's listeners on her live radio programme, *The Big Show*, with a rousing number, forty-seven-year-old Bankhead said of her forty-two-year-old guest, 'Thank you, daaahling, that was wonderful! And, may I say, you don't look a day over sixty!'

Even Merman had to laugh.

Saturday, 28 February 2004

I've always considered myself a working actress, and like about 98 per cent of my fellow thespians spend a great deal of time 'resting' involuntarily. It therefore irks me when great swathes of the media refer to actors disparagingly as 'luvvies' and represent us as parasites and narcissists who love swanning around and dressing up.

I've just started rehearsing *Full Circle* with the nicest, most hard-working and dedicated group of performers you could find, and that is how (with a few exceptions) I've found most working actors to be.

Because they love working in a vastly overcrowded profession they often get paid far too little. For rehearsing six days a week, eight hours a day, and often spending extra hours going to fittings and learning lines, we are all receiving the Equity minimum of just over £300 a week, which is a lot compared to a pensioner's £102 per week, but I believe is on the low average for the nation, and certainly a complete joke when compared to my accountant's rate of £650 an hour!

Thursday, 18 March 2004

I am discovering that travelling in the United States has become more and more tedious, particularly the endless and intrusive security procedures.

I'm often unlucky enough to be picked out for those euphemistically titled 'special searches' (due to my obvious resemblance to Mr Bin Laden, no doubt) and I try to endure them with stoic indifference as I stand there, coatless, shoeless, hatless and sunglass-less, arms akimbo. Meanwhile the officer, wearing the grim, sadistic expression of an Alcatraz security guard, runs what looks very much like a cattle prod far too close for comfort to one's private parts.

It is not what I would term a good look, particularly if some sly soul who's just gone through the procedure takes a couple of snaps sneakily on his cellphone, which he'll probably email to his mates.

Nevertheless, refusing to do a Diana Ross, I close my eyes and think of England as the indignities of having the contents of every piece of carry-on luggage examined minutely are executed.

At one airport in the States last month, an amiable searcher, having examined the contents of my jewellery case in detail, remarked pleasantly if a bit too loudly, 'You got some nice stuff there!'

While his partner nodded in agreement, I yelped, 'It's all fake!' Which it was.

'Looks good to me!' his partner said.

Although I can't blame airport security for being extra vigilant, it can nevertheless be extreme, as demonstrated by the minor horror story I was told when leaving LA this weekend.

A woman was about to walk through the X-ray machine, holding her eighteen-month-old child, when she was stopped by a brusque security guard.

'Can he walk?' he enquired of the infant.

'He's just learning,' she replied.

'If he can walk, then he's got to walk across by himself – that's the rules,' he stated with the authority of a Gestapo commandant. 'Put him down.'

'But he doesn't like walking,' protested the poor woman, as the baby was wrenched from her arms and stood on its feet.

Armageddon ensued. The poor little chap started bawling his little lungs out. The frantic mother was rushed through the sensor to encourage him to follow her, which he steadfastly refused to do, unable to comprehend why he'd been so unceremoniously dumped on the floor. Then in protest he plonked himself down on the ground, still screaming, while a gaggle of adults, including the security guards, tried to coax him through the X-ray machine.

In spite of his mother's continued protestations that he was not ready for this terrifying toddler trial, the officials insisted, and after several minutes of cajoling, the distraught infant managed to cross the barrier under his own steam. At this point the buzzer went off and the sobbing child had to be thoroughly body-searched because the rivets in his little jeans set the sensors off.

Meanwhile several adults were allowed through without the barest flicker of the fairy wand, much less a request to remove their scarves.

Saturday, 29 May 2004

I haven't been on a bus since I was eighteen, but last week in the suburbs of Birmingham I had no choice.

I'd gone to an afternoon movie with Nickolas Grace, who is also in *Full Circle*, and when we came out the temperature had dropped to below freezing (in April).

Gamely braving the frigid air, we searched for a passing taxi while trudging the three miles back to our hotel.

'Niko, I don't even do walking in the summer,' I huffed, the wind so cold that my teeth ached.

'Right, let's grab a bus, then,' said he.

'A *bus*?' Dame Edith Evans would have been proud of my incredulous inflection.

But before I could protest, Niko hauled me on to a passing double-decker and dragged me to the upper regions. My trench coat dragged on the corkscrew stairs as I stumbled up them. A few passengers glanced at me, but red-nosed and baseball-capped I bore scant resemblance to the glamorous creature we passed on the posters plastered all over the town.

Several women were excitedly discussing plans to see the show the following night, as I slid further down into my seat, pulling the cap over my years.

Sunday, 10 October 2004

As soon as we got off the plane at Heathrow, my driver told me the sad news that Christopher Reeve had died. His persistent struggle to recuperate after a tragic accident, which at the height of his career would have left anyone else's morale utterly devastated, was truly inspiring.

He was a true gentleman of the old school, always charming.

When I first met him at a movie premiere in 1983 I was with Katy, who like all girls at her young age was smitten with Superman. He was utterly delightful and took plenty of time to take pictures with her, which she cherishes.

Since then we saw each other here and there, until last year when I attended two events in New York for the Christopher Reeve Foundation for stem-cell research.

He was calmly dignified in his motorised wheelchair, and still full of joie de vivre and charm, in spite of the ravaged state of his body. He gave the most electrifying and moving speech for half an hour, without the aid of breathing apparatus, modulating his mellifluous voice with controlled breathing, and mesmerising us with his piercing blue eyes and sweet smile.

I am thankful I have that last image to remember him by.

Wednesday, 13 October 2004

In the run-up to hailing a new chief, I've been riveted to the three presidential TV debates.

Democratic candidate John Kerry seems to have a kind, Lincolnesque statesmanship, peppered with a hint of 'Lurch' from the Addams family, while Republican incumbent George W. Bush still looks like a smirking jerk.

The late-night chat-show hosts, David Letterman and Jay Leno, make great sport of these two, while on another channel Jimmy Kimmel strikes comic gold by showing clips from the debates and interspacing them with footage that would show someone holding a cue-card from behind the camera, instructing Bush to continue saying 'a . . . a . . . a' ad infinitum or 'blink like a baby bird', which is a strikingly accurate way of describing his shell-shocked facial expression.

Apparently, the female vote is mightily important now, and it is said that women will be voting for the candidate they would most like to wake up with in the morning, which means that with that large cross-section of the population there is still no good choice.

Saturday, 13 November 2004

I broke my toe in Minneapolis. This is far from the glamorous image of leaving my heart in San Francisco, and infinitely more painful. I stubbed it on a faux-Chippendale dining-room table leg, during a breakfast meeting at the hotel.

It was a hot September morning and the traffic on the motorway was gently buzzing outside, when my toe knocked against the raw metal end-claw of the table leg, which was sticking out menacingly, and my howl of pain pierced through the almost bucolic setting.

After an X-ray at the local hospital, the doctor said, 'Yup, it's a severe fracture and the metatarsal [or something like that] is dislocated.'

'What can I do?' I wailed.

'There's nothing you can do with toes except wait. Only time heals toes.'

Hobbling in sandals back to NY and various meetings I soon realised, as autumn cast its gentle glow, that I could not cram my foot into any of my stilettos, flat shoes, boots or even sneakers, since my right foot had swollen hugely. Off I went to Saks for a restock and re-fit.

After two weeks of considerable pain every time I put any weight on my foot, Percy insisted on whisking me off to the number one foot-man in New York, Dr Rock Positano. Anyone with a name like that is bound to rise high in his field, and Dr Rock was no disappointment.

After examining the toe, he told me the doctor in Minneapolis was wrong and should have insisted I keep it iced twice a day and my foot bandaged all the time. Needless to say, with the bandage on, I now need shoes two sizes bigger, and so another shopping rampage was afoot.

2005–2007

Spring 2005

Percy and I meet Ben Sprecher in New York, a producer ac-
quaintance of his. Ben is a short, bald man with what I suspect
is a strong Napoleonic complex. He wants to do a play with me
on tour and then bring it to Broadway. He sent over several of
them, and we finally decided on *Legends*. It was done in 1986
with Carol Channing and Mary Martin and went on a very successful, if difficult, tour which didn't come to Broadway. *Legends*
reads well, although it needs a lot of updating and some major
rewrites.

Over the summer I made several suggestions for revisions,
and Percy and I worked on lines to try and make them funnier.
John Bowab, our director, and Ben said they loved everything we
did, so it was incorporated into the show.

Fall 2005

I wasn't thrilled when Ben suggested Linda Evans should play
Leatrice. I don't think she is a fan of mine, at least if nine years
in *Dynasty* is anything to go by. We never socialised (even when
she gave parties) and seldom spoke on set. Ben assured me that
wasn't true; he'd spoken to Linda, who was 'fond' of me.

'I don't believe her,' I said. 'She needs the work, and for God's sake she's never been on stage at all. Why can't we get Debbie Reynolds, Barbara Eden or Michele Lee, all of whom are dying to do it, or any one of the dozens of names we haven't approached yet?'

'The bookers want her,' Ben said firmly, so that was that. But I had great foreboding. I want this tour to be fun, and I don't think it will be with her.

Spring 2006

Ben asked me if I would be willing to speak to the group that books all the touring Broadway shows. Presenters from all over the country come to buy shows from producers who are trying to sell them. Ben introduced me on stage and the response was audible. I improvised a spiel about how wonderful our show would be, and how much the public will love it. The audience cheered. Ben told us that that afternoon alone he filled all the gaps in the thirty-week tour, with calls from the Niederlanders and the Shuberts – hurrah!

August 2006 – New York

Linda turned up at the first rehearsal with cosmetic surgery tape on top and under her eyelids and under her chin! Naturally, the cast all pretended to ignore it, but it was obvious she'd come straight from either the facelift doctor or a car wreck. She also has plump Botox enhanced lips, epitomising 'trout pout'. It's quite off-putting to have to look at that face, which used to be so pretty, and pretend not to notice.

I scored a *Harper's Bazaar* layout for *Legends* through my friend, editor Glenda Bailey. When the issue came out, I asked Glenda why the pictures had been so heavily retouched. She sighed and said, 'We had to, because Linda's face needed so much retouching and she would have looked like a mannequin next to you if we hadn't retouched you as well.' Everyone who sees Linda is completely shocked by how she's spoiled her beauty, and now she's back in the limelight stories and photos appear in the tabloids showing the bad effects her plastic surgery has caused.

Linda always had a 'jock' attitude on the *Dynasty* set. She's proud of it – 'I love to fight. Barbara Stanwyck taught me to do my own stunts on *Big Valley*. I don't do car wrecks or falling off buildings but fighting with another woman is not a problem for me.' Well, hah-hah and thanks, Linda, but *this* woman was taught by Gene Kelly, who told me: 'Never do your own stunts, kid. First it's dangerous and second, you're putting some poor stunt girl out of work.' I subscribe to Kelly's theory, having been sent to the hospital during an over-enthusiastic bout of catfighting with Krystal on *Dynasty*. 'You can't do the kind of rough-house fighting you do on film on the stage,' I told Ben, 'I'll get hurt.' I voiced my concerns to Ben and John, but they pooh-poohed them.

Ben Sprecher promised to get the best fight director in New York to work on the scene. During rehearsals, I demurred at several things the fight director wanted. I couldn't figure out why we were being asked to run rapidly around the set several times, pushing and shoving each other hard, actually hitting each other over the head with pillows and swatting each other in the face with our wigs, which we rip off each other's heads. Wasn't a fight director supposed to *simulate* all of the above without anyone having to be in danger of falling over on the set? That is an obstacle course. The rug is raised two inches above the ground, and chairs and tables are all over the place. I didn't think we'd get to the first night without an injury, never mind the 300 other performances. I was therefore not surprised to discover that the person our esteemed producer had brought in was not a fight director at all but an attractive choreographer, who was hired at the insistence of our not very attractive director.

I refused to let Linda rip my wig off on stage because the wig is pinned to my real hair and by the end of the run I would have ended up bald! I refused to do anything that I felt was dangerous, so finally things were staged so that neither of us could get hurt. Linda, however, insisted on doing a hard fall off the sofa on to the floor. Let's see how sanguine she is with *that* after thirty weeks!

In New York rehearsals, Linda seemed nice and vulnerable about being on stage for the first time. She actually broke down in tears in front of Percy. The entire cast pulled together around this 'rookie' stage actress and helped her with the million details one has to deal with before going on tour, so she could concentrate on conquering her fears. I helped her with her stage make-up and wig, found her an acting coach, and tried to give her advice about stagecraft and what she should concentrate on. In general, everyone did their best to make things easy for her. I asked the director to help her with her projection, as it was almost impossible for actors to hear her on stage, as there is no microphone support. The audience might hear her, but her fellow actors couldn't!

As time wore on Linda improved and grew in confidence, although the acting coach said, 'Her body language is awful, and she has very little stage presence.' To try and boost her morale, Percy and I invited Linda and her assistant Bunky out for dinner three times, but she declined every time.

September 2006

Once we got on stage in Toronto during technical rehearsals, Linda started to get her sea-legs and her confidence ballooned. This was a welcome sight to the producers, but unfortunately what tends to happen when an unseasoned actor feels comfortable on stage is that they seem to forget that it is a live show. During our first preview, Linda had a piece of blocking which required her to give me a small shove off a coffee table. Stagecraft dictates that the actor creating the physical action is passive and the one receiving is active, so I would act that this 'push' would propel me off the coffee table and on to a chair. Unfortunately, Linda's confidence had grown to the point that she gave me an almighty shove that really sent me flying on to my knees to the floor. The thud was so resounding I heard the audience gasp in sympathy. Percy told me he was standing next to Ben at the time and even he said, 'Ouch!'

I spent the rest of Toronto needing therapy on my left knee, due to the bursitis caused by the impact. The move was restaged, although I noticed nobody was willing to acknowledge the incident, and Linda never even asked if I was OK – it was as if nothing had happened. We had to restage the fight scene to cut down on the running around I had to do, in order not to aggravate my injury. However, the second night, during the fight scene, she threw my wig at me with the accuracy of a sniper – I had to duck to prevent it from striking me in the face.

A few days later, Linda stole a piece of business I had developed. This is an absolute no-no in showbusiness. In one scene I would peel a banana and then take a bite out of it while discussing husbands, which got a big laugh. One night she reached over and took the bite before me, which stole my laugh. Anyway, the director said it was equally funny, so why didn't

346

we just let her do it? Figuring a laugh's a laugh, I agreed.

No one seems to be pointing out to her where she's going astray, so she naturally concludes it's OK to do anything she likes.

I keep trying to think of new business because I realise this play is not as good and 'actor proof' as I'd first thought. John Bowab, the director, *seemed* competent, but he's not giving any of the cast interesting business or interpretation. We are set adrift while he puts all his energies in trying to give Linda help with motivation and projection.

Thank God he is starting to cut some unnecessary dialogue, but it doesn't seem enough. Apparently, the author's estate is keeping a close eye on what changes we make and have given Ben and John (at least, so they tell us) a hard time, and that's why they keep resisting when I tell them a line isn't funny or is not working. There is a *long* way to go to make this play any good.

The audience likes what we're doing but I'm obsessed with the play becoming better and funnier. I'm making suggestions all the time, coming up with things I can do to make it better. Percy keeps saying to me that I can't do it all, but faced with no one else seeming to do anything, I can't help it. Besides, Ben Sprecher keeps saying that a lot is riding on this for me – more than anyone else. Little creep. If he really believes that, why would he put so many obstacles in my way?

Thursday, 14 September 2006 – Toronto

Linda scrapes a spoon across my chin on stage while I'm speaking. How stupid. You *don't* invade another actor's space or touch their face – not without telling them beforehand. This stage is an obstacle course. The carpet is laid on a motorised 'pallet' which brings the set downstage two feet or so. Our carpenter has maintained from the start that this is an unnecessary expense. You have to watch every step so that you don't trip over it – not easy when you're running around in high heels. I said I didn't like the set when they showed us the model, but this is Ben's plaything and he's such a little tyrant he will accept no dissension. I thought the set would look like a glamorous Art Deco/Sutton Place apartment, but it looks more like a cheap antique shop.

Friday, 15 September 2006

Linda and I fly to LA to do a *Larry King Live* promo for the show. I had managed to get us on because they had wanted us the previous spring for the *Dynasty Reunion*, but I was in the UK, so I had suggested that we go on to promote *Legends*. At the studio Linda is with her assistant Bunky and her manager/agent, Mike Greenfield, whom I dislike. He is an ugly, rough man who curses at every opportunity, has the manners of a sloth, and slinks around glaring at everyone. On one occasion he had to leave the *Dynasty Reunion* set because he was cursing and yelling at someone on the phone while we were shooting.

Larry began by asking for our reaction to the death of Aaron Spelling three months earlier.

I said, 'He's done so much great TV, they used to call ABC Aaron's Broadcasting Company.'

We talked about the *Dynasty* reunion and I was nice about John Forsythe, even though I know he wasn't fond of me.

Amazing how every interviewer always asks the same dreary question. 'How did you get the part?'

Well, not on the casting-couch for sure! But I told the same old story about playing Cleopatra on *Fantasy Island*, and Aaron insisting on me for Alexis, even though the 'suits' at ABC didn't want me. They wanted Sophia or Liz Taylor – especially Jessica Walters.

Larry asks us too many questions about *Dynasty* and not enough about *Legends*. He wonders if we had fights on the show. Oh dear me, another original question, but they showed some great clips from *Dynasty*. Wow, those outfits were superb!

Another stupid question: 'What is the appeal of *Dynasty*?' Oh, please! 'It was lush, glamorous entertainment about rich people suffering,' I said.

Linda said, 'We talked about homosexuality, not done then on TV.'

'Are you *Dynasty* divas?' asked Larry. We rolled our eyes.

'Who decides who gets first billing?' he asked. I diplomatically replied, 'Oh, Larry, it's simply alphabetical.'

Larry then read a question from a viewer who admired my hairstyles but wondered whether it is my own hair or all wigs.

I replied, 'I see actresses who always display their own hair, and they have about a quarter of the amount of hair after being in movies for ten or fifteen years that they had at the outset. Working under lights with hairspray and the rollers is the worst thing you can do, so I decided to wear wigs from the start.'

Larry said, 'You're an honest broad'. Ouch! A bit sexist, *n'est-ce pas*?

As we wrapped up the interview, I noticed Greenfield 'the Toad' slinking up to Percy and bending his ear. Afterwards, I ask Percy what he had said. Percy replied, 'He said he wants to talk to me privately. I'll set up a meeting tomorrow.'

Percy didn't tell me the content of his chat with the Toad until after the tour was well under way, because he knew it would upset me and probably lead to me not wanting to share a stage with Linda. The Toad started the conversation by saying, 'Joan was the only client I ever fired.' Percy was taken aback and said, 'I wasn't aware you ever represented her.' [He never did.] He was obviously trying to get under Percy's skin, but Percy didn't bite, because a confrontation with him at this point would have been disastrous, and no doubt exactly what the Toad wanted. He kept goading Percy, saying things like 'Everybody says your wife is beautiful, but I hate her, and she can't act.' Greenfield laid out a variety of ultimatums, boiling down to 'You had better keep your lady in line and not let her pull any diva shit or Linda will be very unhappy.' Percy was furious and said, 'I have worked with Joan for over five years and my wife is nothing but professional, punctual and hard-working – but she will not be bullied.' The Toad left him with a sour aftertaste. Percy told Ben that neither he nor I would have anything more to do with him. I'm aware that Greenfield has always hated me, but I have no idea why.

Late September

Linda and I got in a couple of battles because the fight scene at the end of Act One wasn't working – mainly because she's trying to put her wig back on after I throw it at her. I keep saying this is unfunny (the audience certainly isn't laughing) and is holding up the next action, which is to grab cushions and hit each other over the head, releasing feathers all over the stage (reminiscent of our first *Dynasty* fight – my idea) and prompting the curtain to fall on Act One. One night, fed up with no one telling her to stop doing this, I threw her wig off the balcony so she couldn't get to it. It got an enormous reaction from the audience, but she was understandably pissed off!

In Act Two, Linda was obviously still angry because she

decided to exit the stage while I'm standing alone, delivering my lines. As a result, I was forced to extemporise until she decided to come back. I heard not a peep backstage about her actions, only a weak 'she doesn't know better' from the stage manager.

Saturday, 30 September 2006

Percy convinces me to make a truce with Linda, and so I do, and we become quite 'pally'. For several days we bond, she asks my advice and I give it, we visit each other's dressing rooms to discuss the play and how we could improve it. I keep thinking how great it would be to have another actress like Michele Lee or Barbara Eden, both of whom are theatrical pros and would be up to the quick-fire repartee that our characters should have. Linda's lines trickle out like molasses.

Nevertheless, the audiences seem to love it and it looks like it may be a hit – at the box office anyway.

Thursday, 5 October – one week before opening night

Katy and Peter Charlesworth arrive and come to see the show. Backstage, Linda comes over to Peter and asks, 'Are you Joan's agent?'

'That's me,' Peter replies.

'Well,' she sneers, 'you must have a STRONG constitution!'

I can't give Linda points for original wit, since it's a line from the play, but she gets full marks on bitchiness. So, I shot back, 'You must have a strong constitution yourself to have Mike Greenfield as *your* agent.' Mike Greenfield, the Toad, is still a complete pig.

Sunday, 8 October 2006

It's great to have Katy here but John Bowab, our director, and I have a big fight on the phone as I beg not to have to work near that damn vacuum cleaner whose wires are laid out across the stage like a giant octopus, waiting to tangle me in its tentacles. I send him and Ben a page of suggestions for improvements, which he ignores.

Tuesday, 10 October 2006

Still waiting for Bowab and Scumbag Sprecher's comments on my notes. I feel sidelined. Ben was quite rude to me on the phone – 'I can't be bothered with this actress's attitude.' Considering that a year ago he was consulting me constantly about rewrites and decisions, and sending me flowers, it's a huge shift.

When I told John that my agent PC thought my notes were good, he said cuttingly, 'Well, I'm your director and I don't.' Charming.

At least I managed to get my blocking changed in two scenes. Thank God.

Friday, 13 October 2006

Opening night went really well but the following night, Friday the thirteenth, was a downer as usual. Things are getting tense between Ben Sprecher and Percy, and also between John Bowab and me. He shouldn't be allowed to direct traffic. It's obvious from the way he deals with me that he dislikes me – always talking over me and dismissing *any* observation I have. He cut my new line yesterday – the one where I re-enter holding Linda's wig and quip, 'Plastic hair, plastic face!' Apparently, it was a bit too close to the truth, even though he and Linda have come up with the most awful ageist lines about me, which they throw in without warning.

Sunday, 15 October 2006

We gave a fabulous party after the matinee for the cast and crew, then Percy finally spilled the beans about how appalling Ben and his management have been, and how he doesn't understand why I'm being persecuted. Percy let me read all the stage manager reports and I was shocked and hurt. 'Joan was nervous in the first scene'; 'Joan was testy during rehearsal' (why not mention the director got testy first?) and on it went, making judgements about my personality and performance. A stage manager's report is meant to be a statement of facts, not a critique or psychological evaluation of an actor.

This reinforced my feeling that some people in this company really have it in for me.

Monday, 16 October 2006

The reviews came out. I didn't read them, but Percy told me they were beyond bad. Thankfully, they all seemed to quite like Linda and me, but they were scathing about the 'mothballed script' and the 'ham-handed direction' – and they're right!

How am I going to get through another twenty-five weeks of this? God give me strength.

Tonight, I confronted the stage manager about his constant nit-picking in the reports. He told me that he was asked by Sprecher to report every single infinitesimal detail about my performance. When I ask him why I've been singled out for this and not Linda, he says, 'Because Ben said there's nothing we can do to improve Linda's performance.' I was appalled.

I thought this play was going to be so much fun, but it seems that sides have been drawn. Now, if I don't go *all out* 100 per cent on the performance, Linda goes even slower on hers, and the whole show really goes down the tube, then I get the blame.

Tuesday, 17 October 2006

I was feeling quite sick tonight and the stage manager again reported that I was 'paraphrasing' and missed lines. I may have done, but I certainly wasn't the only one. Linda and another actress admitted to having missed lines. Besides, you could leave the theatre and go have dinner during the pauses she has between lines and there was not a peep about that in the SM report.

Thursday, 19 October 2006

My hand is in agony because Linda kicked it last night. When I pushed her onto the sofa, her pointy boots shot up and smashed into my hand. I had tried to dodge the boot several times in the past, but knew it was just a matter of time before it would connect. I got hit in the elbow once before, and the wrist before that, but I just suffered in silence. I had told Sprecher and Bowab that this was a dangerous move and one of us could get hurt, but they ignored me. I put my foot down and demanded we have a proper fight director to re-choreograph it. Ben called me in a complete rage, saying it was impossible to change this choreography and I had to continue in spite of my injuries – what an unprofessional asshole.

As a result of the injury I had to wear a bandage on my hand for three days. When Linda tried to hold my hand at curtain call, I whispered through clenched teeth, 'I can't.'

'Why?'

'Can't you see my hand is bandaged?'

Linda shrugged and sailed off without even asking if I was OK. When a reporter asked her about my bandaged hand a few days later, she sniffed, 'Well, we didn't have to call the paramedics.'

Little sympathy too from the director and producer about a potentially serious injury, just fury that they have to now hire a proper fight director to make the fight scene work safely.

Tuesday, 24 October – Philadelphia

This theatre has ridiculous backstage arrangements. Apparently, when they built it, they forgot to put in dressing rooms! They had to buy the building next door to make rooms there. The result is that actors have to walk down two flights of stairs, cross a long hallway, then climb up another two flights to get to the stage. The other option is to walk across the alley with gale-force winds and twenty-degree weather outside. Either way it's a misery.

Percy and I travelled to Philly from New York, where I went on three morning shows. Ben is quite upset about the reviews (so am I!). Because they stress the play is so bad and the direction 'inept and limp', Ben is trying to hire a 'play doctor' – please God!

Linda and I are barely speaking. She has never apologised for kicking me in the hand and injuring my finger.

On opening night in Philadelphia, I went out in the alley for a quick cigarette with Laura, my dresser, and I could hear Ben screaming at Percy further down the alley. Apparently, it was one of the nights that I had not given my usual 100 per cent performance and he was beside himself with rage. 'I thought he was going to hit me,' Percy said.

Thursday, 26 October 2006

The stage manager reports still seem to favour Linda. Whenever she does something good it's recorded, yet not a mention when she screws up. By contrast, everything I do wrong is mentioned. Ben will come backstage and say things like – 'You're the engine of the show' or 'You were fantastic, I really love all your choices' or 'Thank you for all the publicity you're doing, the press only really want you', but this never gets reported, only the bad things.

Sunday, 29 October 2006

I just found out that Linda has not been performing the curtain call as directed. I turn upstage while she is taking her bow, then Linda is supposed to do the same when I take mine, however she doesn't! I don't have eyes in the back of my head, so only now do I realise that for the last forty performances she's been standing behind me grinning at the audience while I take my bow – un-fucking-believable.

Monday, 30 October 2006

After Ben came to the first night in Philadelphia, he said he would call me. He still hasn't, one week later. In the meantime, I'm doing a lot of press, which we desperately need. A new company manager was brought in to meet Linda, but not me! John Bowab came to the matinee, went to see Linda, and not me! On top of that I noticed that Ben has deducted one performance from my salary, because we only had seven performances instead of eight last week, but he hasn't touched anyone else's salary! I'm really pissed off about that. He says it's because I'm one of the producers, but he hasn't taken any off his own producer fee – it really shows I'm being singled out for bad treatment.

My friends Randy and Connie Jones came to see the show. After they visited my dressing room, they bumped into Linda backstage. 'Everyone always comes to see Joan, but no one comes to visit me!' she bleated. 'Maybe it's because she hasn't many friends!' said Randy.

Thursday, 2 November 2006

Barry, the new fight director, came to re-direct the fight scene, but Linda and I had a verbal fight on stage. She has no under-standing that physical activity might be difficult for others, so treats me with contempt because I won't duke it out with her. She's always talking about 'motivation' and 'things that are good for the play' as if she's Dame fucking Edith Evans and the play is fucking Ibsen. What a pain she can be – she wasn't like this on *Dynasty*. She's insisting I press the switch on the vacuum cleaner (which we can easily fake to prevent me tripping over the jungle of cords *she's* arranged). Otherwise, she says, it 'hurts the intention of the plot'. Oh, please!

At tonight's performance, Linda tries to upstage me! From little Miss 'Oh, I don't know what I'm doing onstage' to trying to upstage me! She plays the wide-eyed Miss Innocent part, know-ing that people will buy into me being a bitch. She gets a lot of help from her Toad-Manager to promote that fable.

Saturday, 4 November 2006 – last weekend in Philadelphia

Jerry Zacks, one of Broadway's best directors, came to see the show, with the possibility of re-directing it. Afterwards he came backstage and spoke to me at length. We really see eye to eye, and I think he is so right about everything. 'The script sucks, it's not funny enough'; 'The relationship between the two characters has not been explored enough' (indeed, because Bowab was spending all his time with Linda and not any with the rest of us); 'There are no highs and lows, and Linda is very weak.' He wants to gut the show and start again, which I am 100 per cent in favour of. God, I regret ever agreeing to cast Linda. Everyone (critics especially) thinks it's just cashing in on *Dynasty* – and they're right. I wish I hadn't been talked into it and so does Percy.

Tuesday, 7 November 2006 – Hartford

A simply horrible review in the Hartford paper, terrible for the script and direction. Oh, God! twenty-one and a half more weeks of this! I don't understand how the critics can trash it so much, yet the audiences seem to love it.

Saturday, 11 November 2006 – last day in Hartford

I was beginning to think that perhaps Linda wasn't as devious as I thought she was, when she invited the entire cast out to dinner with her – everyone except us! Guess our invitation was lost somewhere backstage. This, after she came to every one of our parties and dinners, was incredibly rude. This is exactly what used to happen during *Dynasty*. I would invite her to all my parties, and she would never, *ever* reciprocate.

On the bright side, a fab review in another paper.

Wednesday, 15 November 2006 – East Lansing, Michigan

What a dump! And freezing cold, and of course I get sick. Don't know what happened but I got shaky and my legs and arms felt like cotton during the show. I was also very upset by an email

Ben sent me, accusing me of 'changing all kinds of lines and dialogue'. I wonder who is misreporting this. I tried *one* new line, *with* the blessing of the stage manager. Am I supposed to call him in London – or wherever the fuck he is kissing Kevin Spacey's ass – every time I come up with an idea? I was really upset with him on the phone, fuming and raging. Poor Percy got the brunt of it from Ben: 'Keep your wife in line.' How dare he! I wish I could quit, but Equity could sue me.

16–17 November 2006

By Thursday I was feeling worse. Staggered to the theatre after spending the day in bed and had the most horrible first act – could barely stand, walk or say my lines. Towards the end of Act One, I almost fainted, then collapsed backstage. Everyone decided I should no longer go on, so I missed Act Two.

On Friday I went back to the doctor. Two doctors examined me and ran tests – apparently I am suffering from a viral infection, probably brought about by utter exhaustion and stress – my battery has run out of gas. Their advice: 'Don't go on tonight.' That way I can maybe, just maybe, do the four shows over the weekend. Relief tinged with some guilt, but frankly I feel Ben Sprecher has done this to me with all his nasty phone calls, emails and generally vile behaviour. Why doesn't he go let some steam off on 'Dame Edith' with her endless pauses, slow delivery and tiny little voice that no actor can hear, much less understand? Ben and Bowab's excuse has always been 'You're right, but there's nothing we can do about her' – I wonder how she ever got to be an actress? It's really sad that Percy and I were so excited about this show and now after only one third of the tour we are thoroughly despondent. The trouble is there's no leader. Bowab has gone (and was useless anyway), and Ben's idea of leadership is to bully everyone into submission. Plus, he's just thrilled to deduct my salary from the performances I miss because I'm sick. Pretty soon it'll be like I'm paying for this show to be on.

Friday, 24 November 2007 – Washington

It's the day after Thanksgiving. My driver doesn't know the way and ends up taking me to downtown DC. It's like that scene from *Bonfire of the Vanities*; we're right in the middle of what looks like bombed-out Beirut when he stops in the middle of traffic and tells me he's lost, which doesn't exactly put me in the best of moods – a complete nightmare. It was the *one* day Percy stayed home to work on another project. I was quite terrified when we had to pull into a gas station where two cars full of young Turks were eyeing me menacingly as I went in to ask for directions to the White House (I knew they wouldn't know where the theatre is). I finally arrived at the theatre five minutes before curtain, after an hour in the car.

My nerves are not helped by 'Dame Edith', who has decided to put in a few extra lines during and at the end of the show. I don't care about the extra lines during the show. I like to be told ahead of time, but apparently, she decided on the spot. This is rude – I always inform stage management if I'm going to add a line – but I handle it.

However, inserting a line just before curtain without warning anybody is downright dangerous, because of what happens after it. The curtain has to come down, I have to step upstage so that it won't hit me in the head, lights have to go out and music needs to go on. Yet everyone is paralysed because no one was expecting another line from Linda. I complained to the stage manager, who said he'd speak to the bitch.

That evening – same thing! Not only that, but this time she even spoke *over* my last line. She certainly has projection when she wants it! When I got off stage I called out, 'Linda!' She ignored me, so I yelled, 'Linda, you can't say an unscripted line before the curtain falls without telling us.' She had the gall to respond, 'Well, you're putting lines in all the time.' We had a contretemps in front of the entire company. 'I think we should sort this out now,' I said, but she replied, 'I've got better things to do!' and stalked off. 'I don't think that's very professional,' I said. She turned back, her face like Linda Blair in *The Exorcist*, and a demonic croak came out of her mouth: 'Well, you're unprofessional!'

I was furious. It's one thing to qualify someone's specific behaviour as not professional, and quite another to call the person unprofessional. I realise now who the snitch has been – Linda! Complaining to Ben for weeks. I remember 'the Toad's' ominous warning to Percy before we started rehearsal – 'Make sure she doesn't pull any of her diva shit!' But Miss Evans is doing just that, *and she ain't no Edith!*

Sunday, 26 November 2006

After a couple of tense days on stage with Linda during which it's all I can do to look at that Botoxed face, I can't remember the word 'ruthless' during one of my speeches, so I pull 'devious' out of thin air and continue with my line. You would think World War III had broken out. John Galo and Ben Sprecher were on the phone immediately to Percy *screaming* how DARE I change lines and make up dialogue. Percy got into a real fight with Ben, defending me: 'She forgot one word, *one word*, Ben!' but apparently it had got into the stage manager's report that I was changing *several* lines.

Ben is trying to intimidate me. I've *never* been treated so horribly in all my years in this business. Percy and Ben had another yelling match on the phone on the *only* day off we have. Ben decides to create a shitstorm then. He takes his own weekends uninterrupted then gets on the phone with either Percy or me on our day off, ensuring that we have no rest and that our only possible time to enjoy it is absolutely ruined.

I was so upset, I feel my health is being compromised. I can't sleep well, and my indigestion is getting worse. There is no other recourse for me than to put a call into Actors' Equity to keep Ben from harassing me. I simply can't take his irrational and threatening behaviour any more. Why, after so many years in the business, am I being picked upon and treated like a villain by management and producer alike? We've got two more weeks before the Christmas break so I'm just going to get the words out and fuck all of them.

December, Christmas break

Equity has ruled that no one but the director is supposed to give an actor notes, thankfully bringing an end to Ben's insane phone calls and emails. If only I'd known sooner!

However, there's a new problem. It turns out that Linda has been stewing that I'm sitting quietly upstage of her during her 'big moment' and John and Ben want me to sit downstage for it. Originally it was staged to get me out of Linda's way, so she could take her moment. But that's not good enough for 'Dame Edith'. Apparently, she needs a face to 'relate' to onstage so that she can get the 'emotional' springboard for her speech. I said I'll sit wherever they want. Whatever keeps the peace.

Sunday, 14 January 2007 – San Diego

Our first big rehearsal after four weeks' break and I'm more than a little apprehensive. I suggest I sit downstage so we can fix Linda's problem and she can look at my face for the emotional scene and, hey presto! – problem solved in two seconds.

Friday, 26 January 2007 – Los Angeles

Director and stage manager summon Percy and me to Linda's dressing room because I'm apparently upsetting her again. I have discovered a funny piece of business, which the director, stage manager and producers praised me for, and it gets a great reaction from the audience. I've been doing it for two weeks and it turns out that Linda's been silently fuming because again, it 'cuts into her moment'. Actually, it's well before 'her moment', but the powers that be have decided that mollifying 'Dame Edith' is more important than making sure the audience enjoy themselves. So the meeting in her dressing room immediately disintegrates into Linda giving me a bollocking. Not one to take kindly to that, it quickly turns into a screaming, slagging match between the two of us. Again, she uses that word 'unprofessional' at least four times (as if she knows what it means). I suggest that she uses the same fervour and passion on the stage, telling her, 'I've seen nothing but your same low-key performance since Toronto, and it's getting boring for me and the rest of the audience.' Well, that infuriated her, so she retorted with: 'Well, you're so unprofessional that Frank Langella slapped you on the stage!'

I was mystified at that point. I *had* worked with Frank Langella, and *I* had slapped *him* on stage, but it had nothing to do with professionalism or unprofessionalism – it was something the director had devised in our drunk scene. I finally saw that this meeting was convened only to pacify Linda. She wants me to give a metronomic performance, with every line, pause and inflection *exactly* the same every night. That's no way to act. You have to keep it fresh and organic within the boundaries of what was directed. I'd talked to Frank Langella about the value of that, and how an element of unpredictability may be necessary to keep things fresh, and agreeing the parameters beforehand. I'm so disgusted with all these so-called professionals who are catering to the demands of an actress who has *never* been on stage before!

I finally asked Linda what I thought was the most pertinent question at this point: 'Why did you do this play? Were you so desperate for work?' She had no answer. Thank God, Percy chose that moment to say to me, 'This is getting nowhere, and we have to get ready for a show.'

I told Percy, 'I can't understand why Linda and John Bowab and John Galo can't just tell me what's bothering them at the time, instead of letting it stew for weeks and having it come out in such unproductive ways. It's like they *want* to aggravate and upset me.' He had no answer but was so great at soothing me.

To make matters worse, I've been asked to play a role in *Desperate Housewives*, which I can't do because of this junk.

Sunday, 11 February 2007 – Denver

Great quote: 'Over sixty-five you understand life is too short. I want to make a vow about people I don't want to see, work I don't want to do. I don't want to throw my life away!' Well, working with 'Dame Edith' is sure a trial. Today at the matinee, during my tender aria about the day my mother caught me looking at my ass in the mirror (hard to do tenderly), Dame Edith kept craning her scrawny neck to look at my ass. This, coupled with that perma-startled look of the surgically enhanced, caused great titters and guffaws in the audience. So much for her respecting my 'moment' – complete upstaging of the kind she accuses me of. She's been told not to do this but every now and then tries to get away with it, so I finally turned and said, 'Had a good look?' She then decides to slap me on the butt! Typical Linda – she isn't smart enough to think of a retort, so she resorts to physicality. I asked Galo to report what happened and back he came with his standard answer whenever Linda misbehaves – 'I didn't see it.' He is completely on her side.

I asked Galo where he got this untrue story about Langella slapping me and he said, 'Ben Sprecher told us.' What a slimy bottom-feeder that man is. I told my agent Peter. When he called Ben to ask him if he was spreading this malicious rumour, Ben replied, 'Yes, I did. So, *what*?' and hung up. This is our alleged producing 'partner'.

Monday, 12 February 2007

Ben deducted money from me arbitrarily in October and is refusing point-blank to pay it back. Every time we bring the subject up, he gets more and more insane. Had a long talk with Barbara Berkowitz, my lawyer, to see if there is any way out. Ben said to my agent the other day, 'I *want* Joan Collins to sue me!' I'm considering it, but frankly it's a sign of his irrational mindset. He even threatened PC with: 'I have partners on the show that would sue Joan just for the fun of it.' What an unprofessional little runt.

Tuesday, 20 March 2007 – Cleveland

My knee aches, my finger throbs and is swollen to twice its size and I've got indigestion due to stress. I look horrible and I've gained seven pounds because I'm too exhausted to even exercise. This experience has almost cured me of my love for live theatre.

My pink silk Nolan Miller suit has shrunk so much from cleaning that I can barely move. The skirt, which was well below my knees is now well above them. I spoke to Nolan, who said that although it's an Equity ruling to have replacement costumes on a long tour, Sprecher refused to allow any replacements to be made. He also snapped at him saying, 'I'm not spending another five dollars on her clothes!!' Funny attitude, considering he cast someone known for glamour and good dressing. Conversely, he overspent $30,000 on the scenery, which the stage manager once told Percy is 'his toy'.

So, Nolan suggested I wear one of my own suits, which I'm now doing.

Unbeknown to Linda, who thinks we're on equal pay, Ben has been paying me $5,000 a week more than Linda, and calling it a 'producer fee'. He's furious because I told him if he didn't give back the money he unjustly deducted, I would let Linda in on the secret arrangement. Well, wouldn't you, dear diary?

Tuesday, 3 April 2007 – opening night, Fort Worth

I wore my own green Yves St Laurent jacket and black skirt, which actually looked better, and I didn't have to keep pulling it down. My black leather gloves are so stretched that they keep falling off my hands, but I'm told by wardrobe they don't have the budget to replace them, for forty dollars! However, the producer reports state that we have a budget of one thousand dollars a week for 'costume replacement' – I wonder where it's going? Up someone's nose?

Tuesday, 17 April 2007 – Memphis

I call Ben Sprecher 'The Spectre'. When PC again requested that he pay me what I'm owed, he told him, 'I will not consider paying JC what I owe her until after the show closes and I've taken care of my investors.' He owes me almost $10,000 between my producer's fee, money I spent personally on alterations and my work permit for the US, which I paid for upfront. Even though he agreed verbally to reimburse us, he is now telling PC that 'it's not in writing so I won't consider it' – what a gent!

However, he has managed to pay himself $7,500 a week every week and has never taken a pay cut even when he made others take cuts. Many of the actors are working for scale – there are no words to describe how ghastly I think he is. I've come across some bastards in my time, but he takes the cake, the icing and the cherry on top.

1–5 May 2007 – Raleigh

The Spectre sends me and Percy an email inviting us to a celebration dinner for the end of *Legends*.

There is no way we would break bread with that man and when my agent told him that, the tiny creature bleated, 'I've never been so insulted in my life.' Frankly, good!

Sadly, a few days before we closed, 'Lips' Evans tried some of her onstage antics again. She would probably call it 'naturalistic' acting, but it's just mimicking of my gestures. If I put my hands behind my head, she does. If I stand up, she does. If I sit down, she does. It's like some bizarre game of 'Simon Says'. Perhaps she's finally become aware that she has done and said everything the same way since we started and is trying to vary things, poor dear.

Another piece of business she's been doing much more recently is to smirk or giggle after *every* line I say. It's driving me crazy and it's dragging the tempo of this show, if it ever had one, to the ground.

During one speech, I waved a chiffon scarf. She grabbed the other end of it and would not let go, glaring at me with a maniacal expression. When I tried to wrest it from her, she hung on for dear life, so I finally had to lunge towards her with both hands and pull it away really hard. She's pissed at me about something again, but God knows, or cares, what or why.

Percy and I threw our own dinner for cast and crew at the best restaurant in Raleigh on the Saturday before the final performance, and it was fabulous. We printed individual menus and dressed the table with gorgeous flowers and candles. I made a witty speech and toasted every single member of the cast and crew – even Linda, of whom I said (rather graciously I thought), 'You are one brave beautiful bitch', quoting a line from the play. Everyone said that the food, ambience and entire tone were far superior, more fun and glamorous than Sprecher's sterile dinner in a steakhouse.

We sent everyone invitations telling them to 'dress glamorous' and everyone, including 'the guys' in the crew made a big effort. Everyone that is, except for Linda, who wore a drab ill-fitting black pantsuit; a battered straw hat and no make-up. Percy overheard one of the wardrobe department whispering to a colleague, 'You'd think she'd have made an effort.'

Linda rose to thank everyone generally, effusively as only she can, sincerity oozing from every pore (she was even complimentary to Percy, and she's hardly said hello to him in six months). She then turned to me and said, 'I must say, Joan, I've never been bored.'

Lucky you, I've been bored stiff every night for nine months!

Sunday, 13 May 2007 – final show, New Haven

FREEDOM! Hurray, hurray and yippee-kay-yay. I threw a small champagne toast in my dressing room with cast and crew and many of us were tearful and sad – I was so fond of them. It could have been marvellous fun, but sadly only when I worked with some of them did it ever really sizzle and take off.

Thursday, 17 May 2007 (four days later) – New York

My finger is so swollen and painful that I haven't been able to wear a ring for six months. My doctor insisted I see a specialist at the NY hospital, he said I had developed a huge cyst on my knuckle from where Linda kicked me. There's only one thing for it – a steroid injection in the knuckle. This was the most painful thing I have ever experienced. As the needle went in, and in front of the doctor, Percy, three internists and one nurse, I let out the most godawful shriek that probably reverberated across the hallowed halls and made EKG machines jump off their marks. Not surprisingly, the *New York Post*'s 'Page Six', that feared gossip column, found out and called us for comment, so I told them I was injured during the play and needed treatment. The story that appeared had Linda choking me! The usual exaggeration, but interestingly enough, a quote from the Toad, Mike Greenfield, who no doubt they found under some old rock, saying 'Joan Collins is the biggest bleeping sack of bleep. She is the single most unprofessional actress working in Hollywood.' Too bad his client isn't working in Hollywood. They also quoted Sprecher as saying he was 'unaware' of any injuries to me or any need for therapy. Since every injury is filed with the stage manager's report, Equity and the Insurance Company, once again he's putting his tiny lying foot in it.

In the movie *The Girl in the Red Velvet Swing*, I had a line which I often quote of people who betray me: 'If you lie down with dogs, you get up with fleas.' That's exactly how I felt about my *Legends* experience. But now, thank God, it's over and I never have to have anything to do with those dreadful people again.*

17 February 2009

It's our seventh wedding anniversary today – who said it wouldn't last?

I've never been happier or more content. Everyone adores Percy, especially Tara, Katy and Jackie, all of whom hated my last husband, 'The Swede', and had a mutual 'hate-on' with my last boyfriend.

We gave a divine seventh anniversary party at the beautiful Hotel Bel-Air, renewing our vows with Reverend José Ferrer (son of the famous actor). Then everyone congregated for drinks in the lovely garden overlooking the pond where elegant swans floated serenely.

We posed for pictures with many friends and family. Sadly,

---

* *Tuesday, 13 August 2019*

Open the *New York Post* to see the following headline: 'Ben Sprecher, Notorious Broadway Producer with Scandal-Scarred Past, Arrested on Federal Child Pornography Charges'. I knew there was something terribly weird about him. The chicken has come home to roost.

Nolan Miller was in a wheelchair but Bill and Hazel, Sacha, his wife Angela and my granddaughter Ava, Jackie and all her children, the Daleys, Betsy Bloomingdale, Wendy Stark, the Schlatters, Barbara Davis, Stefanie Powers, my goddaughter Vic and her husband Rick and their baby Ben, and Judy Quine and Niven Jr.

Last but not least, my 'BFF' Judy Bryer and her husband Max, who had walked me down the aisle seven short years ago.

It was the most magical and perfect of days, and when Percy and I vowed again to 'love and honour until death do us part', I finally believed that that is the way it will be always. I hope we will always love each other, through thick and thin, even if we don't always obey!

Epilogue

May 2021

I have been keeping a daily diary for the past fifteen terrible months of the Coronavirus pandemic. It seems inconceivable to me, having lived such a rich and free life, that so many liberties have been stolen from us. The past fifteen months have been almost other-worldly, a bizarre nightmare that has disrupted all our lives.

But like the great chanteuse, Edith Piaf, sang '*Non, je ne regrette rien*' – I am not one for regrets. I try, in the time-honoured British way, to just get on with it.

In my diary, during those dreary months of lockdown, I've tried to focus on the future and what it might hold, not only for me, but for the rest of the world. What I realised, watching the nasty trolls on social media and the endless news reports, was how much anger and pain there is in the world. So many people in countries, cities and villages seem convulsed by rage. I really feel it's time for the world to 'come together' and show some love. It really does make the world go around.

Percy and I have become even stronger, shut together 24/7 for a year in our London flat. It was a test of our love, and I am delighted that next year we will be celebrating our platinum anniversary – twenty years of marriage – and that we have never been happier.

We were lucky enough to escape the UK's stringent lockdown in February and were thrilled to sample the freedoms that Los Angeles had to offer. I took full advantage of indoor dining, walking on the beach and shopping in malls and department stores, fully vaccinated, of course. I took my first shot on the same day as our Queen!

Despite dire rules and warnings, we gave a gloriously glamorous Oscar party in March to which we were allowed fifty friends in the ravishing Trousdale home of our friend Eugenio Lopez. It was heaven to see so many of those friends who also feature in my unapologetic diaries, like Jeffrey Lane, who has played such a big role in my life, ditto David Niven Jr, Charles Duggan, Jolene and George Schlatter, Wendy Stark, Alan Nevins, Cara Delevingne, Michael Feinstein, Alana Stewart, Robert Kass, Barbara Davis, Michael and Irena Medavoy, Rene Horsch, Mark Zunino, Alice Bamford and so many others, dressed up and celebrating.

I now look forward to 'going forward', to quote the vernacular of the day. I have several irons in the fire and am particularly enthusiastic about a documentary about my life, which I will narrate and which will include a vast selection of home movies, film clips and interviews. After all, after seventy years as an actress and still working I think I'm entitled to blow my own horn!

I hope you have enjoyed my trips down memory lane, and sharing some of my amusing experiences, and some frustrating ones too! But I chose to work in a profession which has no job security and is notorious for dumping people when their shelf life is expired (and often when it hasn't!) so I shall barrel on, always optimistically and always looking on the bright, and fun, side. Onward!